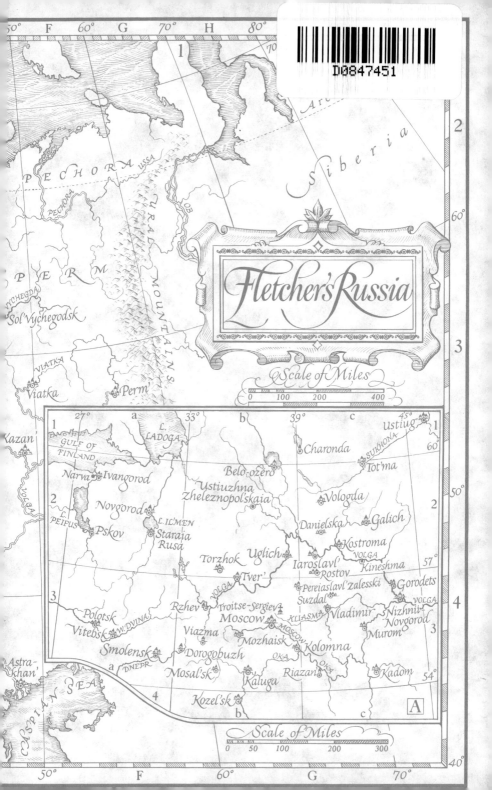

Of the Russe Commonwealth

Of the Russe Commonwealth

BY GILES FLETCHER

1 5 9 1

Facsimile Edition with Variants

WITH AN INTRODUCTION BY RICHARD PIPES
AND A GLOSSARY-INDEX BY JOHN V. A. FINE JR.

HARVARD UNIVERSITY PRESS · 1966
Cambridge · Massachusetts

Preface

The editors of this volume originally intended merely to make available to students of Russian history a scarce and important work on Muscovite Russia. The plan was to publish a facsimile of the first edition of Fletcher's *Of the Russe Commonwealth* (London, 1591) with a brief introduction and a glossary-index. In the course of their work, however, the editors learned of the existence of several manuscripts of Fletcher's book, none of which had been consulted by previous editors. This information induced them to expand somewhat the scope of their undertaking by collating the available texts and listing important variants.

Work on this collation was well under way when Professor Lloyd E. Berry brought out his volume, *The English Works of Giles Fletcher, the Elder* (Madison, Wisconsin, 1964), in which he not only reprinted the 1591 edition of *The Russe Commonwealth* but also provided variant readings from all three extant manuscripts. The publication of this volume at first seemed to make the present enterprise superfluous. But in the end it was decided to proceed with the work, on the grounds that Mr. Berry's edition was prepared mainly for the specialist in Tudor literature rather than for the historian of Russia. The two editions thus complement one another.

The present volume has several parts. Its core consists of a facsimile of the 1591 edition of *The Russe Commonwealth* accompanied by notes giving significant variants from the oldest extant manuscript, presently deposited in the Library of Cam-

Preface

bridge University (Queens College MS 25). Only those variants are noted which alter in some significant manner the meaning of a passage or improve the rendering of Russian proper names. Appended to this text are three other pertinent contemporary documents. These materials are preceded by an introduction, written by Richard Pipes, which outlines the circumstances in which Fletcher composed his book, analyzes its political premises, and discusses its editions. They are followed by a glossary-index, prepared by John Fine, which lists and identifies terms appearing in *The Russe Commonwealth*, and, where necessary, corrects them.

The editors would like to express their thanks to those who have given them assistance, and especially Messrs. J. L. I. Fennell, W. K. Jordan, Thomas Esper, and Edward L. Keenan. They also feel indebted to Mr. Samuel H. Bryant for admirably coping with the task of drafting a map of "Fletcher's Russia."

JOHN V. A. FINE, JR.
RICHARD PIPES

Cambridge, Massachusetts

[vi]

Contents

[vii]

Contents

Maps

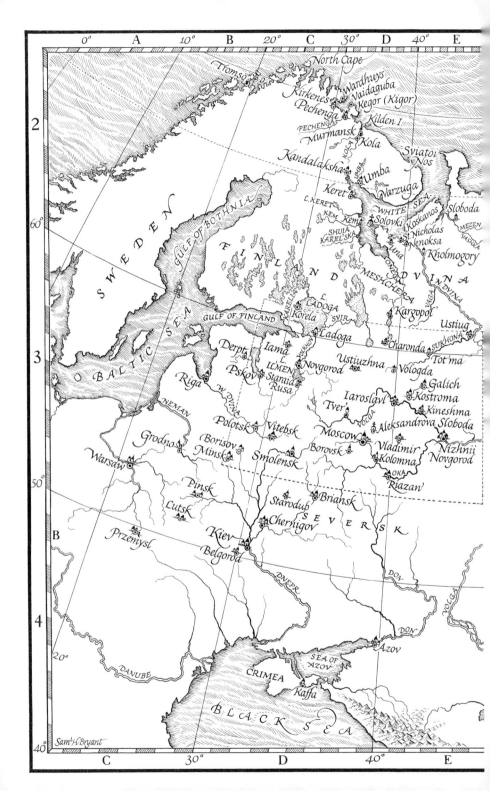

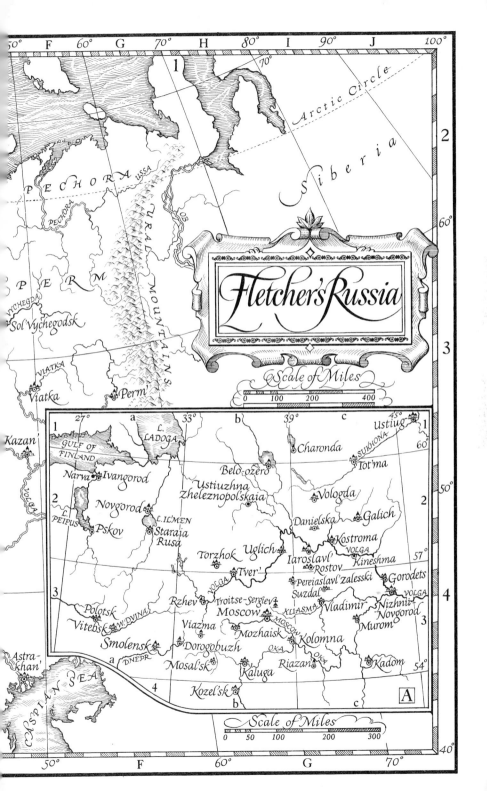

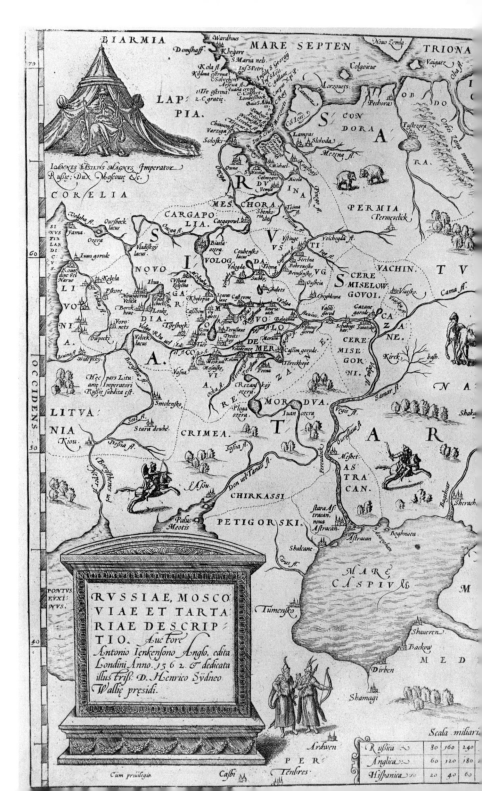

BIARMIA   MARE SEPTEN   TRIONA

Wardhous   Nouo Zemla   Vaigatz

Domshaff   Kegore   Insula S Georgij
            Kola st   Inss S Maria nelif
            Kildma ostroua   Inss S Petri   OB
            Soloetzey   Suana croest   Colgoieue   DO
            Arsiua st   C Comfort   Morzouets   RA
1 Tre ostroua   Lomeiul st   Pechora   Obijs Zona mutis
2 C gratie   Baia S Alba   CS Iohis

LAP
PIA.

        CON
S   DORA
        A

R   Lampas   Sloboda
DV   Mezena fl.
VI
NA   S Michael   Princep fl.

        S Nicola
CORELIA   Colmogro   Toima   PERMIA
        Venta   Permeuelick

Iohannes Basilius Magnus Imperator
Russie, Dux Moscouie &c.

        MES   CHORA   Toima   Shenko   ria
CARGAPO
LIA.   Cargapoul hc   Vstinge   Voichogda fl.

SI   Onega fl.   VS   TI   Vachin.   TV

Valchia R.   Ourshock   Biala   Coubensko   Strelna   Cama fl.
lacus   ozera   lacus   Tosma   Bobrouesko

SI NVS   Yama   VOLOG   Bronsenko   Vslaisko
FIN   Ozera   Vologda   UG
LAN   Vladiskoj   DA   Ousscia
DI   lacus   CERE
CV S   Iuan gorode   NOVO   Choghlema   MISELOW   CAZA
            Iuan Castroma   GOVOI.   NE.
LI   Kexola   GAR   Vasili   Cazane   Cama fl.
VO   Noucorond   DIA   Kholopia   gorod   gorde
NI   Velica   Ium luie   Aculici   Schuboss Suiatoy   CA
A.   Borek   Casshim   MO   Nisnou   har   ZA
houe   Louke   gorod   NE.
Voro   VIlet   Schaleis   CERE
nets   Torshock   VO   Cassim gorode   MISE
        Vologda R lu uel   Morum   GOR
Dwina fl   Widespey   Ek   Tuer   Tereckhoue   NI.   Kirch   bash.
            A CO   Prona
        Vasna   Volock   A   Colom
            lacus   VI   Mosaiske
Hec pars Litu   ocka fl   Rezan   Samar fl.
anie Imperatori   keij
Russie subdita est.   Smolensko   ozera
                Ploga   MORDVA   Vrgis fl.

LITVA   Stara dowhe   CRIMEA.   Iuan ozera   TAR
NIA   Sosha fl.   Oursuline fl.
Kiou.   Disna fl.   Perecolich   Meshet
        Beristhenes uel   Don uel Tanas fl.   ASTRA   Bagshur   Sherach
                    CAN.
            LASsu   stara Asf   Boghnuta
        Palus   tracan   Astracan
        Meotis   CHIRKASSI   noua
                Astracan.
        PETIGORSKI.   Shalcane
                    Cirus fl.   MARE   Shaueren
                            CASPIVM   Backow
                                MED
                        Tumensko   Dirben
PONTVS   M
EVXI   Shamagi
NVS.

RVSSIAE, MOSCO
VIAE ET TARTA
RIAE DESCRIP
TIO. Auctore
Antonio Ienkensono Anglo, edita
Londini Anno. 1562. & dedicata
illus Triss. D. Henrico Sydneo
Wallie presidi.

                    Arkwen
                    PER   TENebres
Cum priuilegio.   Casbi

Scala miliarij
Russica   80   160   240
Anglica   60   120   180
Hispanica   20   40   60

OCCIDENS

70
60
50
40

INTRODUCTION

In the first edition of that encyclopedia of early English travels, Hakluyt's *Principall Navigations, Voiages, and Discoveries of the English Nation* (1589), among descriptions of distant lands in America and Asia, one may find a document dated 1555 which bears the curious title, "Charter of the Merchants of Russia, granted upon the discovery of the said country by King Philip and Queen Mary." That the English of the mid-sixteenth century should have regarded themselves as the discoverers of Russia tells us not only of their provincialism but also of their commercial cunning. Actually, Russia had been "discovered" a good century earlier by continental Europeans, and the English were not entirely unaware of that fact. Their insistence on priority represented, as we shall see, an attempt to buttress an insecure claim to a monopoly on the trade with Russia through the northern route. Nevertheless, the concept of a "discovery" of Russia is not entirely to be dismissed, for it reflects both English and continental feeling of that time. Until the fifteenth century, Russia had indeed been a *terra incognita*, a part of legendary Tartary, the home of Scythians and Sarmatians, about whom Europeans knew no more than about the inhabitants of the continents in fact newly discovered by the great maritime explorers of that age.

There was a time when the principalities of Russia had maintained close commercial and dynastic links with the rest of Christendom. In the eleventh century, Kiev's ruling family married into the royal houses of France, England, and Norway.

Introduction

But a succession of disasters resulting principally from recurrent invasions of Turkic and Mongolian nomads from inner Asia snapped one by one the links connecting Russians with the Catholic world. The final disaster was the great Mongolian invasion of 1236–1241 which ravaged most of Russia and placed it under the sovereignty of the Khan. The Russians were henceforth compelled to turn eastward. It was to the east that their princes had to travel to make their humiliating homage and pay their tribute, and it was there that they learned new means of government and warfare. Between the middle of the thirteenth and the middle of the fifteenth century, Russia was effectively separated from Europe and integrated into the oriental world. Infrequent travelers to Mongolia or China crossed lands once inhabited by Russians in the south and west, but they stayed away from the forests of the upper Volga and Oka, to which regions the center of Russian population and statehood had shifted. Plano Carpini, who journeyed to Mongolia in 1246, left in his account only passing references to the Russians, where he depicts them as abused vassals of the Tatars: any Tatar, he says, no matter how lowly, treats the best born Russian with utter disdain. Willem van Ruysbroek, who repeated Carpini's trip seven years later, speaks of Russia as a province "full of woods in all places . . . [which] has been wasted all over by the Tatars and as yet is daily wasted by them." [1] Given the hazards of medieval travel, there was nothing in these casual references to encourage European interest in Russia.

If Russia lost contact with Europe as a result of Mongol-Turkic conquests, she re-established this contact as soon as she had emancipated herself from the invaders and organized a sovereign state. This event occurred in the second half of the fifteenth century. With startling rapidity what had been an im-

[1] C. R. Beazley, ed., *The Texts and Versions of John de Plano Carpini and William de Rubruquis* (London, 1903), p. 205.

poverished and maltreated frontier area of the Mongol Empire transformed itself into the most powerful eastern Christian kingdom. Some Russian theoreticians even began to claim for the Grand Dukes of Moscow — descendants of princelings who so recently had been humiliated by the Khans — the imperial title which had lapsed with the death of the last Byzantine emperor during the Turkish seizure of Constantinople in 1453. This claim was not very seriously taken by westerners when they first learned of it. But the existence of a large Christian kingdom in the east could not well be ignored by a continent threatened with Ottoman invasion. From the middle of the fifteenth century, Papal and Imperial legates found their way to Moscow in search of diplomatic or military alliances. At the same time, the first Russian missions appeared in western Europe: they arranged for the marriage of Ivan III to the niece of the last Byzantine emperor, then a refugee in Rome (1472), brought to Moscow architects and decorators to construct the new Kremlin, and engaged in a variety of negotiations. In this manner the old links between Russia and the other states of the Western world were gradually reforged.

On the European mind these first contacts produced quite an exotic impression. Owing to long commercial and military dealings with the Tatars, Turks, and Persians, the Russians of the fifteenth and sixteenth centuries presented a completely oriental appearance. Their nobles wore clothes imported from Persia, and their soldiers carried weapons copied from the Tatars. Russian women painted their faces with garish colors quite unlike anything seen in Europe. The visual impression of strangeness, recorded by virtually every early visitor to Russia, was reinforced by curious customs. The practice of kowtowing before superiors, imposed on the Russians by the Tatars and retained after independence, astounded visitors as much as it repelled them. The absolute power of the ruler, the habit of even the highest nobles of referring to themselves as the monarch's "slaves" (*kholopy*), the prevalence of sexual promiscuity — these and many other features of Muscovite Russia amazed all visitors, regardless of background. Russia appeared to them not as a European country, but as what one historian calls "a Christian-exotic country of the New World." [2] This initial impression never quite lost its hold on the European imagination. It continued to influence attitudes many years later, after Russia had become an integral member of the European cultural and political community. When an angry Castlereagh, in 1815, called the thoroughly Frenchified Alexander I a "Calmuck prince," he was unconsciously reverting to this tradition.

The rediscovery of Russia produced a sizeable body of literature which in Russian historiography is known as *skazaniia inostrantsev* (accounts of foreigners). This literature, like the whole body of travel accounts of the age of discovery, has both specific strengths and weaknesses as a historical source. The early explorers were subjective, intolerant, and often uncritical, but they also approached foreign lands with a freshness of vision that comes only once to individual cultures as to individual persons. They saw more sharply and with less preconditioning than did their successors. The picture of Russia which emerges from these accounts is strikingly consistent — so much so that the historian Kliuchevskii felt justified in preparing on their basis a composite description of Muscovy.[3]

The most important of these early accounts was written by the Imperial ambassador, Sigismund von Herberstein, who traveled to Russia twice in the reign of Vassilii III (1517 and 1526). His book, *Commentarii rerum Moscoviticarum*, appeared in Vienna in 1549 and ran through several editions. It was based on good knowledge of the written sources as well as intelligent per-

[2] Karl H. Ruffman, *Das Russlandbild im England Shakespeares* (Göttingen, 1952), p. 176.

[3] V. O. Kliuchevskii, *Skazaniia inostrantsev o Moskovskom gosudarstve* (Moscow, 1918).

[4]

Introduction

sonal observations, and it provided westerners with the first serious description of Russian history, geography, government, and customs.[4] Herberstein's book was the main source of continental knowledge of Russia in the sixteenth century, but by no means the only one.[5]

The English were at first not greatly interested in this body of information. They did not even bother to translate Herberstein's book, which within a few years of publication in Latin had come out in Italian, German, and Czech editions: for in the middle of the sixteenth century they had neither religious, nor diplomatic, nor commercial relations with Russia. England's first encounter with that country was an accidental byproduct of a search for a route to China, and for that reason bore the earmarks of a genuine maritime discovery.

In the 1550's England experienced an economic depression caused by a sudden drop in the export of textiles. The merchants, who had come to depend on foreign markets, were now compelled to undertake in earnest maritime explorations in which England so far had lagged behind both Spain and Portugal. Since the Spanish and Portuguese had prior claim to the best southern routes, the English had to seek other, more risky ones. One of them was a northeast passage to China. Some of the outstanding geographers of the time, such as the cartographer Mercator, the explorer Sebastian Cabot, and the mathematician and astrologer John Dee, believed that such a passage was feasible. Basing their reasoning on the best available evidence,

[4] The handiest edition is that published by the Hakluyt Society, translated and edited by R. H. Major: S. von Herberstein, *Notes upon Russia*, 2 vols. (London, 1851–52).

[5] A good account of foreign travel accounts is by V. Kordt, *Chuzhozemny podorozhny po skhydnyi Evropy do 1700 r.* (Kiev, 1926). The pioneering bibliography by F. Adelung, *Kritisch-literarische Uebersicht der Reisenden in Russland*, 2 vols. (St. Petersburg-Leipzig, 1846), though outdated, is still useful. There is no edition or bibliography of Russian reports on Europe and Europeans, but a selection of the so-called *stateinye spiski*, or formal reports of ambassadors, has been published under the title *Puteshestviia Russkikh Poslov XVI-XVII vv.* (Moscow-Leningrad, 1954).

they concluded that the Asian continent terminated in the vicinity of the river Ob, where the coastline turned sharply south toward China. If that was indeed the case, then by sailing northeast, past the tip of Scandinavia, it would be possible to reach the great Chinese markets in a relatively short time. Encouraged by this prospect, a group of entrepreneurs equipped three vessels and in the summer of 1553 sent them in search of the passage to China by way of the North Sea. The expedition was under the joint command of Sir Hugh Willoughby and Richard Chancellor.

The vessels of this expedition, having rounded the tip of Norway, sailed into waters previously unexplored by westerners. There they soon became separated. Two ships, including the one with Willoughby aboard, encountered adverse winds and decided to drop anchor off the Kola Peninsula. Unprepared for the severity of the northern winter and unable to establish contact with natives, Willoughby and all his companions later froze to death. Their ships, intact but without a sign of life aboard, were discovered the next spring by Laplanders and eventually returned to England. Chancellor, in the meantime, having waited in vain for his companions in the third ship, sailed on into the White Sea, and on August 24, 1553, sighted the Russian monastery of St. Nicholas at the mouth of the Dvina River, where he landed.

The English travelers touched Russian soil at a propitious moment. The country, led by the ambitious and belligerent Ivan IV, was in great need of military supplies and specialists with which to pursue war against the Tatars. Russia's western neighbors had for some time previous imposed an effective embargo on the shipment of European craftsmen and weapons, for they feared that Moscow, having defeated the Tatars, would once more begin to expand in their direction. By opening the northern route, the English had made it possible to break this embargo, and to establish a new and dependable route connecting

Introduction

Russia with the outside world.[6] It is not surprising, therefore, that they were warmly welcomed. As soon as news of Chancellor's landing had reached Ivan, he ordered the visitors brought to him. In Moscow, where he was received with much display of friendliness, Chancellor learned that the Russian government was prepared to open negotiations for the purpose of granting the English merchants commercial privileges. With this assurance, the sponsors of Chancellor's expedition founded, on his return, a regular company, popularly known as the Muscovy Company, which received a royal charter and became the prototype of the great English joint-stock companies for overseas trade. In the same year (1555) the company received liberal privileges from Ivan IV which exempted it from the payment of customs and other dues, and in effect confirmed the monopoly on all English trade with Russia granted it by the English charter. Subsequent grants extended the company's rights to trade with Persia and with the Baltic port of Narva, held by the Russians between 1566 and 1581. The port of St. Nicholas was reserved for the company's exclusive use.[7] Under the auspices of the Company, Russia and England developed a lively maritime trade which greatly contributed to the economic development of the entire Russian north.[8]

The English soon discovered that there was in fact no northeast passage to China: the Asian continent stretched far beyond the river Ob, and in any event the northern waters at a certain degree of longitude (not far east of St. Nicholas) were impassable because of ice. But through Russia English traders unexpectedly found a land route to the commercial centers of the

---

[6] Russian sailors had used the northern route before the arrival of Chancellor, but they did so sporadically and mainly for diplomatic purposes, rather than for regular trade. See Joseph von Hamel, *England and Russia* (London, 1854), pp. 50–54.

[7] The best account of the Company is T. S. Willan's *The Early History of the Russia Company, 1553–1603* (Manchester, 1956).

[8] I. Liubimenko, *Les relations commerciales et politiques de l'Angleterre avec la Russie avant Pierre le Grand* (Paris, 1933), pp. 280–81.

Introduction

Middle East. The establishment of the Muscovy Company co-incided with the conquest by the Russians of the entire length of the Volga River. By capturing Astrakhan, in 1556, the Russians planted themselves on the Caspian Sea, through which there was easy access to Persia and Central Asia. One year after the fall of Astrakhan, Anthony Jenkinson carried out a journey through Moscow to Turkestan and a few years later to Persia. Before long, amazed Englishmen began to receive oriental goods by way of the Northern Sea: "The silks of the Medes to come by Muscovia into England is a strange hearing," Sir Thomas Smith wrote to Sir William Cecil in 1564.[9]

The oriental trade through Russia came to an end in 1580. The route had proved too hazardous, and in that year another group of merchants formed the Turkey (or Levant) Company, which undertook trade with the Middle East through the Mediterranean. The Muscovy Company gave up this part of its business and came to concentrate entirely on an import and export trade with Russia, from which it derived no mean profit. The English brought into Russia manufactured goods (mostly textiles), metals and other mineral products useful for war (tin, lead, saltpeter, sulphur, and gunpowder), and colonial products (sugar, fruits, etc.). They purchased Russian furs, seal oil, tallow, wax, cordage, and even caviar. The Russian monarchy was in general well disposed toward the English merchants, causing by its patronage the displeasure of some high Russian officials. When Ivan died, the head of the foreign office, Andrei Shchelkalov, mocked a member of the Muscovy Company: "And now your English tsar is gone."[10]

Under the protection of the Russian monarchy, the company was allowed to establish in Moscow and several provincial towns permanent agencies staffed by its merchants and clerks. In some

[9] Cited by Willan, *The Early History*, p. 58.
[10] Cited by I. M. Kulisher, *Ocherk istorii russkoi torgovli* (Petrograd, 1923), p. 118.

[8]

instances, agents of the company stayed in Russia for many years, learned fluent Russian, and became first-rate Russian experts. In this manner, within thirty years after Chancellor had stepped ashore at St. Nicholas, England knew more about Russia than did any other country in Europe. This expertise lends British accounts particular value. In general, they are both more factual and less partisan than the accounts of Germans, Poles, or Italians. Some of them are indeed nothing more than intelligence reports prepared by and for merchants who cared only for information helpful in business. They reported distances between towns, measures and weights, coinage, available commodities, the customs and practices of their Russian counterparts, and the institutions of local and central government with which they had to deal.

This fact must be kept in mind in evaluating English accounts, lest they be charged with gross prejudice, for they are virtually unanimous in their condemnation of Russia. Although a number of English residents became thoroughly assimilated, only one of them is known to have chosen to remain — and he was a man who faced prosecution for financial misdeeds. To the English of the time, Russia was a barbarous country, much more so than the other countries of the Orient with which they then entered into relations.[11] Their impressions are well summed up in three rhymed letters which the poet George Turberville sent to his London friends from Moscow, where he was serving in 1568 as Thomas Randolph's secretary:

> Their manners are so Turkie-like, the men so full of guile,
> The women wanton, temples stuffed with idols that defile

[11] It is interesting to note that the Turks were much admired in sixteenth-century English and particularly French literature for their sobriety, discipline, and effective government. See Samuel C. Chew, *The Crescent and the Rose* (New York, 1937), pp. 100–121, and C. D. Rouillard, *The Turk in French History, Thought, and Literature (1520–1660)* (Paris, [1938?]), pp. 376–406.

Introduction

The seats that sacred ought to be, the customs are so quaint
As if I would describe the whole, I fear my pen would faint.
In sum, I say, I never saw a prince that so did reign
Nor people so beset with saints, yet all but vile and vain:
Wild Irish are as civil as the Russies in their kind,
Hard choice which is the best of both, each bloody, rude
and blind.
If thou be wise, as wise thou art, and wilt be ruled by me,
Live still at home, and covet not those barbarous coasts
to see.[12]

Despite the advantages which both sides derived from it, Anglo-Russian trade ran into increasing difficulties. These difficulties stemmed in part from different attitudes towards commerce and in part from growing Russian dissatisfaction with the monopoly enjoyed by the Muscovy Company on the northern route.

To England, trade with Russia was all along purely a business proposition. If Queen Elizabeth granted the Muscovy Company privileges and diplomatic support it was not because she expected to derive from its activities any immediate political advantage, but because in England then, as now, foreign trade and the well-being of the state were inseparable. This was not the case in Russia. Trade in general, and foreign trade in particular, played a small part in the life of the state, whose preoccupation was still with political and military matters. Ivan IV welcomed English merchants and granted them privileges not so much because he was interested in trade as such as because with their help he could break the Polish-German-Swedish blockade isolating him from the west. Although he personally derived a fair profit from doing business with England, as an autocratic ruler

---

[12] Cited in Herberstein, *Notes upon Russia*, vol. I, p. CLVI. A good analysis of the Elizabethan "image" of Russia is to be found in Ruffman's *Das Russlandbild*.

claiming to own everybody and everything in his domain he treated commerce as only one of several ways of enhancing his power and wealth.

These different attitudes led to misunderstandings which, compounded by Ivan's worsening paranoia, caused in 1567 the first crisis in Anglo-Russian relations. In that year, Ivan, feeling menaced by internal and external enemies, requested Elizabeth to enter into an alliance with him and to offer him asylum in England in the event he were forced to flee. The Queen promptly granted the request for asylum, but she hedged on the matter of alliances, for she saw no point in getting involved in Ivan's quarrels with his neighbors. Infuriated by her evasive reply, Ivan began to apply pressure on the Muscovy Company, threatening to open Russia to other English merchants. Under the pressure of the alarmed company, the Queen dispatched an embassy (1568–69) headed by Thomas Randolph which succeeded brilliantly in reconfirming the merchants' privileges and even adding new ones. The Muscovy Company was once more acknowledged the only English organization permitted to trade with Russia both through St. Nicholas and the newly acquired Baltic port of Narva. In addition, its agents and properties were placed under the protection of the *oprichnina*, the part of the government under the tsar's direct control. Ivan, who used trade privileges as diplomatic leverage, apparently hoped that the generous new charter would persuade the Queen to grant his request for an alliance. But when this hope was again disappointed, he began to make new difficulties. In a violent letter which he wrote to the Queen in 1570, he clearly stated his political position:

We thought that you lord it over your domain, and rule by yourself, and seek honor for yourself and profit for your country. And it is for this reason that we wanted to engage in these affairs with you. But now we see that there are men who do rule beside you, and not men but trading boors (*muzhiki torgovye*) who do not think of the profit of our safety, honor, and lands, but seek their own merchant profit. And you remain in your maidenly estate like a common maid . . . And if it be so, then we shall set these affairs to the side. And the trading boors who abandoned our royal heads and our royal honor and the benefit of our lands for their own merchant affairs, they shall see how they will now trade. For the realm of Moscow had not been wanting without their English goods.[13]

To the English ambassador, Anthony Jenkinson, whom the Queen sent in 1572 to patch up relations, Ivan also complained that the English government allowed "merchants' matters" to take precedence over "princely affairs." [14] In this manner, the Company time and again found itself a helpless victim of international diplomacy.

To compound its troubles, the Company had to confront a challenge from independent English merchants who resented its monopoly. Once the trade with Russia got under way in earnest, such merchants sought to persuade the Russian government that it would profit more by opening its ports to all comers. Ivan IV, who in general opposed these interlopers, for a while (in 1568, during his quarrel with Elizabeth) let them have their way. A number of highly placed Russians, moreover, were known to hold anti-monopolistic views, and this explains the Company's constant stress on its "discovery" of Russia. Even more difficult to control was the private trade carried on by the Company's employees. English agents, past and present, clerks,

---

[13] Iurii Tolstoi, *Pervye sorok let snoshenii mezhdu Rossiieiu i Anglieiu, 1553–1593* (St. Petersburg, 1875), pp. 109–110. The original English translation (pp. 114–115), omits the words "rule by yourself" in the first sentence, and renders "trading boors" as "boors and merchants." One cause of Ivan's fury was Elizabeth's failure to request reciprocal rights of asylum in Russia. In her reply she said she had "no manner of doubt of the continuance of our peacable government without danger either of our subjects or of any foreign enemies." Willan, *The Early History*, p. 99. Another, was her coolness to his marriage proposal.

[14] Willan, *The Early History*, p. 119.

and even simple sailors, engaged regularly in a lucrative side business of importing and exporting goods legally reserved to the Company. In some instances, these interlopers entered into partnerships with Russian officials who thereby became personally interested in terminating the Company's monopoly. The Russian government, accustomed to collective responsibility, tended to treat the Company as liable for debts incurred by individual Englishmen, whether or not they were acting on the Company's behalf and in its name. The Company's refusal to honor these debts led to constant recriminations and occasional confiscations of its property.

The death of Ivan IV in 1584 by no means resolved these difficulties. The new government of Fedor Ivanovich, in which effective authority was exercised by Boris Godunov, was less concerned with diplomatic alliances which had so much harmed Russo-English relations under Ivan. But it was unfavorably inclined to the Company's exclusive commercial privileges secured under Ivan which it considered economically detrimental to Russia. In this attitude Godunov was supported by the head of the office of foreign affairs, Andrei Shchelkalov.

In 1586 Elizabeth dispatched to Moscow a new embassy, headed by Jerome Horsey. Horsey was an old Moscow hand, having been there on Company business since 1572. He spoke fluent Russian, a language which he considered "the most copious and elegant in the world." [15] He was also sufficiently close to the Russian court to have been employed a short time before on a delicate and secret diplomatic mission on its behalf in Livonia. Horsey in part re-established the Company's privileges, but immediately new difficulties arose. One of the causes was a financial dispute between Shchelkalov and an English trader by

---

[15] Jerome Horsey, "His Travels," in E. A. Bond, ed., *Russia at the Close of the Sixteenth Century*, Hakluyt Society Publications, vol. XX (London, 1856), p. 156.

Introduction

the name of Anthony Marsh.[16] Clearly, until the powerful minister was placated, the affairs of the Company would not prosper. To settle this matter, as well as to re-negotiate some of the general issues of Anglo-Russian trade, Elizabeth in the summer of 1588 dispatched Giles Fletcher as her ambassador to Moscow.

Fletcher was born in Watford, Hertfordshire, in 1546, the son of a clergyman. He received his initial education at Eton, and in 1565 proceeded to King's College, Cambridge, where he remained for the next twenty years. At the university he took an active part in academic politics, wrote some Latin poetry, and eventually became lecturer in Greek and Dean of Arts at King's.[17] In 1579 he turned to law. In two years he earned his doctorate, and then entered politics, apparently under the patronage of Thomas Randolph. It is known that Fletcher served in Parliament (1584–85), as well as in the treasury of the City of London (1586–87), and participated in embassies to Scotland (1586) and Hamburg (1587), the former headed by Randolph.[18] (It is probably to Randolph, himself an ex-ambassador to Ivan, that Fletcher owed his Moscow appointment.) The combination of literary and academic training with legal and political experience accounts in no small measure for the high quality of his book.

Fletcher received his royal papers on June 6, 1588, and departed, accompanied by twenty Englishmen, a short time afterwards. He carried with him several letters from the Queen, her

---

[16] See below, Appendix A, p. [43]. Documents bearing on the Marsh affair can be found in *Sbornik Imperatorskogo Russkogo Istoricheskogo Obshchestva*, XXXVII (1883), 186–245, *passim*, and Tolstoi, *Pervye sorok let*, pp. 292–340.

[17] Fletcher's life is most fully recounted by Lloyd E. Berry in *The English Works of Giles Fletcher, the Elder* (Madison, Wisconsin, 1963), pp. 3–49.

[18] *Athenae Cantabrigienses*, III (Cambridge, 1913), pp. 36–37; Berry, *The English Works of Giles Fletcher*, pp. 7–25.

ministers, and the Company to the Tsar, his wife, and Boris Godunov, as well as the customary presents.[19]

Fletcher's mission — for a variety of reasons, most of them beyond his control — had a poor beginning. He landed at the Dvina estuary in the middle of September, and then slowly made his way to Moscow. The journey of some 650 miles took over two months. Contrary to accepted custom, the embassy was neither welcomed officially at the gates of Moscow upon its arrival on November 25, nor escorted into the city. The quarters which the Russian authorities assigned the ambassador proved unsatisfactory; Fletcher later described them as "very unhandsome and unwholesome." [20] He was allowed for three weeks to cool his heels under conditions of virtual house arrest before being asked to his first audience at the Kremlin. The audience got off to a bad start when Fletcher refused to pronounce the full title of the Tsar, allegedly because it was too long to be remembered but in fact (as he later admitted) because it was longer than that of the English Queen. The Russians would not allow the audience to proceed until he did so, and eventually he gave in.[21] This incident did not improve relations. They became extremely strained the next day when the gifts Fletcher had brought were returned to his lodgings and unceremoniously dumped at his feet.[22]

The principal reason for Fletcher's unfriendly reception was diplomatic. Shortly before his arrival, the Russian government

---

[19] The official Russian record of Fletcher's embassy is in *Vremennik Imperatorskogo Moskovskogo Obshchestva Istorii i Drevnosti Rossiiskikh*, vol. VIII (1850), Part II/2, pp. 1–96: "Stateinyi spisok Angliiskogo posla Elizara [*sic*] Fletchera byvshego v Moskve v 7097 godu."

[20] See below, Appendix A, p. [45]. The Russian record supports his assertion that he was not welcomed at the city gates ("Stateinyi spisok," p. 2).

[21] See the present edition of the *Russe Commonwealth*, pp. 19–19v, and Appendix A, p. [44].

[22] This episode, described by Fletcher in his report (Appendix A, p. [44]), is also noted in the Russian record ("Stateinyi spisok," p. 3).

had opened negotiations in Moscow with Spanish and German missions which tried to enroll the Russians in an anti-Turkish alliance. They seem to have succeeded in persuading Godunov that England would soon be defeated by Spain and Elizabeth deposed. Apparently, the news of the defeat of the Armada, which had occurred while Fletcher was en route to Russia (August 1588), did not reach Moscow until sometime later that winter. Another factor was the presence in Moscow of the Patriarch of Constantinople, Jeremiah, with whom the government was negotiating the establishment of a Russian Patriarchate. While talks with him were in progress — that is, until January 26, 1589, when Job was named the Patriarch of Moscow — other issues were relegated to the background (cf. Appendix A). The particular indignities and discomforts which the embassy experienced can probably be traced directly to the hostility of Andrei Shchelkalov, who, as head of the foreign office, was in charge of the visitors. The English did not improve matters by returning niggardly gifts for the exceptionally rich ones the Russians had sent Queen Elizabeth the previous year. All these factors hampered and delayed Fletcher's mission. But his loss is our gain, for the many months he spent in idleness permitted him to study closely the country and its inhabitants, and to acquire the information which lends his account permanent importance.

Fletcher was called for a second audience in the middle of January 1589, at which time Shchelkalov raised the issue of English debts. At about this time news of the English triumph over the Armada reached Moscow, and the atmosphere thawed considerably. On April 22, Fletcher went to his third and final audience in the Kremlin. He was given a new charter of privileges, which, without meeting all the Company's demands, was on the whole quite satisfactory. The Company in effect had to give up its monopoly of the northern route, but it won exemption from responsibility for the debts of individual English merchants. Control over its activities was also shifted from the foreign office, headed by the unfriendly Shchelkalov, to the Treasury.[23] There was some additional difficulty with the Office of Foreign Affairs a few days later when Fletcher insisted on delivering personally to the Tsar a note brought in the interval by courier from England. The foreign office refused the request on the grounds that Fletcher had already been formally dismissed. In the end he had to capitulate, and on May 6, 1589 was allowed to depart for Vologda, a major depot of the Company. There he spent two months waiting for the reply from Moscow to the latest note, and for the permit to sail. The permit and reply arrived sometime after July 17, and Fletcher, in the company of Horsey and Marsh, embarked for England soon afterwards.[24] The party arrived in England in late August or early September.

Fletcher's experience in Russia had not been a happy one, and he had good reason to dislike that country. This fact has been noted by historians, and there can be little question that to some extent his critical attitude derives from the treatment he received. Shortly upon his return to England, in a conversation with a Cambridge friend, he is reported to have "heartily expressed his thankfulness to God for his safe return from so great a danger":

for the poets cannot fancy Ulysses more glad to be come out of the den of Polyphemus, than he was to be rid out of the power of such a barbarous prince; who, counting himself by a proud and voluntary mistake emperor of all the nations, cared not for the law of all nations; and who was so habited in blood, that, had he cut off this ambassador's head, he and his friends might have sought their own amends; but the question is, where he would have found it?[25]

---

[23] See Appendix A, pp. [51–52].
[24] "Stateinyi spisok," pp. 41–75.
[25] Thomas Fuller, *The Worthies of England*, edited by John Freeman,

[17]

Introduction

While in Russia, Fletcher kept a journal [26] which furnished the basis of his book. We know from Fletcher himself that he composed a draft of the *Russe Commonwealth* during the return voyage from Russia (see below, *Of the Russe Commonwealth*, "The Epistle Dedicatorie," p. A3). Unfortunately, neither the journal nor this first draft seems to have survived, and all the texts known to us are edited versions, prepared during the interval between Fletcher's arrival in England and the appearance of the book some two years later.

The earliest reference to the *Russe Commonwealth* can be found in the first edition of Hakluyt's *Principall Navigations*, which came out toward the end of 1589. Hakluyt provides a brief description of Fletcher's embassy, enumerates certain terms of the treaty signed by Fletcher in Moscow, and adds: "The said Ambassador . . . as I understand, hath drawn a book, intituled *Of the Russe Commonwealth*," the chapters of which he then recapitulates. Hakluyt's list contains 24 chapters, four less than are to be found in the published edition of 1591. Actually, since one of the chapters of the 1591 version (chapter 22) is divided in the Hakluyt list into two separate chapters (one on the liturgy and another on the sacraments), the Hakluyt list is five chapters shorter. The missing chapters are 4 through 6, 20, and 26. At the end of his notice, Hakluyt adds: "The book it selfe he [Giles Fletcher] thought not good, for divers considerations, to make publike at this time." [27]

What these "considerations" were it is not difficult to surmise in view of what happened after the *Russe Commonwealth* did appear in 1591. The Muscovy Company must have exerted considerable pressure on Fletcher not to publish his account, so critical of Russia, from fear that it would further jeopardize its

---

(London, 1952), p. 279. Bond, citing this passage (*Russia*, p. cxxiii) wonders how a dead man could have sought amends for his own murder.

[26] See below, *Of the Russe Commonwealth* (1591), p. 2v.

[27] Richard Hakluyt, *Principall Navigations*, London, 1589. In some copies Fletcher's account is on pp. 502–504, in others on pp. 498–500.

trading privileges. For the time being, Fletcher had to content himself with two reports to the Queen, one describing the course of his embassy and the other suggesting the means of improving the position of English traders in Russia (see Appendices A and B). In 1590, his scholarly interests turned to native history, and he conceived a plan of writing a Latin account of the reign of Elizabeth. We have a letter of his to Lord Burghley (William Cecil) dated November 3, 1590, in which he outlines his project and requests patronage as well as access to state papers.[28] For some reason, however, the project fell through, and Fletcher returned to his Russian manuscript.

In the Library of Cambridge University (Queens College MS 25) there is a manuscript of Fletcher's *Of the Russe Commonwealth* prefaced by an autograph dedication to the Queen. The table of contents of this manuscript lists the same number of chapters as does Hakluyt, that is, twenty-four, but with the difference that the two chapters on liturgy and sacraments are now consolidated into one, and a new chapter (corresponding to chapter 26 in the 1591 edition) on "The Emperours domestiqve or priuat behaviour" is added. The captions of the chapters in the Hakluyt list and Cambridge manuscript are virtually identical. Chapters 4, 5, 6, and 20 of the 1591 edition are still missing, and so are many scattered passages, short and long, found in the 1591 edition. The Cambridge manuscript thus seems to be a slightly expanded version of the original draft.[29]

A comparison of the Cambridge manuscript and the book published in 1591 reveals one fact of particular interest. Nearly

---

[28] Berry, *The English Works of Giles Fletcher, the Elder*, pp. 383–384.

[29] Two other manuscripts are known. One is at the Bodleian Library in Oxford (MS. Univ. E. 144), the other at the University of Minnesota Library. Lloyd Berry, who has studied all three, considers the Oxford and Minnesota manuscripts posterior to the Cambridge one. His collation indicates that they contain no significant information not found in the Cambridge manuscript. The Cambridge manuscript, as being closest to the original version produced immediately upon Fletcher's departure from Russia, is by all accounts the most important and therefore it is the one we have selected for our collation.

Introduction

all the references to historical sources made in the 1591 edition, and indeed virtually all the historical background of that edition, are missing from the manuscript. This fact strongly suggests that Fletcher did the bulk of his research on Russia after he had returned to England, during the interval which elapsed between the writing of the Cambridge manuscript and the publication of his book. On the basis of this research he now wrote chapters 4, 5, 6 and 20, and inserted numerous shorter historical passages in the other chapters.

The Russian historian S. M. Seredonin identifies the following sources as having been consulted by Fletcher:[30] Herberstein's *Commentaries*; Pachymeres' *History of the Paleologues*;[31] Martin Kromer's *History of Poland*;[32] Nicephorus Gregoras, *History of Byzantium*;[33] A. Bonfinius' *History of Hungary*;[34] the so-called *Berossus Babilonicus*,[35] and Saxo Grammaticus' *History of the Danes*.[36] The following table provides references to the most important passages added to the Cambridge manuscript:

Passage	Fletcher's pages	Probable source
Origin of Slavs and Russians	1–2	Kromer, Book i, ch. vii–viii
Description of the Russian winter	4v	Herberstein, vol. II, p. 2

[30] S. M. Seredonin, *Sochinenie Dzhil'sa Fletchera 'Of the Russe Commonwealth' kak istoricheskii istochnik* (St. Petersburg, 1891), pp. 45–56.

[31] *Georgii Pachymeris De Michaele et Andronico Paleologis Libri Tredecim* (cf. ed. Bonn, 1835).

[32] Martin Kromer, *De origine et rebus gestis Polonorum libri XXX*, Basileae, 1555.

[33] Nicephorus Gregoras, *Romanae, hoc est Byzantinae historiae Libri XI*, probably in the Basel 1562 edition, which contains also L. Chalcocondylas' account, *De origine ac rebus Gestis Turcorum*, which Fletcher cites.

[34] *Antoni Bonfinii Rerum Ungaricarum Decades Quatuor*, Basileae, 1568.

[35] *Berosus Babilonicus*, Paris, 1510.

[36] Saxo Grammaticus, *Gesta Danorum* (cf. Holder edition, Strassburg, 1886).

Introduction

Introduction

Fletcher, it may be noted, was neither a profound nor an accurate scholar. His research is much inferior to his powers of observation, and the parts of his book based on study of other histories have been most severely criticized. There are a number of other differences between the manuscript and the book. Fletcher's printer made many errors, especially in setting proper names and numbers. For this reason, the manuscript is more accurate in rendering Russian terms. In the book version, Fletcher occasionally softened some opinions, especially as concerns Russian religion.

Fletcher's life after 1591 was not particularly eventful. He wrote a volume of mediocre verse, *Licia, or Poems on Love* (probably 1593), and *Israel redux* (published posthumously in 1667) in which he argued that the Caspian Tatars were descendants of the ten tribes of Israel. Having served for a while as treasurer of St. Paul's Church in London, he obtained a lease on a provincial rectory. He had some trouble during the Essex rebellion, but was found innocent and released. He died in February 1611, shortly after he had carried out diplomatic negotiations with Denmark on behalf of the Eastland merchants. Fletcher's sons, Giles the Younger and Phineas, were also poets, both somewhat more prominent than he. Even more famous is the son of his brother Richard, the dramatist John Fletcher. His own reputation today rests entirely on the *Russe Commonwealth*, a book which occupies a unique place in the entire foreign literature on Muscovite Russia.

Of the Russe Commonwealth consists of three unequal parts. The first (chapters 1–4) contains a geographic description, the second (chapters 5–25) an analysis of the state and its institutions, and the third (chapters 26–28) an account of customs and manners. The first and third parts are short, and the bulk of the narrative (184 of the 232 pages) is devoted to the second, which

Introduction

in turn can be divided into four subsections: the government (including the nobility and fiscal apparatus), the judiciary, the armed forces, and the church. This structure, as outlined by Fletcher himself in the table of contents (p. A4v), indicates that he intended his book as a systematic treatise. This feature alone distinguishes it from all other foreign accounts.

Seredonin, having analyzed the sources Fletcher used, concluded that he was "undoubtedly the most erudite of all the foreigners who in the sixteenth and seventeenth centuries had written about Russia."[37] Of course, the real value of his book derives not from his reading, done, as we now know, mostly after his return, but from the knowledge obtained either from personal observation or from conversations with agents of the Muscovy Company resident in Russia. He seems to have profited especially from talks with Horsey, who accompanied him on the return voyage. Indeed, Horsey afterwards claimed that he had furnished Fletcher with "all" the information for his book.[38] Another informant may have been Marsh, who had traded with Siberia and may have supplied Fletcher with facts about the Tatars and the eastern borderlands in general. Fletcher's account may be said to represent the cumulative knowledge and experience which the agents of the Muscovy Company had acquired over thirty-five years of commercial contact with Russians and their government.

Fletcher was not content, however, to rely on information supplied by others, and went out of the way to learn on his

[37] Seredonin, *Sochinenie Dzhil'sa Fletchera*, p. 56.
[38] Bond, *Russia at the Close of the Sixteenth Century*, p. 256. Fletcher's indebtedness to Horsey is a matter of dispute among historians. Hamel (*England and Russia*, p. 225) and Seredonin (*Sochinenie Dzhil'sa Fletchera*, p. 67) support Horsey's claim. Others reject it on the grounds that Horsey, judged by his own account, lacked both the education and the understanding to do more for Fletcher than supplement the information Fletcher had obtained on his own (Bond, p. cxxii; Ruffman, *Das Russlandbild*, p. 54; Berry, p. 148). Horsey's account, in which he admits to being "but a plain grammarian," is reproduced in Bond, pp. 153–266.

[23]

own.[39] His descriptions are sometimes introduced by "I saw," "I heard," or "I talked to." He subjects a Russian clergyman to an examination on the Bible and the essentials of Christian doctrine. He asks a Russian merchant the reason for his reluctance to display his goods. He talks to his servant about a conversation the latter has had with a Russian. All this information Fletcher noted down, and he did so with considerable accuracy. How reliable he is may be judged from those parts of his narrative which lend themselves to verification from independent sources. His rendering of Russian words, names, and even sentences is precise, as are his accounts of Russian customs and dress. Some of the statements about his treatment in Moscow are also confirmed by contemporary Russian records. He reports rumors circulating in Moscow that the young prince Dimitrii, the sole successor, is in danger of being assassinated by persons interested in seizing the throne.[40] If this statement does not solve the mystery of Dimitrii's death, which occurred two years after Fletcher's departure from Moscow, it does explain why Russian opinion should have immediately blamed Boris Godunov for it. Anyone who read *Of the Russe Commonwealth* at the time of its appearance should have been prepared both for Godunov's succession to the throne (1598), and the civil war which broke out shortly after his death (1605).[41] Naturally, Fletcher is somewhat less dependable when dealing with subjects which fall in the category of state secrets, such as the revenues or military capabilities of the Russian state. But even on these matters he reports so intelligently that his information constitutes to this day an indispensable historic source.[42]

---

[39] Fletcher had at his disposal an English-Russian interpreter named John Sowter (Tolstoi, *Pervye sorok let*, p. 397; see also *Of the Russe Commonwealth*, 1591 ed., p. 89).

[40] *Of the Russe Commonwealth*, pp. 16–16v.

[41] *Ibid.*, pp. 21–21v, 27, 28 and 26.

[42] Seredonin, who subjected Fletcher's book to a detailed analysis as a historical source, was himself a conservative and nationalist Russian and con-

Introduction

From the point of view of the modern historian, the least useful contributions of Fletcher's book are the geographic and historical facts reported in the opening five chapters, most of which he seems to have learned after his return from Russia. The British merchants were well acquainted with the northern territories linking Moscow with the Dvina estuary, along which they traveled and traded, but the rest of the vast country they knew largely from hearsay. Their information, such as depicted in Jenkinson's map of Russia of 1562, which Fletcher used extensively, has long since been superseded.[43] Much of the same holds true of the historical background which Fletcher sketches in chapter 5.

The central part of the book devoted to the state and its institutions (chapters 6–20) represents the first systematic study of the Russian political and social system ever undertaken. Its superiority over all preceding foreign accounts, Herberstein's included, lies in the fact that Fletcher was not content to describe the surface appearance of things, but insisted on finding and laying bare the inner mechanism of the system. He grasps the relations between various, seemingly disparate institutions and practices which other early travelers had missed entirely. That Russia was a "tyranny" and that its tsar had absolute authority to dispose of the lives and properties of his subjects was a commonplace in the literature of the time.[44] But only Fletcher among

---

sidered Fletcher prejudiced toward Russians and incapable of "understanding" them. Seredonin's treatment of Fletcher, therefore, must be accepted with some caution. He considers the most important parts those dealing with commodities (chapter 3), the armed forces (chapters 15–17), the borderlands (chapters 18–20), and everyday life (chapters 26 and 27). The sections dealing with politics and fiscal policies are in his opinion useful but full of errors, owing in part to what Seredonin considers Fletcher's regrettable tendency toward over-systematizing. Fletcher's geographic and historical descriptions, as well as his chapters on religion, he dismisses as useless.

[43] A detail from Jenkinson's map is reproduced on p. xii above; an accurate map, incorporating information supplied by Fletcher in his book, on pp. x–xi.

[44] See, e.g., Ruffman, *Das Russlandbild*, 81–87.

the travelers bothered to ask how such a government functioned and by what means it retained power. He perceives a connection between the authority of the monarchy, the position of the estates, and the general cultural level of the nation. He understands the political significance of the fiscal measures devised by the Russian government, as well as the various techniques employed to keep control of the conquered borderland regions. His whole analysis of political institutions is conceived in suprisingly modern, one may almost say sociological, terms. Indeed, if one were not afraid of modernizing, one could describe *Of the Russe Commonwealth* as a pioneering study of what today is called totalitarianism. His concern with the exercise of political power in all its aspects makes his book a very important document in the history of European political thought.

Before dealing with Fletcher's account of the Russian political system it is necessary to say a few words about the premises from which he proceeds.

Fletcher was an Elizabethan, the product of an age which was keenly interested in itself and engaged, as it were, in constant self-discovery.[45] The emergence of Tudor absolutism on the one hand, and increased relations with other lands on the other, awakened a desire to know how England was ruled and what were the reasons that her government was so different from that of any other country with which Englishmen came in contact. The result was a body of literature, relatively small in the sixteenth century and voluminous in the seventeenth, which contributed greatly to the subsequent formulation of the English constitution. Fletcher's book must be viewed not only as one of the foreign accounts of Russia, but also, and perhaps above all, as a document of this genre. What it says of Russia tells us indirectly what Fletcher thinks of England, for, rightly or wrongly, he seems to have considered the two countries antithetical.

Fletcher viewed the English constitution from the position

[45] A. L. Rowse, *The England of Elizabeth* (New York, 1961), chapter ii.

of a proponent of parliamentary monarchy, a position best expounded in the most famous work of Tudor political thought, Sir Thomas Smith's *The Commonwealth of England*.[46] Although Smith belonged to an earlier generation than Fletcher (he was thirty-three years Fletcher's senior), the two men had much in common. Like Fletcher, Smith was a Cantabrigian and a lawyer, one of the great lights of the university where he acquired a great reputation and left many disciples. Both combined literary pursuits with civil service, and both served on foreign embassies. Their respective books had a similar origin. While on a mission to France in the 1560's Smith conceived, as he put it, "a yearning for our commonwealth," and composed his treatise in order "to set forth almost the whole of its form, especially those points in which it differs from the others." [47] His book, like Fletcher's, was thus inspired by contact with a foreign state in which royal absolutism was the accepted form of government.

Smith's treatise, composed in 1565, first appeared in print in 1583, that is, at the very time when Fletcher entered government service. Its principal thesis was that the government of England was a fusion of the interests and rights of the king, lords, and commons as formally embodied in the institution of the parliament. In parliament rested full sovereignty, or, as Smith called it, "the most high and absolute power." In Smith's view, parliament was not a counterweight to the monarchy, but the common ground on which the monarchic, aristocratic, and democratic forces met. The sovereignty of the king was that of the king-in-parliament. In certain respects—foreign policy, military affairs, and the appointment of chief officials — the king acted independently; in others, such as passing laws, raising revenue, and dispensing justice, he acted in concert with the

---

[46] *De republica Anglorum* (London, 1583); see the edition by L. Alston (Cambridge, 1906).
[47] *Ibid.*, p. XIII.

Introduction

nobles and commons represented in parliament. In Smith's view, the nation and monarchy were joined in an indissoluble community of interest. From this assumption followed a definition of a good and a bad king. A good king comes to power, "with the good will of the people," administers the commonwealth "by the laws of the same and by equity," and seeks "the profit of the people as much as his own." A tyrant, by contrast, "by force comes to the monarchy against the will of the people, breaks laws already made at his pleasure, makes others without the advice and consent of the people, and regards not the wealth of his communes but the advancement of himself, his faction, and kindred." [48] According to Smith, a ruler may qualify as a tyrant by being guilty of any one of these three malpractices.

Whether Smith was accurately portraying or idealizing Tudor practices is a matter which need not concern us here. The important fact is that his book acquired immediate popularity, running through several editions in quick succession. Many Englishmen saw in it a true description of their constitution, and it came to be treated as something of a manual for persons entering state service. [49] It is virtually certain that Fletcher, who in the 1580's had held a variety of political posts including membership in parliament, and who was also a scholar of wide interests, had read Smith's treatise. It is even probable that his *Of the Russe Commonwealth, or Maner of Governement by the Russe Emperour* was consciously conceived as a counterpart to Smith's *The Commonwealth of England, and manner of government thereof.* [50] If Smith wished to present what he understood as a genuine, that is, parliamentary monarchy, Fletcher wanted to depict its opposite: "a true and strange face of a tyrannical state,

---

[48] *Ibid.*, pp. 14–15.

[49] M. Dewar, *Sir Thomas Smith; a Tudor intellectual in office* ([London], 1964), p. 112.

[50] This is the title under which Smith's book appeared in 1589 and thereafter.

most unlike your own," as he wrote in the dedication to Queen Elizabeth, "without true knowledge of God, without written law, without common justice."

Fletcher, like Smith, assumes a good government to be a partnership between crown and nation. In Russia he finds no such relation. There the monarch does not, as Smith would want him to, "seek the profit of the people as much as his own." The Russian government is "plain tyrannical," for everything must work "to the behoof [i.e., advantage] of the Prince," the nobility and commons alike being "but storers for the Prince, all running in the end into the Emperors coffers" (pp. 20–20v). This is the central accusation Fletcher levies against the tsarist government; from this evil flow all its other vices. In his account, the tsarist government resembles as it were a monstrous vampire which sucks from the nation all wealth and robs it of all initiative.

Fletcher begins his description of Russian absolutism by pointing out that the tsar concentrates in his hands all "the principal points and matters of state wherein Sovereignty consists." He is the sole legislator, he appoints all officials and judges, and he has control over the country's foreign affairs. He is the framer of laws and their executor, and he carries out both functions without being held accountable to any genuine parliamentary institution. The Russian councils, whether the Boyar Duma, or what he calls the "Sobor," [51] he dismisses as impotent. Their function is not to initiate, influence, or even discuss pending laws, but merely to confirm laws which the monarch and his closest advisers had previously decided upon. All laws, he says, are "ever determined of before any public assembly or parliament be summoned" (p. 20v). "To propound bills what

[51] Seredonin points out (*Sochinenie Dzhil'sa Fletchera*, pp. 230–233), citing Kliuchevskii, that the institution which Fletcher calls "Zabore" (p. 22v) is not the so-called Zemskii sobor, or Assembly of the Land, but the "Dumnyi Sobor," a joint meeting of the Boyar Duma and clergy.

every man thinks good for the public benefit (as the manner is in England) the Rus Parliament allows no such custom nor liberty to subjects" (p. 23). Fletcher considers the Boyar Duma so intrinsic a part of the monarchical machinery that he places its description in the section devoted to the administration (chapter 11).

Fletcher attaches much importance to the position of the nobility, for he believes that a powerful noble estate with firm rights is essential to prevent the monarchy from degenerating into despotism. One of the central features of the Russian constitution, as he interprets it, is that the nobles, including those of the highest degree (that is, the descendants of the former appanage princes) are completely subordinated to the crown. In a penetrating analysis in chapter 11, Fletcher describes the various means used to undermine the Russian nobility.

The first, and in his opinion most efficacious, of these means is to prevent the fusion of titles with offices. "As touching the public offices and magistracies of the realm, there is none hereditary, neither any so great nor so little in that country, but the bestowing of it is done immediately by the Emperor himself" (p. 21). The fact that many of the high officials are members of the great noble families does not deceive him, for he notes that every governor (or duke) has at his side a *d'iak* or secretary "to assist him or rather to direct him; for in executing of their commission, the diak does all" (p. 31). Furthermore, he observes, the government makes certain that no official is given an opportunity to ensconce himself in office. The "dukes and diaks are . . . changed ordinarily at every year's end . . . They are men of themselves of no credit nor favor with the people where they govern, being neither born nor brought up among them, nor yet having inheritance of their own there or elsewhere" (pp. 31v–32). Any Englishman of the 1590's reading these lines would instantly compare the situation with that prevailing in his own country, where the local government was as a rule entrusted to officials (lieutenant-governors and the deputies) who were native to the region, and held in it extensive properties.

In the second place, the Russian monarchy by a great variety of means assures the disintegration of the great noble families. Among these, Fletcher mentions measures which historians have come to regard as instrumental in the monarchy's triumph over the old aristocracy: preferential treatment of the service gentry, the establishment of the *oprichnina*,[52] and the forceful transfer of nobles from their patrimonial estates to distant provinces "where they might have neither favor, nor authority, not being native nor well known there" (p. 26v). The tsar also forces noble women into convents "to keep them unmarried from continuing the blood or stock which he would have extinguished" (p. 89v).

By these measures, partly political and partly social, the Russian monarchy has reduced the nobility to a condition in which it poses no threat. "Now [the nobles] hold their authorities, lands, lives and all at the Emperor's pleasure, as the rest do" (p. 25; cf. p. 46). The contrast with the vigorous and self-confident English nobility of Elizabethan times is as obvious as it must have been intentional.

As for the clergy and commons, Fletcher does not see much possibility of either group challenging the authority of the tsar.

[52] In dealing with the *oprichnina* Fletcher says that "nobles" were enrolled in both the *oprichnina* and *zemshchina*, the criterion being loyalty to the tsar (p. 25v). This view contrasts with that dominant until recently in Russian historiography which held that the *oprichnina* had been established as an institution formed of the gentry to destroy the great nobility assigned to the *zemshchina*. It is interesting to note that most recent research confirms Fletcher's interpretation. Monographs by S. B. Veselovskii (*Issledovaniia po istorii oprichniny*, Moscow, 1963) and A. A. Zimin (*Oprichnina Ivana Groznogo*, Moscow, 1964) show that the *oprichnina* contained both nobles and gentry, and was directed not against the upper nobility as such but against all persons regarded as disloyal by Ivan IV. The prevailing earlier opinion rested in part on a misreading of Fletcher. Cf. Zimin, p. 344.

Introduction

In a long and in part very biased account of Russian religion and the Russian church, he depicts the clergy as too rich and too ignorant to participate seriously in public life. It devotes all its energies to the management of its great landed properties and the pursuit of trade, and prefers to suffer in silence occasional spoliation rather than to stand up to the monarchy and risk losing all it has (p. 42v). "The clergy of Russia," Fletcher says, "as well concerning their lands and revenues, as their authority and jurisdiction, are altogether ordered and over-ruled by the Emperor and his council, and have so much, and no more of both as their pleasure does permit them." (p. 83v) Fletcher's characterization of the Russian clergy as preoccupied with agricultural management and trade, ignorant, depraved, and ready to back the autocracy to the hilt as the price of preserving its wealth, conforms in general with the picture we obtain from contemporary Russian sources.

The merchants do not appear as a separate category in Fletcher's narrative; nor are they so treated in other sixteenth-century English accounts of Russia.[53] As may be gathered from Ivan's contemptuous reference to them in a letter to Elizabeth (cited above, pp. 11–12), they were then considered merely a low breed of commoners. The term *muzhiki torgovye* — "trading boors" — indicates that clearly enough. As far as the English were concerned, the only important traders in Russia were the tsar, who accumulated merchandise from tribute, and the monasteries.

The whole massive structure whose ultimate purpose is the exploitation of the country for the benefit of the monarch rests, in Fletcher's view, on the ignorance and depravity of the common people. His devastating description of Russian manners and morals has earned him a bad reputation among some Russians and in large measure accounts for the troubles his book subse-

[53] Ruffman, *Das Russlandbild*, pp. 110–111.

[32]

quently had with Imperial as well as Soviet censorship. He has been accused of being hostile to the Russians and giving an unfair picture of their intellectual and moral condition.[54] The charge of antipathy toward Russians is not quite just. Certainly, Fletcher had his reasons to dislike the country. Yet it must be noted that his antipathy was invariably directed against the regime, and never against the people. He speaks of the Russians as a nation "of reasonable capacities," "of natural wit," and regrets their lack of opportunities "that some other nations have to train up their wits in good nurture [i.e., education] and learning" (p. 48 and 115v). He shows much sympathy for the "poor people . . . now so oppressed with intolerable servitude" and hopes they may some day be given a government "of some better temper and milder constitution" (p. 17). Fletcher nowhere states that the Russians have a tyrannical government because they are uncivilized, but, on the contrary, explicitly says that they are uncivilized because they have a tyrannical government. One of the principal premises and conclusions of his account is that tyranny breeds barbarism.

Furthermore, what Fletcher has to say about the general cultural level of the population finds ample confirmation in other contemporary accounts, native as well as foreign. One late nineteenth-century historian, drawing on a large body of sixteenth-century literature — much of it of Russian origin — drew a picture of Russian society of that time every bit as devastating as Fletcher's.[55] The picture which emerges from other English accounts is similar.[56] The concensus is so overwhelming — one

[54] The charge was first levied by Slavophile publicists, from whom Fletcher was defended by the westerners. See the anonymous article (written by A. Pypin), "Dzhil's Fletcher," *Sovremennik*, No. 3 (1865), Part 1, pp. 105–132.

[55] I. Preobrazhenskii, *Nravstvennoe sostoianie russkogo obshchestva v XVI veke po sochineniiam Maksima Greka i sovremennym emu pamiatnikam* (Moscow, 1881). Russian sources, in conceding the low moral level of the population, often blamed it on foreign (i.e., western) influences. See Seredonin, *Sochinenie Dzhil'sa Fletchera*, pp. 160–162.

[56] Ruffman, *Das Russlandbild*, 135–144.

may almost say, unanimous — that it cannot be ascribed simply to prejudice or misunderstanding.

The ordinary sixteenth-century Russian, as he emerges from the narrative of Fletcher and other contemporaries, is given to lying and cheating, idleness, and inveterate 'round-the-clock drinking. He is also addicted to a variety of "sins": "whoredoms, adulteries, and like uncleanness of life" (p. 116v). The distinction of Fletcher here, as in other parts of his narrative, is that he goes beyond mere condemnation to the causes. He raises the question why a people of "reasonable capacities" and "national wit" should sink into so barbarous a condition. He places the blame directly on the government, which he accuses of having an interest in keeping the people ignorant "that they may be fitter for the servile condition wherein now they are, and have neither reason nor valor to attempt innovation": for "a man of spirit and understanding, helped by learning and liberal education can hardly endure a tyrannical government" (pp. 48 and 85v). The monarchy, assisted by the nobility and clergy, enter, in Fletcher's view, into a deliberate conspiracy to maintain the population in ignorance and to prevent it from learning of life abroad.

This end is furthered by the policy of relentless fiscal exaction by the government and its agents, which breeds duplicity, indolence, and the habit of living at mere subsistence level:

The great oppression over the poor commons makes them to have no courage in following their trades: for that the more they have the more danger they are in, not only of their goods but of their lives also. And if they have anything, they conceal it all they can . . . I have seen them sometimes when they have laid open their commodities for a liking [for approval] . . . to look still behind them and towards every door, as men in some fear that looked to be set upon and surprised by some enemy. Whereof asking the cause, I found it to be this, that they have doubted lest some nobleman or *syn boiarskii* of the Emperor had been in company, and so laid a train for them to pray upon their commodities perforce. This makes the people (though otherwise hardened to bear any toil) to give themselves much to idleness and drinking, as passing for no more than from hand to mouth. (pp. 46v–47v).

Fletcher calls attention to two additional features which reinforce the grip of the monarchy over the nation. First is the rigidity of the social system. He notes with great insight that it is virtually impossible for a Russian to change his social status, and ascribes this practice to political considerations: "This order that binds every man to keep his rank and several degree[s] wherein his forefathers lived before him is more meet to keep [the Emperor's] subjects in servile subjection . . . than to advance any virtue or to breed any rare or excellent quality in nobility or commons, as having no farther reward nor preferment whereunto they may bend their endeavors" (p. 49).

The second is lawlessness. Fletcher correctly states that Russia had no written laws "save only a small book" (p. 53) — meaning the Code of Ivan IV, issued in 1550 — and rightly stresses the great importance of spoken or customary law. As an Englishman and a lawyer he was shocked by the submissiveness of judges, and the authority of the tsar and his council to give verdicts and to grant pardons (p. 21v).

The total picture of Russian society as it emerges from Fletcher's description is of an interlocking system of economic exploitation, the ultimate aim of which is, regardless of the consequences, to enrich the monarch. The words which Fletcher puts in the mouth of Ivan IV, whether true or apocryphal, describe Fletcher's own view of the matter as practiced in Russia: that the nation is like a beard or like a flock of sheep "that must needs be shorn once a year at the least to keep them from being overladen with their wool" (p. 14). The fleecing is done directly and indirectly: directly by an elaborate system of exactions, which Fletcher

[35]

enumerates in detail (chapter 12), and indirectly by first allowing the officials to rob the people, and then arresting these officials and confiscating their ill-gotten gains. The low level of culture combined with lawlessness which breeds social conflict assures the preservation of this despotic regime.

The whole system is so firmly consolidated in its political, social, and cultural elements that there is little possibility of Russia evolving toward that government of "better temper and milder constitution" which he hoped Russians would some day secure. In a passage which is one of the most remarkable in a book abounding in remarkable passages, Fletcher addresses himself to a question which has much vexed political thought in the twentieth century: whether an all-embracing absolutism is capable of peaceful evolution toward a more liberal system. His answer is negative. He says it would be "a hard matter to alter the state of the Russe government as it now stands," and justifies this view as follows (pp. 33v–34v):

First, because they have none of the nobility able to make head. As for the lords of the four *chetverti* or *tetrarchies* they are men of no nobility, but diaks advanced by the Emperor, depending on his favor, and attending only about his own person. And for the dukes that are appointed to govern under them, they are but men of a titular dignity . . . of no power, authority, nor credit, save that which they have out of the office for the time they enjoy it. Which does purchase them no favor but rather hatred of the people, for as much as they see that they are set over them not so much for any care to do them right and justice as to keep them under in a miserable subjection, and to take the fleece from them not once in the year (as the owner from his sheep) but to pull and clip them all the year long. Besides the authority and rule which they bear is rent and divided into many small pieces, being divers of them in every great shire, limited besides with a very short time; which gives them no scope to make any strength nor to contrive such an enterprise if happily they intended any matter of innovation. As for the common people . . .

besides their want of armor and practice of war (which they are kept from of purpose) they are robbed continually both of their hearts and money (besides other means), sometimes by pretence of some service to be done for the common defence, sometimes without any show at all of any necessity of Commonwealth or Prince. So that there is no means either for [the] nobility or people to attempt any innovation, so long as the military forces of the Emperor (which are the number 8000[o] at the least in continual pay) hold themselves fast and sure unto him and to the present state. Which needs they must do being of the quality of soldiers and enjoying withal that free liberty of wronging and spoiling of the commons at their pleasure which is permitted them of purpose, to make them have a liking of the present state. As for the agreement of the soldiers and commons, it is a thing not to be feared, being of so opposite and contrary practice much one to the other. This desperate state of things at home makes the people for the most part to wish for some foreign invasion which they suppose to be the only means to rid them of the heavy yoke of this tyrannous government.

The country, desolate and apathetic, "so full of grudge and mortal hatreds, . . . will not be quenched (as it seems now) til it burn [out] into a civil flame" (p. 26). The foreign invasion and the civil war which Fletcher expected came to Russia fifteen years later.

Of the Russe Commonwealth ran into difficulties from the moment of its appearance.

The Muscovy Company had had enough trouble with the Russian government to be acutely disturbed by a book written by an ambassador who had acted in Moscow on its behalf in which Russia and its country were described in the blackest colors. It feared in particular that the Russians would seize upon passages casting aspersions on Tsar Fedor and his protector Boris Godunov to cancel its surviving rights. As soon as the book was out, therefore, the company formally petitioned William Cecil to suppress it. In their petition the merchants nowhere accused Fletcher either of falsehoods or of inaccuracies, but merely of making statements offensive to the Russians. The request was granted, and the book was withdrawn from circulation.[57]

Of the Russe Commonwealth was reprinted in its entirety in 1643, at the height of the controversy between parliament and king and on the eve of the English civil war. At that time Fletcher's account acquired particular relevance as a protest against royal absolutism. This version was published again in 1657. Afterwards, the book fell into oblivion. Since all these integral versions became very rare, the public knew Fletcher's account mostly from expurgated versions which appeared in various compendia of travel accounts.[58]

Of the Russe Commonwealth came back into circulation early in the nineteenth century when it was discovered by Russian historians. Karamzin located a copy of the 1591 edition in the archive of the Ministry of Foreign Affairs, and referred to it frequently in the ninth and tenth volumes of his *History*, published in the 1820's. In his opinion, Fletcher gave on the whole a just estimate of sixteenth-century Russia.[59] Karamzin's severe condemnation of Ivan IV, which earned him the disapproval of Russian reactionaries, was in no small measure due to Fletcher's evidence. Sergei Solov'ev, another great nineteenth-century historian, also relied heavily on Fletcher, as did every subsequent historian writing on the sixteenth century. But much as it was used by specialists, the book itself remained inaccessible to the general public.

An attempt to remedy this situation was made in 1845 by a

---

[57] See Appendix C. Evidence that the book was in fact suppressed can be found in Berry, *The English Works of Giles Fletcher*, p. 153.

[58] See bibliography below.

[59] N. Karamzin, *Istoriia gosudarstva Rossiiskogo*, volume X, note 343.

group of archivists working in the Russian Ministry of Foreign Affairs. The Archive of this ministry was in the first half of the nineteenth century an active center of intellectual and scholarly life, in part thanks to its unique collection of books and documents on Russian relations with the West. With the encouragement of the enlightened director of the Archive, Prince M. A. Obolenskii, the archivists undertook to translate into Russian some of the most important foreign accounts of Muscovite Russia, beginning with Herberstein's and Fletcher's. In so doing they took advantage of a regulation which exempted from censorship materials bearing on the period antedating the Romanov dynasty, that is, prior to 1613. Fletcher's book was translated by one D. I. Gippius, and edited by the legal historian N. V. Kalachov. The text was ready in 1847, at which time Obolenskii made arrangements with the Imperial Moscow Society of Russian History and Antiquities to have the translation as well as the full original English text come out in its quarterly Proceedings (*Chteniia*).[60] The Gippius-Kalachov translation appeared under Obolenskii's editorship in the twenty-third number of the Proceedings, issued in September 1848.

One can hardly conceive of a less oportune time for the publication of a book as critical of Russia as Fletcher's. Nicholas I, always a conservative, had been thrown into panic by the revolutionary wave which had swept Europe in the spring of 1848, and had adopted a policy of extreme reaction. The government now made a genuine effort to base its internal policy on the ambiguous triad which the Minister of Education, Count S. S. Uvarov, had casually formulated in 1832 in his annual report: Orthodoxy, Autocracy, Nationality. One of the unwritten axioms

[60] S. A. Belokurov, " 'Delo Fletchera,' 1848–1864 gg.," *Chteniia Imperatorskogo Moskovskogo Obshchestva Istorii i Drevnosti Rossiiskikh*, vol. 3 (234), 1910, Section II, pp. 1–40; A. A. Titov, "Istoriia pervogo perevoda sochineniia Fletchera," in *O gosudarstve russkom — sochinenie Fletchera*, 3rd ed. (St. Petersburg, 1906), pp. vii–xiv.

of this doctrine was the sanctity of Russia's past. Only a year before, the censors had prohibited the publication of a Russian translation of Herberstein's *Commentaries*, an innocuous work compared to Fletcher's.[61]

It was apparently no coincidence that the very first recipient of the Proceedings containing Fletcher's work was Count Uvarov himself. Uvarov had been engaged in a personal feud with the chairman of the Imperial Moscow Society which sponsored the edition, at whose hands he had suffered the previous year a humiliating defeat in a bureaucratic squabble. Some well-wisher (rumor blamed the writer Shevyrev or the historian Pogodin) brought the issue to his attention, and the minister could now enjoy his revenge. Uvarov quickly perused the text, learned the names of the persons responsible for the publication, and within an hour notified Nicholas. The punishment was swift. The publication of the Proceedings was suspended, the chairman of the society was reprimanded by Nicholas personally and forced to resign, and the wholly innocent secretary to the society temporarily was deprived of his professorship at Moscow and was ordered to Kazan. Curiously, Obolenskii himself suffered no harmful consequences. All of the nearly one thousand copies of the Proceedings with the offending text which had been distributed to subscribers were recalled, except for four left in the possession of eminent and trusted persons. The impounded copies of the journal, as well as proofs of the English text scheduled for future publication, were placed under seal in storage. Efforts to lift the ban on Fletcher in the more enlightened reign of Nicholas's successor, Alexander II, were unavailing. But somehow the impounded copies disappeared, and when early in the present century a search was made for them in the

---

[61] V. S. Ikonnikov, *Opyt Russkoi istoriografii*, Vol. I, Pt. 2 (Kiev, 1892), p. 1430; Kliuchevskii, *Skazaniia inostrantsev*, p. 315.

storage where they had been placed in 1848, not a single one could be found.[62]

Of the Russe Commonwealth was republished in its integral form by the Hakluyt Society in 1856, under the editorship of E. A. Bond. The first legal Russian edition appeared in the midst of the Revolution of 1905.

RICHARD PIPES

[62] Belokurov, " 'Delo Fletchera,' " pp. 37–38.

OF
THE RVSSE
Common Wealth.

O R

MANER OF GO-

uernement by the Ruſſe
Emperour, (commonly called the
Emperour of *Moskouia)* with
the manners, and faſhions
of the people of that
Countrey.

⁂

The Contents are noted in the Table, ſet downe before the beginning of the Booke.

AT LONDON

Printed by T. D. for
Thomas Charde.
1591.

To the Queenes moſt ex-
cellent Maieſtie.

 Oſt gracious Soueraigne, beeyng employed in your Maieſties ſeruice to the Emperour of *Ruſſia*, I obſerued the State, and manners of that Countrey . And hauing reduced the ſame into ſome order , by the way as I returned, I haue preſumed to offer it in this ſmal Booke to your moſt excellent Maieſtie. My meaning was to note thinges for mine owne experience, of more importaunce then delight, and rather true then ſtrange . In

A 3   their

Most gratious soveraign, beeing employed in your Highnes service in the Countrey of *Russia*, I did what I could to learn the state of that common wealth, and their manner of Government. Whearof having gott soom good and true intelligence, I have reduced the same into order, and presumed to offer it to your Highnes, if it please yow to bee

their maner of gouernment, your Highnesse may see both: A true and strange face of a *Tyrannical state*, (most vnlike to your own) with out true knowledge of G O D, without written Lawe, without common iustice: saue that which proceedeth from their *Speaking Lawe*, to wit, the Magistrate who hath most neede of a Lawe, to restraine his owne iniustice. The practise hereof as it is heauy, and grieuous to the poore oppressed people, that liue within those Countreyes: so it may giue iust cause to my selfe, and other your Maiesties faithfull subiects, to acknowledge our happines on this behalfe, and to giue God thankes for your Maiesties most Princelike, and gracious gouernment: as also

DEDICATORIE.

also to your Highnesse more ioy,
and contentment in your royall
estate, in that you are a Prince of
subiectes, not of slaues, that are
kept within duetie by loue, not
by feare. The Almightie stil blesse
your Highnes with a most long,
and happy reigne in this life,
and with Christ Iesus in
the life to come.

*Your Maiesties most humble
subiect, and seruant*

G. Fletcher.

allso to your Maiestie cawse of reioycing, in that yow are a Prince of subiects not of
slaves, that are tied to their obedience with love, not with fear. The Lord allmightie
bless your Highnes with all his good blessinges.
   Your Maiesties most humble subiect, and servant.
                                                        G. Fletcher.

[from the manuscript]

The order of the Discourse

1. The description of the Contrey.

> 1. The bredth, length, and Shyres of Russia.
> 2. The Soyle, and Clymat.
> 3. The natiue commodities of the Contrey.

2. Their policye.

> 1. The setting or ordering of their State.
>> 4. The state or manner of their gouerment vnder the Prynce.
>> 5. Their Parliaments, and manner of holding them.
>> 6. The Russe Nobilitie, and meanes whereby it is kept in an vnder proportion agreeable to that State.
>> 7. The manner of gouerning their Proiuinces or Shyres.
>> 8. The Emperours priuie Counsell.
>> 9. The Emperours Customes, and other reuenewes, and what they amount vnto with the Sophismes practised for the encreasing of them.
>> 10. The Russe Communaltie, and their state or condition.
>
> 2. Their iudiciall proceeding.
>> 11. Their Judiciall Offices with theire manner of proceedinge.
>
> 3. Their prouision for warres.
>> 12. The Emperours forces for his warres, with their chiefe officers, and theire Salary.
>> 13. Their manner of mustering, armour, prouision for vittaile, and encampinge.
>> 14. Theire order in marching, charging, and martiall discipline.
>> 15. Theire Colonies and pollicie in maynteyninge theire purchases by Conquest.
>> 16. Theire Borderers, with whome they haue most to doe in warre and peace.
>
> 4. Theyre church gouerment.
>> 17. The Church offices and degrees.
>> 18. Theire Leiturgie, and forme of Church seruice, with theire manner of administring the Sacraments.
>> 19. The doctrine of the Russe Churche.
>> 20. Their manner of solempnizing Mariages.
>> 21. The other Ceremonyes of the Russe Churche.

3. Their Oeconomie, or priuat behauiour.
> 22. The Emperours domestique or priuat behauiour.
> 23. The Emperors houshold, and offices of his house.
> 24. The priuat behauior, and manners of the Russe People.

The sum of this discourse conteining the

1. Cosmographie of the Countrie.
1. The breadth and length of the Countrie, with the names of the Shires.
2. The Soyle and Clymate.
3. The natiue commodities of the Countrie.
4. The chiefe cities of Russia.

2. Policie.

1. The ordering of their State.
5. The house or stocke of the Russe Emperour.
6. The maner of inauguration of the Russe Emperours.
7. The forme or manner of their publique gouernment.
8. Their Parliamentes and manner of holding them.
9. The Russe Nobilitie, and meanes whereby it is kept in an vnder proportion agreeable to that State.
10. The manner of gouerning their Prouinces, or Shires.
11. The Emperours priuie Counsell.
12. The Emperours Customes and other Reuenues, & what they amount vnto, with the Sophismes practised for the encrease of them.
13. The Russe communaltie & their condition.

2. Their iudicial proceeding.
14. Their publique Iustice and manner of proceeding therein.

3. Their warlike prouisions.
15. The Emperours forces for his warres, with the officers and their Salaries.
16. Their manner of mustering, armour, prouision for vittaile, encamping, &c.
17. Their order in marching, charging, and their martiall discipline.
18. Their colonies and pollicie in mainteyning their purchases by conquest.
19. Their borderers, with whom they haue to doo in warre and peace.
20. most

4. Their Ecclesiastical State.
21. Their Church offices, and degrees.
22. Their Leiturgie or forme of Church seruice, with their manner of administring the Sacraments.
23. The doctrine of the Russe Church.
24. Their manner of solemnizing marriages.
25. The other Ceremonies of the Russe Church.

3. Oeconomie or priuat behauiour.
26. The Emperours domestique or priuate behauiour.
27. The Emperours houshold, and offices of his house.
28. The priuate behauiour, and manners of the Russe people.

NOTE: This outline appeared on page A4v in the 1591 edition, facing the first page of the first chapter. Its position has been changed in the present edition to facilitate comparison with the variant.

*The defcription of the Countrie of Rufia,
with the breadth, length, and names
of the Shires.*

The 1. Chapter,

 He countrie
of *Ruffia* was
fometimes cal-
led *Sarmatia.* It
chaunged the
name (as fome
do fuppofe) for
that it was par-
ted into diuerfe
fmall, and yet abfolute gouernments, not
depending, nor being fubiect the one to the
other. For *Ruffe* in that tongue doth fig-
nifie afmuch as to parte, or diuide. The
Ruffe reporteth that foure brethren, *Tru-
bor*, *Rurico*, *Sinees*, and *Variuus*, diuided
among them the North parts of the countrie. Likewife that the Southpartes were
poffeffed by foure other, *Kio*, *Scieko*, *Cho-
ranus*, and their fifter *Libeda:* each calling
B   his

● (24–25) The *Russe* reporteth . . . [to end of paragraph on p. 1v] *omitted.*

his territorie after his owne name . Of
this partition it was called *Ruffia*, about the
yeare from Chrift 860 . As for the coniecture which I find in fome Cofmographers,
that the *Ruffe* nation borrowed the name of
the people called *Roxellani*, and were the very fame nation with them, it is without all
good probabilitie: both in refpect of the ety-
mologie of the word (which is very far fet)
Strabo in his and efpecially for the feat and dwelling of
7. booke of that people, which was betwixt the two ri-
Geogr. uers of *Tanais* and *Borifthenes*,(as *Strabo* reporteth) quite an other way from the coun-
trey of *Ruffia*.

When it bare the name of *Sarmatia*, it was
diuided into two chiefe parts: the *White*, and
the *Blacke*. The *White Sarmatia* was all that
part that lieth towardes the North, and on
the fide of *Liefland:* as the Prouinces now
called *Duyna*, *Vagha*, *Vftick*, *Vologda*, *Cargapolia*, *Nouogradia*, &c: whereof *Nouograd velica* was the Metropolite, or chiefe cittie.
Blacke Sarmatia was all that countrey that
lieth Southward, towards the *Euxin*, or *Black
Sea:* as the dukedome of *Volodemer* of *Mofko*, *Rezan*, &c. Some haue thought that the
Gen.10. name of *Sarmatia* was firft taken, from one
Iofeph.l.1. *Sarmates*, whom *Mofes* and *Iofephus* call *A-
cap.14.* *farmathes*, fonne to *Ioktan*, and nephew to
Heber, of the pofteritie of *Sem*. But this feemeth

(1–14) *omitted*. (26–30) Some haue thought . . . [to end of paragraph on p. 2]
omitted.

meth to be nothing but a coniecture taken
out of the likenes of the name *Asarmathes.*
For the dwelling of all *Ioktans* posteritie is
described by *Moses,* to haue beene betwixt
Mescha or *Masius* (an hill of the *Amonites*)
and *Sephace* , neare to the riuer *Euphrates.*
Which maketh it very vnlikely ,that *Asar-*
mathes should plant any colonies so far off
in the North and Northwest countries. It is
bounded Northward by the *Lappes* and the
North *Ocean.* On the Southside by the *Tar-*
*tars,*called *Chrimes* . Eastward they haue the
Nagaian Tartar, that possesseth all the countrie on the East side of *Volgha,*towards the
Caspian sea,On the West and Southwest border lie *Lituania, Liuonia* and *Polonia.*

   The whole country being now reduced vnder the gouernment of one,coteyneth thefe
chief Prouinces or Shires. *Volodemer,*(which
beareth the first place in the Emperours stile,
becaufe their houfe came of the Dukes of
that countrey) *Mosko , Nisnouogrod, Plesko,*
Smolensko , Nouogrod velica (or *Nouogrod* of
the low countrey) *Rostoue, Yaruslaue, Bealo-*
zera, Bezan, Duyna, Cargapolia, Mefchora, Va-
gha, Vstuga, Ghaletfa. Thefe are the naturall
shires perteyning to *Ruffia,* but far greater &
larger then the shires of England , though
not fo well peopled. The other countries or
prouinces which the *Ruffe* Emperours haue

         B 2   gotten

The borders of Ruffia.

The shires of Ruffia.

5

10

15

20

25

30

The breadth, length, and

The Prouinces or countries got by conquest. gotten perforce added of late to their other dominion, are thefe which follow *Twerra, Youghoria, Permia, Vadska, Boulghoria, Chernigo, Oudoria, Obdoria, Condora,* with a great part of *Siberia :* where the people though they be not natural *Ruffes,* yet obey the Emperour of *Ruffia,* and are ruled by the lawes of his countrie, paying cuftomes and taxes, as his owne people doe. Befides thefe hee hath vnder him the kingdomes of *Cazan* and *Aftracan,* gotten by conqueft not long fince. As for all his poffefsion in *Lituania* (to the number of 30. great townes and more,) with *Narue* and *Dorp* in *Liuonia,* they are quite gone, beyng furprifed of late yeares by the kinges of *Poland* and *Sweden.* Thefe Shires and Prouinces are reduced all into foure *IurifdiEtions,* which they call *Chetfyrds* (that is) *Tetrarchies,* or *Fourthparts.* Wherof we are to fpeake in the title or chapter, concerning the Prouinces , and their manner of gouernment.

The bredth and length ofthe countrie. The whole countrie is of great length and breadth. From the North to the South (if you meafure from *Cola* to *Aftracan* which bendeth fomewhat Eaftwarde) it reacheth in length about 4260. verft, or miles. Notwithftanding the Emperour of *Ruffia* hath more territorie Northward, far beyond *Cola* vnto the riuer of *Tromfchua,* that runneth a 1000. **verft**

(1–2) gotten . . . follow/Whereto are added   (21–22) manner of government./manner of government. It is bordered Northward by the *Lappes* and the North Ocean: On the Southside by the *Tartars* called *Chimmes.* Eastward they have the *Nagaian* Tartar it possesseth all the contrey on the East side of *Volgha* toward the *Caspian* Sea. On the west and Southwest border lieth *Lituania* and *Polonia.*   (27) verst, or miles./verse or Myles, as may appeare by the Journall sett downe in the end of this booke.   (30) *Tromschua/Tromscua*

verſt,welnie beyód *Pechinga,*neare to *Ward-
bouſe,* but not intire nor clearly limited ,by
reaſon of the kings of *Sweden* and *Denmark,*
that haue diuers townes there , aſwell as the
Ruſſe , plotted togither the one with the o-
ther : euery one of them claiming the whole
of thoſe North parts as his owne right. The
breadth (if you go from that part of his territorie that lieth fartheſt Weſtwarde on the
Narue ſide,to the parts of *Siberia* eaſtward,
where the Emperour hath his garriſons) is
4400.verſt or thereabouts. A verſt(by their
reckoning)is a 1000.paſes, yet leſſe by one
quarter then an Engliſh mile. If the whole
dominion of the *Ruſſe* Emperour were all
habitable , and peopled in all places, as it is
in ſome , hee would either hardly hold it all
within one regiment,or be ouer mightie for
all his neighbour Princes.

Of the Soyle and Climate.

The 2. Chapter.

He ſoyle of the countrie for
the moſt part is of a ſleight
ſandie moulde , yet very
much different one place
from another,for the yeeld
of ſuch thinges as grow out
B 3 of

(1) verſt . . . *Pechinga/*verse from beyond *Pechingha* (1–2) *Wardbouse/Wardhows*
(14) an English mile./an English mile. The countrye hath many deserts and wast
growndes within yt especiallye beetwixt *Perme* and *Siberia* and on the north syde betwixt *Cargapolia* and Cola.

of the earth. The countrie Northwards towards the partes of S. *Nicolas* and *Cola*, and Northeaft towards *Siberia*, is all very barren, and full of defert woods by reafon of the clymat, and extremitie of the colde in winter time. So likewife along the riuer *Volgha* betwixt the countries of *Cazan*, and *Aftracan*: where (notwithftanding the foyle is very fruitefull) it is all vnhabited, fauing that vpon the riuer *Volgha* on the weft fide, the Emperour hath fome fewe caftels with garrifons in them. This hapneth by means of the *Chrim Tartar*, that will neyther himfelfe plant townes to dwell there, (liuing a wilde and vagrant life) nor fuffer the *Ruffe* (that is farre off with the ftrength of his countrie) to people thofe partes. From *Vologda* (which lieth almoft 1700. verft from the porte of S. *Nicholas*) downe towardes *Mosko*, and fo towardes the fouth parte that bordereth vpon the *Chrim*, (which conteineth the like fpace of 1700. verft or there abouts) is a very fruitfull and pleafant countrie, yeelding pafture, and corne, with woods & waters in very great plentie. The like is betwixt *Rezan* (that lieth foutheaft frõ *Mosko*) to *Nouograd* and *Vobsko*, that reach fartheft towards the northweft. So betwixt *Mosko*, and *Smolensko* (that lieth fouthweft towards *Lituania*) is a very fruitful and pleafant foile.

The

The whole countrie differeth very much from it felfe, by reafon of the yeare; fo that a man would meruaile to fee the great alteration and difference betwixte the winter, and the fommer *Ruſſia* . The whole countrie in the winter lyeth vnder fnow, which falleth continually, and is fometime of a yarde or two thicke, but greater towardes the north . The riuers and other waters are all frofen vp a yarde or more thicke, how fwifte or broade fo euer they bee . And this continueth commonly fiue moneths, vz, from the beginning of Nouember till towardes the ende of March, what time the fnow beginneth to melte. So that it would breede a froft in a man to looke abroad at that time, and fee the winter face of that countrie. The fharpenefle of the ayre you may iudge of by this: for that water dropped downe or caft vp into the ayre, congealeth into Ife before it come to the ground. In the extremitie of winter, if you holde a pewter difhe or pot in your hand, or any other mettall (except in fome chamber where their warme ftoaues bee) your fingers will friefe fafte vnto it, and drawe of the fkinne at the parting. When you pafle out of a warme roome into a colde, you fhall fenfibly feele your breath to waxe ftarke, and euen ftifeling with the colde, as you draw it

The cold of Ruſſia.

in

in and out . Diuers not onely that trauell
abroad, but in the very markets, and ftreats
of their townes, are mortally pinched and
killed withall : fo that you fhall fee many
drop downe in the ftreates, many trauel-
lers brought into the townes fitting dead
and ftiffe in their fleddes. Diuers lofe their
nofes, the tippes of their eares, and the bals
of their cheekes, their toes, feete, &c. Many times when (the winter is very harde
and extreame) the beares and woolfes iffue
by troupes out of the woodes driuen by
hunger, and enter the villages, tearing and
rauening all they can finde: fo that the inhabitants are faine to flie for fafegard of their
liues. And yet in the Sommer time you fhall
fee fuch a new hew and face of a countrie, the
woods (for the moft part which are all of fir
and birch)fo frefh and fo fweet, the paftures
and medowes fo greene and well grow en,(&
that vpõ the fudden)fuch varietie of flowres,
fuch noyfe of birdes (fpecially of Nightin-
gales, that feeme to be more lowde and of a
more variable note then in other countries)
that a man fhall not lightly trauell in a more
pleafant countrie.

And this frefh and fpeedy grouth of the
fpring there, feemeth to proceede from the
benefite of the fnow : which all the winter
time being fpred ouer the whole countrie as

a

(9–16) Many times . . . of their liues *omitted.*

a white robe, & keeping it warme from the
rigour of the froſt, in the ſpring time (when
the ſunne waxeth warme, and diſſolueth it
into water) doth ſo throughly drench and
ſoake the ground, that is ſomewhat of a
ſleight and ſandy mould, & then ſhineth ſo
hotely vpon it againe, that it draweth the
hearbes and plants forth in great plenty and
varietie, in a very ſhort time. As the winter
exceedeth in colde, ſo the ſommer inclineth
to ouer much heat, ſpecially in the moneths
of Iune, Iuly, and Auguſt, being much war-
mer then the ſommer ayre in England.

The countrie throughout is very well watred with ſprings, riuers, & ozeraes, or lakes.
Wherein the prouidence of God is to bee
noted, for that much of the countrie beyng
ſo farre inland, as that ſome parte lieth a
1000. miles and more euery way from any
ſea yet it is ſerued with faire riuers, and that
in very great number, that emptiyng themſelues one into an other, runne all into the
ſea. Their lakes are many and large, ſome of
60. 80. 100. and 200. miles long, with
breadth proportionate.

The chief riuers are theſe 1. *Uolgha,* that
hath his head or ſpring at the roote of an
Aldertree, about 200. verſt aboue *Yaruſlaue,*
& groweth ſo big by the encreaſe of other
riuers by that time it commeth thither, that
it

The chief riuers of Ruſſia.

it is broad an Englifh mile and more, and fo runneth into the *Cafpian* fea, about 2800, verft or miles of length.

The next is *Borifthenes* (now called *Ne-per*) that diuideth the counrrie from *Litua-nia*, and falleth into the *Euxin* fea.

The third *Tanais* or *Don*, (the auncient bounder betwixt *Europe* and *Afia*) that ta-keth his head out of *Rezan Ozera*, and fo running through the countrie of the *Chrim Tartar*, falleth into the great fea lake, or meare, (called *Mæotis*) by the Citie of *Azou*. By this riuer (as the *Ruffe* reporteth) you may paffe from their citie *Mosko* to *Conftanti-nople*, and fo into all thofe partes of the world by water, drawing your boate (as their manner is) ouer a little *Ifthmus* or narrow flippe of lande, a fewe verfts ouerthwart. Which was proued not long fince by an Am-baffadour fent to *Conftantinople*, who paffed the riuer of *Moskua* and fo into an other cal-led *Ocka*, whence he drew his boate ouer in-to *Tanais*, and thence paffed the whole way by water.

The fourth is called *Duyna*, many hun-dred miles long, that falleth Northward in-to the Baye of Saint *Nicholas*, and hath great Alabafter rockes on the bankes towards the fea fide.

The fifth *Duna*, that emptieth into the
Baltick

---

(1) and more *omitted*. (7–8) *parenthetical phrase omitted*. (11) *Tartar omitted*.

Baltick fea by the towne *Riga.*

The fixt *Onega,* that falleth into the Bay at *Solouetsko* 90, verft from the port of Saint *Nicholas.* This riuer below the towne *Cargapolia* meeteth with the riuer *Volock,* that falleth into the *Finland* fea by the towne *Yama.* So that from the port of S. *Nicholas* into the *Finland* fea, and fo into the Sound, you may paffe all by water, as hath bene tried by the *Ruffe.*

The feuenth S*uchana,* that floweth into *Duyna,* and fo into the North fea.

The eight *Ocka,* that fetcheth his head from the borders of the *Chrim,* & ftreameth into *Volgha.*

The ninth *Moskua,* that runneth thorough the citie *Mosko,* and giueth it the name.

There is *Wichida* alfo a very large and long riuer that rifeth out of *Permia,* and falleth into *Volgha.* All thefe are riuers of very large ftreames, the leaft to be compared to the *Thames* in bigneffe, and in length farre more, befides diuers other. The Pole at *Mofko* is 55. degrees 10. minutes. At the porte of S.*Nicholas* towards the North 63. degrees and 50 minutes.

The

The 3. Chapter.

Or kindes of fruites, they haue Appels , Peares, plummes, cheries, redde and blacke, (but the blacke wild) a deene like a muske, millian , but more sweete & pleasant, cucumbers & goords (which they call *Arbouse*) rasps, strawberies, and hurtilberies , with many other bearies in great quantitie in euery wood and hedge. Their kindes of graine are wheat, rie, barley, oates, pease, buckway, psnytha , that in taste is somewhat like to rice. Of all these graynes the countrie yeeldeth very sufficient with an ouerplus quantitie , so that wheate is solde sometime for two alteens or ten pence starling the *Chetfird*, which maketh almost three English bushels.

Their rye is sowed before the winter, all their other graine in the spring time , & for the most parte in May. The *Permians* and some other that dwell far north, and in desert

fert places, are ferued from the partes that
lye more Southward, and are forced to make
bread fometimes of a kinde of roote (called
Vaghnoy) and of the middle rine of the firre
tree. If there be any dearth(as they accounted this laſt yeare, *An.* 1588. wheat and rye
beyng at 13. *alteens*, or 5. ſhillings 5. pence
ſtarling the *Chetfird*)the fault is rather in the
praɛtiſe of their Nobilitie that vſe to en-
groſſe it, then in the countrie it felfe.

    The natiue commodities of the coun-
trie (wherewith they ſerue both their owne
turnes, and ſende much abroad to the great
enriching of the Emperour, and his people)
are many and ſubſtantiall. Firſt, furres of
all ſortes. Wherein the prouidence of God
is to be noted,that prouideth a naturall remedie for them,to helpe the naturall inconuenience of their countrie by the colde of
the Clymat. Their chiefe furres are theſe,
Blacke fox,Sables,Luſernes, Dunne fox, Mar-
trones, Gurneſtalles or Armins, Laſets or Mi-
niuer, Beuer, Wuluerins, the skin of a great wa-
ter Ratte that ſmelleth naturally like muske,Ca-
laber or Gray ſquirrell,red ſquirrell,red,& white
Foxe. Beſides the great quantitie ſpent
within the countrie (the people beyng clad
all in furres the whole winter) there are
tranſported out of the countrie ſome yeares
by the marchants of *Turkie,Perſia,Bougharia,*
Georgia,

The chiefe commodities of the countria.

1.Furres.

5

10

15

20

25

30

(7) 13. *alteens*/15 alteens (7–8) or 5. shillings 5. pence starling *omitted*. (21)
Sables omitted. (25–26) *red, and white Foxe* . . . quantitie spent/redd & white Fox,
bysydes the furr of white *Sea wolves, white Beares, white hares* etc. Of theise kyndes of
Furres their store is soe great that bysydes the great quantitye spent

Georgia, *Armenia*, and some other of Chriſtendome to the value of foure or fiue hundred thouſand rubbels, as I haue heard of the Marchants. The beſt Sable furre groweth in the countrie of *Pechora*, *Momgoſorſkoy* and *Obdorskoy*, the worſer ſort in *Siberia*, *Perm*, and other places. The blacke fox and redde come out of *Siberia*, white & dun from *Pechora*, whence alſo come the white wolfe, and white Beare skin. The beſt Wuluerin alſo thence and from *Perm*. The beſt Martrons are from *Syberia*, *Cadam*, *Morum*, *Perm*, and *Cazan*. Lyſerns, Mineuer, and Armins, the beſt ar out of *Gallets*, and *Ouglites*, many from *Nouogrod*, and *Perm*. The Beauer of the beſt ſort breedeth in *Murmonskey* by *Cola*. Other cōmon furres, and moſt of theſe kindes grow in many, and ſome in all partes of the countrie.

2. Waxe. The ſecond cōmoditie is of Wax, whereof hath bene ſhipped into forraine countries (as I haue heard it reported by thoſe that beſt know it) the ſumme of 50000. pood yearlie, euery pood conteyning 40. pound, but now about 10000. pood a yeare.

3. Hony. The third is their Hony, whereof beſides an exceeding great quantitie ſpent in their ordinary drinks (which is *mead* of al ſorts) & their other vſes, ſome good quantitie is carried out of the countrie. The chiefe encreaſe

of

---

(5) countrie/countries (14) *Ouglites/Ougletsa* (26-27) Hony . . . quantitie/Hony whereof ther is carried out of the country some store besydes an excedinge great quantitye

of honie is in *Mordua* & *Cadam* neare to the
Cheremiſſen Tartar : much out of *Seuerskoy,*
Rezan, Morum, Cazan, Dorogoboſe, & *Vaſma,*

Fourthly, of Tallow they afoord a great 4. Tallow.
waight for tranſportation : not only for that 5
their countrie hath very much good ground
apt for paſturage of cattaile, but alſo by reaſon of their many Lents and other faſtes :
and partly becauſe their greater menne vſe
much waxe for their lightes, the poorer and 10
meaner ſorte birch dried in their ſtoaues,
and cut into long ſhiuers, which they call
Luchineos. Of tallow there hath bene ſhipped out of the realme a fewe yeares ſince a-
bout a 100000, pood yearely, now not paſt 15
300co. or thereabonts, The beſt yeeld of tallow is in the parts & territories of *Smolensko,*
Yaruſlaue, Ouglits, Nouogrod, and *Vologda, Ot-*
fer, and *Gorodetskey.*

An other principall commoditie is their 5. Hide. 20
Loſh and Cowe hide. Their Loſh or Buffe
hide is very faire and large. Their bull and
cowe hide (for oxen they make none, neyther yet weather) is of a ſmall ſiſe. There
hath bene tranſported by Marchants ſtran- 25
gers ſome yeares, a 100000. hydes, Now it is
decreaſed to a 30000, or thereabouts. Beſides great ſtore of goates skinnes, whereof
great numbers are ſhipped out of the countrie, The largeſt kind of Loſh or Buffe bree- 30
deth

(21-24) Their Losh or Buffe . . . small sise/The *Losh* hide very fair and large, the
O*x* hide but small

deth about *Roſtoue*, *Wichida*, *Nouogrod*, *Mo-rum*, and *Perm*, The leſſer ſorte within the kingdome of *Cazan*.

An other very great and principall com-moditie is their *Trane oyle*, drawen out of the ſeal fiſh . Where it will not bee impertinent to ſhewe the manner of their hunting the ſeal, which they make this oyle of : which is in this ſort . Towardes the ende of ſommer (before the froſt begin) they go downe with their boates into the Bay of S. *Nicholas*, to a cape called *Cuſconeſſe* or *Foxnoſe*, where they leaue their boates till the next ſpring tide. When the ſunne waxeth warme towarde the ſpring, and yet the yſe not melted with-in the Bay, they returne thither againe. Then drawing their boates ouer the ſea yſe, they vſe them for houſes to reſt and lodge in . There are commonly about 17. or 18. fleete of them , of great large boates, which diuide themſelues into diuers companies, fiue or ſix boates in a conſort.

They that firſt finde the haunt, fire a bea-con , which they carry with them for the nonce. Which being eſpied by the other co-panies, by ſuch among them as are appoyn-ted of purpoſe , they come altogither and compaſſe the ſeales round about in a ring, that lye ſunning themſelues togither vpon the yſe, comonly foure or fiue thouſand in a ſhole,

5   **6. Trane oyle.**

The man-ner of hun-ting the Seal fiſh.

10

15

20

25

30

(12) *Cuſconeſſe/Cuſkoneſs*   (22) boates in a conſort./boates in a conſort. Beinge thus divided they ſeeke up and downe for the haunt of the ſeales uppon the Iſe.

ſhoale, and ſo they inuade them euery man with his clubbe in his hand, if they hit them on the noſe, they are ſoone killed. If on the ſides or backe they beare out the blow,and many times ſo catche and holde downe the club with their teeth by main force, that the party is forced to cal for help to his fellowes. The manner of the Seals is, when they ſee themſelues beſet,to gather all cloſe together in a throng or plumpe , to ſway downe the yſe,and to breakit(if they can) which ſo ben-deth the yſe that many times it taketh the ſea water vpon it, and maketh the hunters to wade a foot or more deepe. After the ſlaugh-ter,when they haue killed what they can they fall to ſharing euery boate his part in equall portions: and ſo they flay them,taking from the body the skin,and the lard or fat withall that cleaueth to the skin.This they take with them,leauing the bodies behind,and ſo goe to ſhore. Where they digge pits in the groūd of a fadome and an halfe deepe, or there a-bout, and ſo taking the fat or larde off from the skinne,they throw it into the pit, and caſt in among it hoat burning ſtones to melt it withall. The vppermoſt and pureſt is ſolde & vſed to oyle wooll for cloth,the groſſer(that is of a red colour)they ſell to make ſope.

Likewiſe of *Ickary* or *Cauery*,a great quan-titie is made vpon the riuer of *Volgha* out of Ickary.
C   the

(26) ſolde & *omitted.*

the fiſh called *Bellougina*, the *Sturgeon*, the *Se-ueriga* & the *Sterledey*. Wherof the moſt part is ſhipped by *French* and *Netherlandiſh* marchants for *Italy* and *Spaine*, ſome by Engliſh marchants.

8. Hempe and flaxe. The next is of Flaxe and Hempe, whereof there hath bin ſhipped (as I haue heard marchants ſay) at the port of *Narue* a great part of a 100 ſhips ſmal & great yerely. Now, not paſt fiue. The reaſon of this abating and decreaſe of this & other cōmodities, that were wont to be tranſported in a greater quantitie, is the ſhutting vp of the port of the *Narue* towards the *Finland* ſea, which now is in the hands & poſſeſsion of the *Sweaden.* Likewiſe the ſtopping of the paſſage ouerland by the way of *Smolensko*, and *Plotsko*, by reaſō of their warres with the *Polonian*, which cauſeth the people to be leſſe prouidēt in mainteining and gathering theſe & like commodities, for that they lack ſales. Partly alſo for that the marchāts & Mouſicks (for ſo they cal the cōmon ſort of people) are very much diſcouraged by many heauy & intollerable exactions, that of late time haue bin impoſed vpon them: no man accounting that which he hathto be ſure his own. And therfore regard not to lay vp any thing, or to haue it before hand, for that it cauſèth thē many times to be fleeſed & ſpoiled not only of their goods, but

(15–17) *Sweaden . . . Plotsko/Sweden.* Lykewise the former passage by the way of *Smolensko* and *Plotsko*

but alfo of their liues. For the grouth of flaxe the prouince of *Uobsko* and the countrey about is the chiefe and only place. For hemp *Smolensko, Dorogobofe* and *Uafma.*

The countrey befides maketh great ftore of falt. Their beft falt is made at *Stararonfe* in very great quãtity, where they haue great ftore of falt wels, about 250. verft frõ the fea. At *Aftracan* falt is made naturally by the fea water, that cafteth it vp into great hils, and fo it is digged down, and caried away by the marchants & other that wil fetch it from thence. They pay to the Emperor for acknowledgement or cuftome 3. d. *Ruffe* vpon euery hundred weight. Befides thefe two, they make falt in many other places of the Realme, as in *Perm, Wichida, Totma, Kenitfma, Solouetske, Ocona, Bõbafey, & Nonocks.* al out of falt pits, faue at *Solouetskey,* which lieth neere to the fea. — 9. Salt. 5

Likewife of tarre they make a great quãtity out of their firre trees in the countrie of *Duyna & Smolensko,* whereof much is fent abroad. Befides thefe (which are all good and fubftantial commodities) they haue diuers other of fmaller account, that are natural and proper to that countrey : as the fifhe tooth (which they cal *Ribazuba* which is vfed both among thēfelues & the *Perfians & Bougariãs* that fetcht it from thence for beads, kniues, & fword hafts of Noblemen, & gentlemē, & for — 10. Tarre. 20 / 11. Ribazuba.

C 2

for diuers other vſes. Some vſe the powder of it againſt poyſon, as the Vnicornes horne. The fiſh that weareth it is called a *Morſe*, & is caught about *Pechora*. Theſe fiſhe teeth ſome of them, are almoſt two foote of length, and weigh eleuen or twelue pound apiece.

12. Slude.

In the prouince of *Corelia*, and about the riuer *Duyna* towardes the North ſea, there groweth a ſoft rocke which they call *Slude*. This they cut into pieces, and ſo teare it into thin flakes, which naturally it is apt for and ſo vſe it for glaſſe-lanthorns and ſuch like. It giueth both inwards and outwards a clearer light then glaſſe, and for this reſpect is better then either glaſſe or horne: for that it nei

13. Saltpeeter & brimſtone.

ther breaketh like glaſſe, nor yet will burne like the lanthorne. Saltpeter they make in many places, as at *Onglites*, *Yaruslaue* and *Vſtug*, and ſome ſmall ſtore of brimſtone vpon the riuer *Volgha*, but want skill to refine it.

14. Iron.

Their iron is ſomewhat brittle, but a great weight of it is made in *Corelia*, *Cargapolia*, and *Vſtug Theleſna*. Other myne they haue none growing within the Realme.

The ſtrãge beaſts, fiſh, foule, &c. that breed in *Ruſſia*.

Their beaſts of ſtrange kinds are the Loſh, the Ollen, the wilde Horſe, the Beare, the Woluering, or wood dogge, the Lyſerne, the Beauer the Sable, the Martron the blacke and dunne Foxe, the white Beare towardes the Sea coaſt of *Pechora*, the Gurnſtale, the Laſet

(23) Vstug Thelesna/*vstiug zshelesna* (30) Gurnstale,/*Gurnistall* or Armins

fet or Mineuer. They haue a kinde of Squir-
rel that hath growing on the pinion of the
fhoulder bone, a long tuft of haire, much like
vnto feathers with a farre broader tayle then
haue any other fquirrels, which they moue &
fhake as they leape from tree to tree, much
like vnto a wing. They skife a large fpace, and
feeme for to flie withall and therefore they
call them *Letach Vechfhe*, that is, the flying
fquirrels. Their hares and fquirrels in Sommer are of the fame colour with ours, in winter the Hare changeth her coate into milke
white, the fquirrell into gray, whereof commeth the *Calaber*.

They haue fallow Deere, the roe Bucke,
and goates very great ftore. Their horfes are
but fmall, but very fwift and harde, they trauell them vnfhod both winter and Sommer,
without all regard of pace. Their fheepe are
but fmall and beare coorfe, and harfh wooll.
Of foule, they haue diuers of the principall
kindes: Firft, great ftore of Hawkes, the Ea-
gle, the Gerfaulcon, the Slightfaulcon, the
Gofhawke, the Taffel, the Sparhawk, &c. But
the principall hawke that breedeth in the
countrey, is counted the Gerfaulcon.

Of other foules their principall kinds are
the fwanne tame and wilde, (whereof they
haue great ftore) the Storke, the Crane, the
Tedder, of the colour of a Feafant, but farre

C 3   bigger

5

10

15

20

25

30

(9) *Letach Vechshe/Letache vechshe* (15) roe Bucke/Roe, Bucke

bigger and liueth in the firre woods. Of Fealant and Partridge they haue very great plentie. An owle there is of a very great bignesse, more vglie to beholde then the owles of this countrey, with a broade face, & eares much like vnto a man.

For fresh water fish besides the common forts (as Carpe, Pikes Pearch, Tench, Roach, &c.) they haue diuers kinds very good & delicate: as the *Bellouga*, or *Bellougina* of 4. or 5. elnes long, the *Ositrina* or *Sturgeõ*, the *Seueriga*, & *Sterledy* somewhat in fashion and taste like to the *Sturgeon*, but not so thicke nor long. These 4. kinds of fish breed in the *volgha*, & are catched in great plenty, & serued thence into the whole Realme for a great food. Of the Roes of these foure kinds they make very great store of *Icary* or *Caueary* as was said before.

They haue besides these that breed in the *volgha* a fish called the *Riba bela*, or white salmon, which they account more delicate thẽ they do the redde salmon wherof also they haue exceeding great plentie in the riuers northward, as in *Duyna* the riuer of *Cola*, &c. In the Ozera or lake neere a towne called *Perislaue*, not far frõ the *Mosko*, they haue a smal fish which they call the fresh herring, of the fashion, and somewhat of the taste of a Sea-hearing. Their chiefe townes for
fish

---

(11) elnes/els (21) *Ribabela/Beaela Riba* (28–30) smal fish . . . Sea-hearing./ small Fishe of the Fashion and somewhat also of the tast of a Herringe which they call the *Selde* or Freshe water Heringe.

fiſh are, *Yaruſlaue*, *Bealozera*, *Nouogrod*, *A-ſtracan*, and *Cazan* : which all yeeld a large cuſtome to the Emperour euery yeere for their trades of fiſhing, which they practiſe in Sommer , but ſend it frozen in the Winter time into all partes of the Realme.

The chiefe Cities of Ruſia.

The 4, Chapter.

HE chiefe Cities of *Ruſſia* are, *Mosko* , *Nouograd*, *Roſtoue*, *Volodomer* , *Plesko*, *Smolensko*, *Iaruſlaue* , *Periſlaue*, *Niſnouograd*, *vologda* , *Uſtiuck* , *Golmigroe* , *Ca-zan*, *Aſtracan*, *Cargapolia*, *Columna.*

The citie of *Mosko* is ſuppoſed to be of *Mosko.* great antiquitie, though the firſt founder be vnknowen to the *Ruſſe.* It ſeemeth to haue takē the name from the riuer that runeth on the one ſide of the town. *Beroſus* the *Chaldean* in his 5. book telleth that *Nimroa* (whom other prophane ſtories cal *Saturn*)ſēt *Aſſyrius*, *Medus*, *Moſcus*, & *Magog* into *Aſia* to plant
C 4   colonies

Colonies there, and that *Moſcus* planted both in *Aſia* and *Europe*. Which may make ſome probability, that the city, or rather the riuer whereon it is built, tooke the denomination from this *Moſcus*: the rather bicauſe of the climate or ſituation, which is in the very fartheſt part and liſt of *Europe*, bordering vpon *Aſia*. The citie was much enlarged by one *Euan* or *Iohn*, ſonne to *Daniel*, that firſt changed his title of Duke into King: though that honour continued not to his poſterity: the rather becauſe he was inueſted into it by the Popes Legate, who at that time was *Innocentius* the fourth about the yeere 1 2 4 6. which was very much miſliked by the *Ruſſe* people, being then a part of the Eaſterne or Greeke Church Since that time the nameof this citie hath growen more famous, and better knowen to the worlde: inſomuch that not onely the prouince, but the whole countrey of *Ruſſia* is tearmed by ſome by the name of *Moſcouia* the Metropolite citie. The forme of this citie is in a manner round with three ſtrong walles, circuling the one within the other, and ſtreets lying betweene, wherof the inmoſt wall, and the buildings cloſed within it (lying ſafeſt as the heart within the bodie, fenced and watred with the riuer *Moskua*, that runneth cloſe by it) is all accounted the Emperours caſtle. The number of

houſes

houſes (as I haue heard)through the whole
citie being reckoned by the Emperour a
little before it was fired by the *Chrim*) was
41500. in all. Since the *Tartar* beſieged and
fired the town(which was in the yeare 1571.)
there lieth waſte of it a great breadth of
ground,which before was well ſet and planted with buildings, ſpecially that part on the
ſouth ſide of *Moskua*,built not long before
by *Baſilius* the Emperour for his garriſon of
ſouldiours, to whom he gaue priuiledge to
drinke Mead, & Beer at the drye or prohibited times , when other *Ruſſes* may drinke
nothing but water , and for that cauſe called
this newe citie by the name of *Naloi*, that is,
skinck or *poure in .* So that now the Citie of
Mosko is not much bigger then the citie of
London. The next in greatnes,and in a manner as large,is the citie *Nouograde*:where was
committed (as the *Ruſſe* ſaith) the memorable warre ſo much ſpoke of in ſtories of the
Scythian ſeruants, that tooke armes againſt
their maiſters : which they report in this
ſort : vz. That the *Boiarens* or Gentlemen of
Nouograde and the territorie about (which
onely are ſouldiers after the diſcipline of
thoſe countries) had warre with the *Tartars.*
Which being well perfourmed and ended by
the,they returned homewards. Where they
vnderſtood by the way that their *Cholopey*

or

Noungrad]

or bondſlaues whome they left at home, had in their abſence poſſeſſed their townes, lands, houſes, wiues, and all. At which newes being ſomewhat amaſed, and yet diſdayning the villanie of their ſeruants, they made the more ſpeed home: and ſo not farre from *Nouograd* met them in warlike manner marching againſt them. Whereupon aduiſing what was beſt to bee done, they agreed all to ſet vpon them with no other ſhewe of weapon but with their horſe whips (which as their manner is euery man rideth with all) to put them in remembrance of their ſeruile condition, thereby to terrifie them, & abate their courage. And ſo marching on & laſhing altogither with their whips in their hands they gaue the onſet. Which ſeemed ſo terrible in the eares of their villaines, and ſtroke ſuch a ſenſe into them of the ſmart of the whip which they had felt before, that they fled altogether like ſheepe before the driuers. In memory of this victory the *Nouogradiās* euer ſince haue ſtāped their coine(which they cal a *dingoe Nouogrodskoy* currāt through al *Ruſ-ſia*)with the figure of a horſeman ſhaking a whip a loft in his hand. Theſe two cities exceed the reſt in greatnes. For ſtrength their chieftownes are *Vobsko, Smolensko, Cazan* & *Aſtracan*, as liyng vpon the borders. But for

Iaruſlaue. ſituation *Iaruſlaue* farre exceedeth the reſt.

For

For befides the commodities that the foyle yeeldeth of pafture & corne, it lieth vpon the famous riuer *Volgha*, & looketh ouer it frō a high banke very faire & ftately to behold: wherof the towne taketh the name. For *Iaruflaue* in that tongue fignifieth as much as a faire or famous bake. In this towne (as may be ghefled by the name) dwelt the *Ruffe* king *vlademir* firnamed *Iaruflaue*, that married the daughter of *Harald* king of England, by mediation of *Sueno* the *Dane*, as is noted in the *Danifh* ftorie about the yeare 1067.

The other townes haue nothing that is greatly memorable, faue many ruines within their walles. Which fheweth the decreafe of the *Ruffe* people, vnder this gouernment. The ftreates of their cities and townes in fteed of pauing are planked with firre trees, plained and layed euen clofe the one to the other. Their houfes are of wood without any lime or ftone, built very clofe and warm with firre trees plained and piled one vpon an other. They are faftened together with dentes or notches at euery corner, and fo clafped faft together. Betwixt the trees or timber they thruft in moffe (whereof they gather plentie in their woods) to keepe out the ayre. Euery houfe hath a paire of ftaiers that lead vp into the chambers out of the yarde or ftreat after the Scottifh manner.

The manner of *Ruffe* buylding.

This

This building ſeemeth farre better for their countrie, then that of ſtone and bricke : as being colder and more dampiſh then their woodden houſes, ſpecially of firre, that is a dry and warme wood . Whereof the prouidence of God hath giuen them ſuch ſtore, as that you may build a faire houſe for twentie or thirtie rubbels or little more, where wood is moſt ſcant. The greateſt inconuenience of their woodden building is the aptnes for firing, which happeneth very oft and in very fearful ſort, by reaſon of the drineſſe and fatneſſe of the firre, that being once fired, burneth like a torch, and is hardly quenched till all be burnt vp.

Of the houſe or ſtocke of the *Ruſſe Emperours.*

The 5. Chapter.

He ſyrname of the imperiall houſe of *Ruſsia*, is called *Beala*. It tooke the originall (as is ſuppoſed) from the Kinges of *Hungarie*. Which may ſeeme the more probable for that the *Hungarian* Kings many yeares agoe haue borne that name : as appeareth by *Bonfinius* and

and other ſtories written of that countrie.
For about the yeare 1 o 5 9 mention is made
of one *Beala* that ſucceeded his brother *An-*
dreas, who reduced the *Hungarians* to the
Chriſtian faith from whence they were fallen
by atheiſme and Turkiſh perſwaſion before.
The ſecond of that name was called *Beala the*
blinde, after whom ſucceeded diuers of the
ſame name.

That their aunceſtrie came not of the *Ruſſe*   The houſe
nation, *Iuan vaſilowich* father to this Empe-   *Beala* not
rour would many times boaſt, diſdaining (as   naturall
ſhould ſeeme) to haue his progenie deriued   *Ruſſe.*
from the *Ruſſe* bloud. As namely to an Engliſh man his goldſmith,that had receiued bul-
lion of him to make certain plate: whom the
Emperour commaunded to looke well to his
waight. For my *Ruſſes* (ſayd he) are theeues
all . Whereat the workeman looking vpon
the Emperour, began to ſmile. The Emperour being of quicke conceipt, charged him
to tell him what he ſmiled at . If your Maieſtie will pardon me (quoth the goldſmith)
I will tell you. Your highneſſe ſaid that the
Ruſſes were all theeues, and forgot in the
meane while that your ſelfe was a *Ruſſe* . I
thought ſo (quoth the Emperour) but thou
art deceiued. For I am no *Ruſſe*,my aunceſtors
were *Germanes* (for ſo they account of the
Hungarians to be part of the *Germane* natio
though

though in deed they come of the *Hunnes.*
That inuaded thoſe countries and reſted in
thoſe parts of *Pannonia,*now called *Hungary.*
How they aſpired to the Dukedome of
Volodemer(which was their firſt degree,and
ingrafting into *Ruſsia*) and whether it were
by cóqueſt,or by marriage, or by what other
meanes, I could not learne any certentie a-
mong them. That from theſe beginnings of
a ſmall Dukedome (that bare notwithſtanding an abſolute gouernment with it, as at
that time did alſo the other Shires or Prouinces of *Ruſsia*)this houſe of *Beala* ſpred it
ſelfe foorth, and aſpired by degrees to the
monarchie of the whole countrie, is a thing
well knowen,and of very late memorie. The
chiefe of that houſe that aduaunced the
ſtocke,and enlarged their dominions, were
the three laſt that raigned before this Emperour,to wit,*Iuan Baſileus,*& *Iuan* father to
the other that raigneth at this time.Wherof
the firſt that tooke vnto him the name and
title of Emperour.was *Baſileus* father to *Iuan,*
& grandfather to this man. For before that
time they were contented to be called great
Dukes of *Mosko.* What hath bene done by
either of theſe three, and how much they
haue added to their firſt eſtate by conqueſt or
otherwiſe, may bee ſeene in the chapter of
their colonies, or purchaſes perforce. For
the

*The ad-
uancement
of the houſe
of Beala.*

the cótinuance of the race, this houſe of *Bea-la* at this preſent is in like caſe as are many of the greateſt houſes of Chriſtendome vz, the whole ſtocke and race concluded in one, two or ſome fewe of the bloud. For beſides the Emperour that now is, who hath no childe (neither is like euer to haue for ought that may be conieftured by the conſtitution of his body, and the barenneſſe of his wife af-ter ſo many yeares marriage)there is but one more vz. a child of ſixe or ſeuen yeares old, in whom reſteth all the hope of the ſucceſ-ſion, and the poſteritie of that houſe. As for the other brother that was eldeſt of the three, and of the beſt towardneſſe, he died of a blowe giuen him by his father vpon the head in his furie with his walking ſtaffe, or (as ſome ſay) of a thruſt with the prong of it driuen deepe into his head. That he meant him no ſuch mortall harme when hee gaue him the blow, may appeare by his mourning and paſsion after his ſonnes death, which ne-uer left him till it brought him to the graue. Wherein may be marked the iuſtice of God, that puniſhed his delight in ſhedding of bloud with this murder of his ſonne by his owne hand, and ſo ended his dayes and ty-rannie together, with the murdering of him-ſelfe by extreame griefe, for this his vnhap-pie and vnnaturall faft.

The

The Emperours yonger brother of ſixe or ſeuen years old (as was ſaid before) is kept in a remote place from the *Moſko*, vnder the tuition of his mother and hir kinred of the houſe of the *Nagaies*: yet not ſafe (as I haue heard) from attempts of making away by pra-ctiſe of ſome that aſpire to the ſuccesſion, if this Emperour die without any iſſue. The nurſe that taſted before him of certaine meat (as I haue heard) died preſently. That hee is naturall ſonne to *Ioan Vaſilowich*, the *Ruſſe* people warrant it, by the Fathers qualitie that beginneth to appeare already in his tender yeares. He is delighted (they ſay) to ſee ſheepe and other cattel killed, and to looke on their throtes while they are bleeding (which com-monly children are afraid to beholde) and to beate geeſe and hennes with a ſtaffe till he ſee them lie dead. Beſides theſe of the male kind, there is a widdow, that hath right in the ſuccesſion, ſiſter to the old Emperour, and aunt to this man, ſomtime wife to *Mag-nus* Duke of *Holſt*, brother to the king of *Denmarke*, by whom ſhee had one daughter. This woman ſince the death of hir husband hath bene allured again into *Ruſsia*, by ſome that loue the ſuccesſion better then hir ſelfe, which appeareth by the ſequele. For hir ſelfe with hir daughter ſo ſoone as they were re-turned into *Ruſsia* were thruſt into a Nunne-rie,

rie, where hir daughter died this laft yeare
while I was in the countrie, of no naturall
difeafe as was fuppofed. The mother remaineth ftill in the Nunnerie, where (as I haue
heard) fhee bewayleth hir felfe, and curfeth   5
the time when fhe returned into *Rufsia*, en-
tifed with the hope of marriage, and other
fayre promifes in the Emperours name:
Thus it ftandeth with the imperiall ftock of
Rufsia of the houfe of *Beala*, which is like to   10
determine in thofe that now are, & to make
a conuerfion of the *Ruffe* eftate. If it be into
a gouernment of fome better temper, and
milder conftitution, it will be happy for the
poore people that are now oppreffed with   15
intollerable feruitude.

Of the manner of crowning or inaugu-ration of the Ruffe Emperours.   20

The 6. Chapter.

He folemnities vfed at the   25
Ruffe Emperours coronatiō,
are on this manner. In the
great Church of *Prechefte* (or
our Lady) within the Empe-
rours caftle is erected a ftage,   30
D   whereon

whereon ftandeth a fcrine that beareth ypon
it the *Imperiall cappe* and robe of very riche
ftuffe. When the day of the Inauguration is
come, there reforte thither, firft the Patriarch with the Metropolitanes, Archbifhops,
Bifhops, Abbots, and Priors, all richly clad
in their Pontificalibus. Then enter the Deacons with the quier of fingers. Who fo foone
as the Emperour fetteth foote into the
Church, beginne to fing: *Many yeares may
liue noble Theodore Iuanowich &c*: Whereunto the Patriarch and Metropolite with the
reft of the Cleargie, anfwere with a certaine
Hymne, in forme of a prayer, finging it all
together with a great noyfe. The hymne beyng ended, the Patriarch with the Emperour mount vp the ftage, where ftandeth a
feat ready for the Emperour. Whereupon the
Patriarch willeth him to fit downe, and then
placing himfelfe by him vpon an other feate
prouided for that purpofe, boweth downe
his head towardes the ground, and fayeth
this prayer: *Oh Lord God King of Kinges,
Lord of Lordes, which by thy prophet Samuel
diddeft choofe thy feruant Dauid, and annoint
him for King ouer thy people Ifraell, heare now
our prayers, and looke from thy fanctuarie vpon this thy feruant Theodore, whome thou haft
chofen and exalted for King ouer thefe thy holy Nations, annoint him with the oyle of glad-
neffe*

neffe, *proteEt him by thy power, put vpon his head a crowne of golde and pretious ftones, giue him length of dayes, place him in the feate of* Iuftice, *ftrengthen his arme, make fubieEt vnto him all the barbarous nations.* Lette thy feare bee in his whole heart, turne him from an euill faith, and from all errour, and fhewe him the faluation of thy holy and vniuerfall Church, that hee may iudge thy people with Iuftice, and proteEt the children of the poore, and finally atteyne euerlafting lyfe. This prayer hee fpeaketh with a lowe voyce, and then pronounceth a lowde : *All prayfe and power to God the Father, the Sonne, and the holy Ghoft.* The prayer beyng ended, hee commaundeth certaine Abbots to reach the imperiall roabe and cappe: whiche is done verie decently, and with great folemnitie, the Patriarch withall pronouncing alowde : *Peace be vnto all.* And fo he beginneth an other praier to this effeEt : *Bowe your felues together with vs, and pray to him that reigneth ouer all. Preferue him (oh Lord) vnder thy holy proteEtion, keepe him that hee may doo good and holy thinges, let iuftice fhine foorth in his dayes, that wee may liue quietly without ftrife and malice.* This is pronounced fomewhat foftly by the Patriarch, whereto hee addeth againe alowd : *Thou art the King of the whole worlde, and the fauiour of our foules, to thee the Father,*

Sonne

5

10

15

20

25

30

Sonne and Holy ghoſt, be all prayſe for euer, and euer, Amen. *Then putting on the roabe and the cappe, he bleſſeth the Emperour with the ſigne of the croſſe: ſaying withall, in the name of the Father, the Sonne, and the Holy ghoſt.* The like is done by the Metropolites, Archbiſhops, and Biſhops: who all in their order come to the chaire, and one after an other bleſſe the Emperour with their two forefingers. Then is ſayed by the Patriarch an other prayer, that beginneth : *O moſt holy virgin mother of God,&c* After which a Deacon pronounceth with an high lowde voice: *Many yeares to Noble Theodore, good, honourable, beloued of God, great Duke of Volodemer of Mosko, Emperour, and Monarch of all Ruſsia,&c.* Whereto the other Prieſtes and Deacons that ſtand ſomewhat farre of by the altar or table, anſweare ſinging : *Many yeares, many yeares, to the noble Theodore.* The ſame note is taken vp by the Prieſtes and Deacons, that are placed at the right and left ſide of the Church, and then all together, they chaunt and thunder out, ſinging : *Many yeares to the noble Theodore, good, honaurable, beloued of God, great Duke of Volodemer, Mosko, Emperour of all Ruſsia,&c.* Theſe ſolemnities beyng ended, firſt commeth the Patriarch with the Metropolites, Archbiſhops, and Biſhops, then the Nobi-
l.tie,

ſtie, and the whole companie in their order,
to doo homage to the Emperour, bending
downe their heads and knocking them at
his feete to the ver ground.

The ſtile wherewith he is in-
ueſted at his Coronation, runneth
after this manner.

THeodore *Iuanowich, by the grace of God
great Lord and Emperour of all Ruſsia,
great Duke of Volodemer, Moskо and Nouо-
grad, King of Cazan, King of Aſtracan, Lord
of Plesko, and great duke of Smolensko, of Twer-
ria, Ioughoria, Permia, Vadska, Bulghoria,
and others, Lord and great duke of Nouograd
of the Low countrie, of Chernigo, Rezan, Po-
lotskoy, Roſtoue, Yaruflaueley, Bealozera, Liefland, Oudoria, Obdoria, and Condenſa, Commaunder of all Siberia, and of the North partes,
and Lord of many other Countries, &c.*
This ſtile conteyneth in it all the Emperours Prouinces, and ſetteth foorth his
greatneſſe. And therefore they haue a great
delight and pride in it, forcing not onely
there owne people but alſo ſtraungers that
haue any matter to deliuer to the Emperour by ſpeach or writing) to repeate the
whole forme from the beginning to the end.
Which breedeth much cauill, and ſome-

times

times quarrell betwixt them and the *Tartar*, and Poland Ambaſſadours : who refuſe to call him *Czar*, that is Emperour, and to repeat the other partes of his long ſtile. My ſelfe when I had audience of the Emperour, thought good to ſalute him onely with thus much vz. *Emperour of all Ruſſia, great Duke of Volodemer, Mosko and Nouograd, King of Cazan, King of Aſtracan.* The reſt I omitted of purpoſe, becauſe I knew they gloried, to haue their ſtile appeare to bee of a larger volume then the Queenes of England. But this was taken in ſo ill part, that the Chauncellor(who then attended the Emperour, with the reſt of the Nobilitie)with a lowde chafing voice called ſtill vpon mee to ſay out the reſt. Whereto I anſwered, that the Emperours ſtile was very long,and could not ſo well be remembred by ſtraungers, that I had repeated ſo much of it, as might ſhewe that I gaue honour to the reſt &c: But all would not ſerue till I commaunded my Interpreter to ſay it all out.

The State or forme of their Gouernment.

The 7. Chapter.

He manner of their gouernment is much after the Turkiſh faſhiō: which they ſeeme to imitate as neare as the coūtrie, and reach of their capacities in pollitique affayres will giue them leaue to doo.

The State and forme of their gouernment is plaine tyrannicall, as applying all to the behoofe of the Prince, and that after a moſt open and barbarous manner : as may appeare by the *Sophiſmata* or ſecretes of their gouernment afterwards ſet downe, aſwell for the keeping of the Nobilitie and Commons in an vnder proportion, & far vneuen ballance in their ſeuerall degrees, as alſo in their impoſitions and exactions, wherein they exceede all iuſt meaſure without any regard of Nobilitie or people : farther then it giueth the Nobilitie a kinde of iniuſt and vnmeaſured libertie, to commaund and exact vpon the commons and baſer ſort of people in all partes of the realme where ſo euer they come, ſpecially in the place where their

The margin: The *Ruſſe* gouernment tyrannicall.

D 4   **landes**

(15) plaine/meare   (16) behoofe of the Prince/behoofe of the *Prince*, without all regard of Nobilitye or Commons   (18) by/in secretes/*secreats*   (27) unmeasured/unreasonable

landes lye , or where they are appoynted
by the Emperonr to gouerne vnder him.
Alfo to the Commons fome fmall contentment, in that they paffe ouer their landes
by difcent of inheritance to whither fonne
they will ; which commonly they doo after
our *Gauillkinde*, and difpofe of their goods
by gifte or Teftament without any controlment. Wherein notwithftanding both Nobilitie and Commons are but ftoarers for
the Prince , all running in the ende into the
Emperonrs coffers : as may appeare by the
practife of enriching his treafurie , and the
manner of exactions fet downe in the title
of his cuftomes,and reuenues.

Concerning the principall pointes and
matters of State , wherein the Soueraintie
confifteth (as the *making and annulling of publike Lawes, the making of Magiftrates, power
to make warre or league with any forraine State,
to execute or to pardon life , with the right of
appeale in all matters, both ciuill and criminall*)
they doo fo wholy and abfolutely pertaine
to the Emperour , and his Counfell vnder
him . as that hee may be faide to be both
the Soueraine commaunder , and the exe-
cutioner of all thefe . For as touching any
Lawe or publique order of the Realme, it
is euer determined of before any publique
affemblie or Parliament bee fummoned.
Where

(12) coffers/Treasury

Where befides his Councell, hee hath none other to confult with him of fuch matters as are concluded before hand, but onely a fewe Bifhops, Abbots, and Friers : to no other end then to make aduantage of the peoples fuperftitions, euen againft themfelues, which thinke all to bee holy and iuft , that paffeth with confent of their Bifhops and Cleargie men, whatfoeuer it be. For which purpofe the Emperours are content to make much of the corrupt ftate of the Church, as now it is among them , and to nourifh the fame by extraordinarie fauours, and immunities to the Bifhops feas, Abbeies and Frieries : as knowing fuperftition and falfe religion beft to agree with a tyrannicall ftate , and to be a fpeciall meanes to vphold and mainteyne the fame.

Secondly, as touching the publike offices and magiftracies of the realme, there is none hereditarie, neither any fo great nor fo litle in that countrie, but the beftowing of it is done immediatly by the Emperour himfelf. Infomuch that the very Diacks or clearkes in euery head towne, are for the moft part afsigned by himfelfe. Notwithftanding, the Emperour that now is (the better to entend his deuotions) referreth al fuch matters per-teyning to the State, wholly to the ordering of his wiues brother, the L. *Borris Federo-wich*

(6) euen against themselves *omitted.* (14) seas *omitted.* (15) false religion/false perswasions of religion (25) for the most part *omitted.*

Thirdly, the like is to be said of the iurisdiction concerning matters iudiciall, specially such as concerne life and death. Wherein there is none that hath anie authoritie or publike iurisdiction that goeth by discent, or is held by charter, but all at the appoyntment and pleasure of the Emperour, and the same practised by the iudges with such awe and restraint, as that they dare not determine vpon anie speciall matter, but must referre the same wholly vp to the *Mosko* to the Emperours Councell. To shewe his Soueraintie ouer the liues of his subiects, the late Emperour *Iuan Vasilowich* in his walkes or progresses, if hee had misliked the face or person of any man who hee met by the way, or that looked vpon him, would command his head to be strook off. Which was presently done, and the head cast before him.

Fourthly, for the soueraigne appeale, and giuing of pardons in criminall matters to such as are conuicted, it is wholly at the pleasure and grace of the Emperour Wherin also the Empresse that nowe is, being a woman of great clemencie, and withall delighting to deale in publike affaires of the Realme, (the rather to supply the defect of her husband)doeth behaue her selfe after an absolute

(14–21) To shewe his Soueraintie . . . cast before him *omitted.* (29–30) *parenthetical phrase omitted.*

abfolute manner, giuing out pardon (fpe-
cically on hir byrth day and other folemne
imes) in her owne name, by open proclamation, without any mention at all of the
Emperour. Some there haue beene of late
of the auncient Nobilitie, that haue held
diuers prouinces by right of inheritaunce,
with an abfolute authoritie and iurisdiction
ouer them, to order and determine all matters within their owne precinct without all
appeale, or controlment of the Emperour.
But this was all annulled and wrung cleane
from them by *Iuan Vafilowich* father to this
Emperour.

The manner of holding their Par-·
liaments.

The 8. Chapter.

Heir higheſt Court of pub- The States
like confultation for matter of Parlia-
of State, is called the *Zabore,* ment.
that is, the *Publike Aſſembly.*
The ſtates & degrees of perſons that are prefent at their
Parliaments, are thefe in order. 1. The Emperour himfelfe. 2. Some of his Nobilitie a-
bout the number of twentie being all of his
Councel. 3. Certain of the cleargy men,&c.
about

(12) wrung cleane/taken quite (23) *Zabore/Zobore* (24) *Publike Assembly*/pub-
lique *Assemblie* or Parliament (29–30) being all of his Councel *omitted.* (30)
Certain *omitted.*

about the fame number. As for Burghers o.
other to reprefent the comunaltie, they haue
no place there: the people being of no better
account with them then as feruants or bond
flaues that are to obey, not to make lawes,
nor to knowe any thing of publike matters
before they are concluded.

The Court of Parliament (called *Zabore*)
The order
of the fum-
mons or af-
fembling. is held in this manner. The Emperour caufeth to be fummoned fuch of his Nobilitie as
himfelfe thinketh meete, being (as was faid)
all of his Councell : together with the Patriarch, who calleth his Cleargie, to wit, the
two Metropolites, the two Archbifhops,
with fuch Bifhops, Abbots, and Friers as are
of beft account and reputation among the.
When they are all affembled at the Emperours court, the day is intimated when the
fefsion fhal begin. Which commonly is vpon
fome friday, for the religion of that day.

When the day is come, the cleargie men
affemble before at the time & place appointed, which is called the *Stollie.* And when the
Emperour commeth attended by his Nobilitie, they arife all, and meete him in an out
roome, following their Patriarch, who bleffeth the Emperor with his two forefingers,
laying them on his forehead, and the fides
of his face, and then kiffeth him on the right
fide of his breft. So they paffe on into their
Parlia-

(4-7) seruants . . . concluded/servaunts or slaves that are to knowe nothinge of
publique matters and to have no parte in makinge but in obeyinge of Lawes   (8) The/
This   (11-12) himselfe . . . Councell/himselfe thinketh meet which for the most
parte are all of his counsell   (23) *Stollie/Stolloy* or Parliament howse

Parliament houſe, where they ſit in this order. The Emperor is enthronized on the one
ſide of the chamber. In the next place not far
from him at a ſmal ſquare table (that giueth
roome to twelue perſons or thereabouts)
ſitteth the Patriarche with the Metropolites and Biſhops, and certeine of the principall Nobilitie of the Emperours Councel,
together with two Diacks or Secretaries (cal-
leo *Dumnoy dyakey*) that enact that which
paſſeth. The reſt place themſelues on benches round about the roome, euery man in
his ranck after his degree. Then is there propounded by one of the Secretaries (who re-
preſenteth the ſpeaker) the cauſe of their aſ-
ſemblie, and the principall matters that they
are to conſider of. For to propund bils what
euery man thinketh good for the publike be-
nefice (as the maner is in England) the *Ruſſe*
Parliament alloweth no ſuch cuſtome , nor
libertie to ſubiects.

The poynts being opened, the Patriarch
with his Cleargie men haue the prerogatiue
to be firſt asked their vote, or opinion, what
they thinke of the poyntes propounded by
the Secretarie. Whereto they anſwere in order, according to their degrees, but al in one
forme without any diſcourſe: as hauing learned their leſſon before , that ſerueth their
turnes at all Parliaments alike, whatſoeuer is
propoun-

*Their diſ-
courſe at
Parliamēt.*

5

10

15

20

25

30

---

(8) Nobilitie . . . Councel/Nobilitie beinge of the Emperours Counsell (as was
sayed beefore) (21) to subiects *omitted*. (29) before *omitted*.

Their manner of holding
propounded. Commonly it is to this effeᵈ. *That the Emperour and his Councell are of great wisedome, and experience, touchiug the pollicies and publike affaires of the Realme, and farre bet- ter able to iudge what is profitable for the com- mon wealth, then they are, which attend vpon the seruice of God onlie, and matters of religion. And therefore it may pleaſe them to proceede. That insteede of their aduiſe, they will aide them with their prayers, as their dueties and vocations doe require, &c .* To this or like effeᵈ hauing made their anſweres euery man in his courſe, vp ſtandeth ſome Abbot or Frier more bold then the reſt (yet appointed before hand as a matter of forme) and deſireth the Empe- rour it would pleaſe his Maieſtie, to com- maund to be deliuered vnto them what his Maieſties owne iudgement and determinate pleaſure is , as touching thoſe matters pro- pounded by his *Deiake.*

Whereto is replied by the ſaide Secreta- rie in the Emperours name. *That his High- neſſe with thoſe of his noble Councell, vpon good and ſound aduiſe haue found the matters propo- ſed to be verie good and neceſſarie for the com- mon wealth of his Realme . Notwithſtanding, foraſmuch as they as religious men, & know what is right, his ᴄMaieſtie requireth their godlie o- pinions, yea and their cenſures too, for the appro- uing or correcting of the ſaide propoſitions. ᴄAnd therefore*

(4) *publike* omitted. (4–5) *and farre better*/and so farre better (11) *&c* omitted. (24–25) *proposed*/propounded (27) *as they as*/*as they are* (29–30) *approuing or*/ *proouinge and*

therefore defireth them againe to fpeake their mindes freely. And if they fhal like to giue thfir confents, that then the matters may paffe to a full conclufion.

Hereunto when the Cleargie men haue giuen their confents (which they vfe to do without any great paufing) they take their leaues with blefsing of the Emperour: who bringeth the Patriarch on his way fo farre as the next roome, and fo returneth to his feat, till all be made readie for his returne homeward. The actes that thus are paffed by the *Zabore* or Parliament, the *Deiakeis* or Secretaries draw into a forme of proclamation, which they fend abroad into euery Prouince, and head towne of the Realme, to be publifhed there by the Dukes and *Diakeis*, or Secretaries of thofe places . The fefsion of Parliament being fully ended , the Emperour inuiteth the Cleargie men to a folemne dinner. And fo they depart euery man to his home.

5

10

15

20

25

Of

*Of the Nobilitie, and by what meanes it is
kept in an vnder proportion agreeable to to that State.*

5

The 9. Chapter.

The *Vdelney Knazey* chiefe of the Nobilitie,

10

He degrees of perſons or eſtates of *Ruſſia* , beſides the ſoueraigne State or Emperour himſelfe) are theſe in their order. 1. The *Nobilitie* which is of foure ſortes. Whereof the chiefe

15 for birth, authoritie, and reuenue are called the *Vdelney Knazey*, that is, the exempt or priuiledged Dukes. Theſe held ſometime a ſeueral iurisdiction, and abſolute authorite within their precincts , much like vnto the

20 States or Nobles of *Germany*. But afterwards (reſeruing their rights vpon compoſition) they yeelded themſelues to this houſe of *Beala*, when it began to waxe mightie, and to enlarge it ſelf by ouermatching their neigh-bours. Onely they were bound to ſerue the Emperour in his warres with a certain num-

25 ber of horſe. But the late Emperour *Iuan Va-ſilowich* father to this prince, being a man of high ſpirit, and ſubtill in his kind meaning

30 to reduce his gouernmēt into a more ſtrickt forme,

---

(17) priuiledged/absolute   (17-19) These . . . precincts/These helde an absolute and severall iurisdiccion within their precinctes

forme beganne by degrees to clip of their
greatnes,& to bring it downe to a leſſer proportion : till in the end he made them not
onely his vaſſals, but his *Kolophey*,that is,his
very villains or bódſlaues. For ſo they terme   5
and write themſelues in anie publike in-
ſtrument or priuate petition which they
make to the Emperour . So that now they
holde their authorities , landes , liues and
all at the Emperours pleaſure, as the reſt   10
doe.

The meanes and practiſe whereby hee
wrought this to effect againſt thoſe, & other
of the Nobility (ſo well as I could note out
of the report of his doings) were theſe, and   15
ſuch like. Firſt, he caſt priuate emulations
among them about preroragatiue of their
titles, and dignities. Wherein hee vſed to
ſet on the inferiours, to preferre or equall
themſelues to thoſe that were accounted to   20
bee of the nobler houſes. Where he made
his aduanntage of their malice and con-
tentions, the one againſt the other,by receiuing deuiſed matter,and accuſations of
ſecrete practiſe and conſpiracies to be in-   25
tended againſt his perſon, and ſtate. And
ſo hauing ſingled out the greateſt of them,
and cut them off with the good liking of
the reſt , hee fell at laſt to open practiſe,
by forcing of the other to yeeld their rights   30
            E   vnto

---

(4) *Kolophey/kholopey* (5–6) terme and *omitted*. (13–14) against those, & other
of the Nobility *omitted*. (19) or equall *omitted*. (22–23) contentions/accusacions
(23–24) by receiuing deuiſed matter, and accusations *omitted*. (26) against his person,
and state/againste himselfe and suche like

vnto him.

2 Hee deuided his fubiectes into two partes or factions by a general fchifme. The one part hee called the *Oppreſſini* or *Select men.* Thefe were fuch of the Nobilitie and Gentrie as he tooke to his owne part, to protect and mainteyne them as his faithful fubiects. The other hee called *Zemskey*, or the *Commons.* The *Zemskey* conteyned the bafe and vulgar fort, with fuch Noblemen and Gentlemen as he meant to cut off, as fufpected to miflike his gouernment, and to haue a meaning to practife againft him. Wherein he prouided that the *Oppreſſini* for number and qualitie of valure, money, armour, &c: farre exceeded the other of the *Zempskey* fide, whom he put (as it were) from vnder his protection: fo that if any of them were fpoiled or killed by thofe of the *Oppreſſini* (which hee accounted of his owne part) there was no amendes to bee fought for by way of publike iuftice, or by complaint to the Emperour.

The whole number of both partes was orderly regiftred and kept in a booke : fo that euery man knewe who was a *Zempskey* man, and who of the *Oppreſſini* . And this libertie of the one part to fpoyle and kill the other without anie helpe of Magiftrate, or lawe (that continued feuen yeeres) enriched that

The factiō of *Oppreſſini* & *Zempskey* deuifed by the Emperour.

(11) as he meant to cut off *omitted.*

that fide, and the Emperours treafurie and wrought that withall which hee intended by this pra&tife, viz.to take out of the way fuch of the Nobilitie, as himfelfc mifliked: whereof were flayne within one weeke to the number of three hundred within the citie of *Mosko*. This tyrannicall pra&tife of making a generall Schifmie, and publike diuifion among the fubie&ts of his whole Realme, proceeded (as fhould feeme)from an extreame doubt, and defperate feare, which hee had conceiued of moft of his Nobilitie,and Gentlemen of his Realme, in his warres with the *Polonian* and *Chrim Tartar*. What time hee grewe into a vehement fufpition (conceiued of the ill fucceffe of his affayres)that they pra&tifed treafon with the *Polonian* and *Chrim*.Whereupon he executed fome,and deuifed this way to be ridde of the reft.

And this wicked pollicy & tyrannous pra&tife(though now it be ceaffed)hath fo troubled that countrey, and filled it fo full of grudge & mortall hatred euer fince, that it wil not be quenched (as it feemeth now) till it burne againe into a ciuill flame.

3   Hauing thus pulled them and feafed all their inheritaunce, landes, priuiledges, &c. faue fome verie fmall part which he left to their name, hee gaue them other

E 2   landes

5

10

15

20

25

30

(24) euer since/ever since that tyme   (26) againe/owte

landes of the tenour of *Pomestnoy* (as they call it) that are helde at the Emperours pleasure , lying farre of in an other countrey , and so remoued them into other of his Prouinces , where they might haue neyther fauour , nor authoritie , not being natiue nor well knowen there. So that now these of the chiefe Nobilitie (called *Udelney Knazey*) are equalled with the rest: saue that in the opinion and fauour of the people they are of more account, and keepe stil the prerogatiue of their place in al their publike meetings.

Their practise to keepe downe these houses from rising againe and recouering their dignities are these, and such like. First, many of their heires are kept vnmaried perforce, that the stocke may die with thē. Some are sent into *Siberia, Cazan* and *Astracan*, vnder pretence of seruice, and there either made away, or else fast clapped vp Some are put into Abbeyes , and shire themselues Friers by pretence of a vowe to be made voluntary, and of their owne accord , but indeede forced vnto it by feare vpon some pretensed crime obiected against them. Where they are so garded by some of special trust, and the Couent it selfe (vpon whose head it standeth that they make no escape) as that they haue no hope but to ende their liues there.

Of

(1) tenour/tenure   (1) *Pomestnoy/pomestye*   (2) that are helde/that are to bee heild   (23) shire/shear

Of this kinde there are manie of verie great Nobilitie . Thefe and fuch like wayes begunne by the Emperour *Iuan Vafilowich* are ftill practifed by the *Godonoes,* who beyng aduaunced by the mariage of the Empreffe their kinfewoman, rule both the Emperour, and his Realme, (fpecially *Borris Federo ich Godonoe*, brother to the Empreffe) and endeuour by all meanes to cut of, or keepe downe all of the beft and auncienteft Nobilitie. Whereof diuers alreadie they haue taken away, whom they thought likelieft to make head againft them and to hinder their purpofe, as *Knez Andreas Guraken Bulgatkoue* , a man of great byrth and authoritie in the Countrey . The like they haue done with *Peeter Gollauni* (whom they put into a dungeon where he ended his life) with *Knez Vafilie Vrywich Golloohen;* with *Andrieu Iuanowich Suskoy* accounted among them for a man of a great wifedome. So this laft yeere was killed in a Monafterie , (whither they had thruft him) on *Knez Iuan Petrowich Suskoy* a man of great valure and feruice in that Countrey : who about fiue or fixe yeeres fince, bare out the fiege of the Citie *Vobsko* made by *Stepan Batore* King of *Polonia*, with a 100000. men, and repulfed him verie valiantly, with great honour to himfelfe, and his countrey,

E 3   and

(2) Nobilitie/Nobilitie as *Knes Methysthosky* [name added and crossed out]   (3–4) begunne by . . . practised/are practized   (4) *Godonoes/Godonoves*   (13–14) and to hinder their purpose *omitted*.   (14–15) *Knez Andreas Guraken Bulgatkoue/knes Andrew Guraken Bulgatkove*   (16–17) The like they have done with *omitted*.   (17) *Peeter Gollauni/Peter Gollavin*   (18–19) put . . . life/putt into a dungeon and thear killed him   (19) *Golloohen/Gollochen*   (22) So/Among other   (22–23) was killed . . . thrust him *omitted*.   (26) or sixe *omitted*.   (28) 100000/500000

and difgrace to the *Polonian.* Alfo *Micheta Romanowich* vnckle to the Emperour by the mothers fide, was fuppofed to haue dyed of poyfon, or fome like practife.

The names of thefe families of greateft Nobility are thefe in their order. The firft is of *Knez Volodemer*, which refteth at this time in one daughter a widow, and without children (mentioned before) fometime wife to *Hartock Magnus* brother to the king of *Denmark*, now clofed within a nunery. The 2. *knez Metheloskey* thruft into a Friery, and his only fonne kept frō mariage, to decay the houfe. The 3. *Glimskoy.* But one left of his houfe, & he without children faue one daughter. The 4. *Suskoy*, wherof there are 4. brethren yong men, & vnmaried al. The 5. *Hubetskoy.* Cf this houfe are 4. liuing. The 6. *Bulgaloy* now called *Guletchey* houfe, whereof are fiue liuing, but youths al. The 7. *Vorallinskoy.* Two left of that ftock. The 8. *Odgoskey.* Two. The 9. *Tellerskoy.* One. The 10. *Taytoue*, three. Thefe are the names of the chiefe families called *Vdelney Knazey:* that in effect haue loft all now, faue the very name it felfe, and fauour of the people, which is like one day to reftore them againe, if any be left.

The 2. degree of Nobility is of the *Boiarens.* Thefe are fuch as the Emperour honoureth (befides their nobility) with the title of coun-
fellers.

(3–4) was supposed . . . practice/was supposed to have died of a violent death by the *Godonoes* meanes (11) now closed within a nunnery *omitted.* (12) *Metheloskey/ Mesthisloskey* (14) *Glimskoy/Glinskoy* (19) *Guletchey/Golitchey* (21) *Teller-skoy/Telletskoy*

fellers. The reuenue of thefe 2. forts of their
Nobles that rifeth out of their lands afsigned
thē by the Emperour, & held at his pleafure
(for of their owne inheritaunce there is little
left them as was faid before is about a thoufand marks a yeere: befides penfion which
they receiue of the Emperour for their feruice in his warres, to the fumme of 700. rubbels a yeere, and none aboue that fumme.

But in this number the lorde *Borris Fe-*
derowich Godenoe is not to be reckoned, that
is like a *Tranfendent*, and in no fuch predica-
ment with the reft, being the Emperors brother in law, his protectour for direction, for
commaund and authority Emperour of *Ruf-*
fia. His yerely reuenue in land & penfion, a-
mounteth to the fumme of 93700. rubbels
and more, as appeareth by the particulars.
He hath of inheritance (which himfelfe hath
augmentēted in *Vafma Dorogobofe* fixe thoufand rubbels a yeere. For his office of *Con-*
nick, or Mafter of the Horfe 12000. rubbels, or markes, raifed out of the *Conaflue*
Sloboday, or the liberties pertayning to that
Office, which are certeyne Landes and
Townes neere about the *Mosko*. Befides,
all the meddowe and pafture grounde on
both fides the banke of the riuer *Mosko*,
thirtie verft vp the ftreame, aod fourtie verft
downwards. For his penfion of the Empe-

E 4   rour

(1–2) The reuenue . . . that riseth/The revenue of the chiefest Nobilitie that riseth
(5–6) a thousand marks/2000 Rub.   (13) with the rest, being/with the rest of the
Nobilitie beeing   (15) *commaund and* omitted.   (15–16) Emperour . . . reuenue/
Emperour of *Russia* him self, and for riches and revenue farr passing all the rest. His
yearlie revenue   (17–18) 93700. rubbels and more/a hundred Fortie & seven thowsand
Rubbells and more   (22) 12000/1200   (24) *Sloboday/Sloboda*   (29) aod/and

rout (befides the other for his office) 15000.
rubbels. Out of the Prouince or Shire of
Vagha, there is giuen him for a peculiar exempted out of the *Chetfird* of *Pofolskoy*
32000. rubbels, befides a rent of furres.
Out of *Rezan* and *Seuer*, (an other peculiar) 30000. rubbels, Out of *Otfer* and *Tu-
riock* an other exempt place 8000. rubbels.
For rent of Bathftoaues and Bathing houfes without the walles of *Moske* 1500. rubbels. Befides his pomeft, or lands which hee
holdeth at the Emperours pleafure, which
farre exceedeth the proportion of land allotted to the reft of the Nobility.

One other there is of the houfe of
Glinskoy that difpendeth in land and penfion
about 40000. rubbels yeerely. Which hee is
fuffered to enioy becaufe hee hath married
Borris his wiues fifter, being himfelfe verie
fimple, and almoft a naturall. The ordering
of him & his landes are committed to *Borris*.

The 3 fort
of Nobili-
tie.

In the third rank are the *Voyauodey* or fuch
Nobles as are, or haue bin generals in the Emperours warres. Which deliuer the honour
of their title to their pofterities alfo : who
take their place aboue the other Dukes and
Nobles that are not of the two former
forts, vz. of the *Vdelney knazey*, nor of the *Boiarens*.

Thefe three degrees of their Nobilitie (to
wit)

(3–4) peculiar exempted/peculiar and exempted (10) 1500/15000 (15) One other
. . . house of/One other thear is of the Nobilitie of the Howse of (19–21) his wiues
sister . . . *Borris*/his wives sister and augmenteth well *Boris* his cofers being him self
verie simple and allmost a naturall. And so the ordering of him self & his lands [are]
permitted to *Boris* (27–28) of the two former sorts, vz. *omitted*.

wit) the *Vdelney knazey*, the *Boiarens*, and the *Voiauodey* haue the addition of *vich*, put vnto their firname as *Borris Federowich*, &c: which is a note of honour that the reft may not vfurpe. And in cafe it be not added in the naming of them, they may fue the *Beft-cheft* or penaltie of difhonour vpon them, that otherwife fhall terme them.

The fourth and loweft degree of Nobili-tie with them, is of fuch as beare the name of *Knazey* or Dukes, but come of the yonger brothers of thofe chiefe houfes, through many difcents, and haue no inheritance of their owne, faue the bare name or title of Duke onely. For their order is to deliuer their names and titles of their dignities ouer to all their children alike, what foeuer elfe they leaue them. So that the fonnes of a *Voiauodey* or Generall in the field, are called *Voiauodey* though they neuer faw the field, and the fons of a *Knez* or Duke are called *Knazey*. though they haue not one groat of Inheritance or liuelyhood to mainteine themfelues withall. Of this fort there are fo many that the plen-tie maketh them cheap : fo that you fhall fee Dukes glad to ferue a meane man for fiue or fix rubbels or marks a yeare, & yet they will ftand highly vpon their *Beftcheft* or reputa-tion of their Honours. And thefe are their feuerall degrees of Nobilitie.

The

5

10

15

20

25

30

(23) themfelues withall/them   (26) fiue or *omitted*.   (28) *Beftcheft/Beffchest*.

The second degree of persons. The second degree of persons is of their *Sina Boiarskey*, or the sonnes of Gentlemen: which all are preferred,& hold that name by their seruice in the Emperours warres,being souldiers by their very st·cke and birth . To which order are referred their Dyacks or Secretaries, that serue the Emperour in euery head towne , being ioyned in Commission with the Dukes of that place

The third degree. The last are their Commons,whom they call *Mousicks*. In which number they reckon their Marchants, & their common artificers. The very lowest and basest sort of this kind (which are held in no degree)are their coū-trie people whom they call *Christianeis* . Of the *Sina boiarskey*(which are all souldiers)we are to see in the description of their forces,& military prouisions.Concerning their *Mou-sicks*,what their condition & behauiour is,in the title or chapter *Of the common people.*

Of the gouernment of their Pro-uinces and Shires.

The 10.Chapter.

THe whole countrie of *Russia* (as was said before) is diuided into foure parts,which they call *Chet-firds*,or *Tetrarchies*.Euery *Chetfird* contei-

---

(1–2) is . . . *Sina Boiarskey*/is of their Gentlemen which they call *Sina Boiarskey* (13–15) basest sort . . . *Christianeis*/basest sort of all their Countrey people they call *Christianeys* (30) *Tetrarchies*/*Tetrarchies* or *Fowrthparts*

côteineth diuers shires, & is annexed to a seuerall office, whereof it takes the name. The
firft *Chetfird* or *Tetrarchie* beareth the name
of *Pofoskoy Chetfird*, or the *Iurifdiction* of the
office of *Ambaffages*, and at this time is vnder
the chiefe Secretarie and officer of the Ambaffages called *Andreas Shalcaloue*. The ftâ-
ding fee or ftipend that he receiueth yearely
of the Emperour for this feruice. is 100.rub-
bels or markes.

The foure
chetfirds.

The fecond is called the *Roferadney Chetfird*, becaufe it is proper to the *Roferade* or
high Conftable. At this time it perteineth by
vertue of office to *Bafilie Shalcaloue*, brother
to the Chancellor, but it is executed by one
Zapon Abramoue. His penfion is an hundred
rubbels yearely.

The third is the *Chetfird* of *Pomeftnoy*, as
perteining to that office. This keepeth a Re-
gifter of all lands giuen by the Emperour for
feruice to his Noblemê, Gentlemê, & others,
giueth out & taketh in all affurances for thê.
The officer at this time is called *Eleazar wel-
lufgine*. His ftipend is 500. rubbels a yeare.

The fourth is called *Caffanskoy dvorets*, as
being appropriat to the office that hath the
iurifdiction of the kingdomes of *Cazan* and
Aftracan, with the other townes lying vpon
the *Volgha*, now ordered by one *Druzhine
Penteleoue*, a man of very fpeciall account
among

---

(4) *Pososkoy/Posolskoy* (5-6) vnder . . . Secretarie/vnder the Channcellor or cheef
Secreatarie

among them, for his wifdome, and prompt-
nes in matters of pollicie, His penfion is 150.
rubbels a yeare.

From thefe *Chetfirds* or *Tetarchies* is exempted the Emperors inheritance or *Vochin*
(as they cal it) for that it perteined from auncient time to the houfe of *Beala* , which is
the firname of the imperiall bloud. This ftã-
deth of 36. townes with their bounds or territories. Befides diuers peculiar iurifdicti-
ons, which ar likewife deducted out of thofe
Chetfirds, as the Shire of *Vagha* (belonging
to the Lord *Borrife Federcwich Godonoe*) and
fuch like.

Thefe are the chiefe gouernours or officers of the Prouinces , not refident at their
charge abroad , but attending the Emperour
whether foeuer he goeth, and carriyng their
offices about with them, which for the moft
part they hold at *Mosko*, as the Emperours
chiefe feat.

The parts and practife of thefe foure offices, is to receiue all complaints and actions
what foeuer, that are brought out of their
feuerall *Chetfirds*, and quarters, & to informe
them to the Emperours counfell. Likewife
to fend direction again to thofe that are vnder them in their faid Prouinces, for all matters giuen in charge by the Emperour and
his Counfell, to be done or put in execution
within

---

(5) or *Vochin* omitted. (7) *Beala/Beaela* (12–14) *Vagha* . . . such like/*Vaga* and
other to Lord *Borise Federowich Godonoe* (18) whether/whither (25) and quarters/
or quarters (26) Emperours *omitted*. (28–30) for all matters . . . [to end of
sentence on p. 31]/for all matters to bee doon by them or put in execution within their
provinces.

within their precincts.

For the ordering of euery particular Prouince of thefe foure *Chetfirds*, there is appointed one of thefe Dukes, which were reckoned before in the loweſt degree of their Nobilitie, which are reſident in the head townes of the ſaid Prouinces. Whereof euery one hath ioyned with him in Commiſſion a Dyack or Secretarie to aſſiſt him, or rather to direct him. For in the executing of their commiſsion, the Dyack doth all.

The parts of their Commiſsion are thefe in effect. Firſt to heare and determine in all ciuil matters within their precinct To which purpofe they haue vnder them certeine officers, as *Gubnoy Starets* or Coroners, who beſides the triall of ſelfe murders, are to attach fellons: and the *Soudiæ* or vnder Iuſtices, who themſelues alſo may heare and determine in all matters of the ſame nature, among the countrie people of their owne wardes or bayliwicks: but ſo that in cafe either partie diſſent, they may appeale, and goe farther to the Duke and Dyack that reſide within the head towne. From whom alſo they may remoue the matter to the higher court at *Mafko* of the Emperours Counſell, where lie all appeales. They haue vnder them alfo *Sotfkoy Starets*, that is Aldermen, or Baliues of the hundreds.

The Commiſſion of the Dukes or Preſidents of Shires.

5

10

15

20

25

30

Secondly

(20) all matters/all Civill matters

Secondly in all criminall matters,as theft, murder, treafon &c. they haue authoritie to apprehend,to examine and to emprifon the malefactor;and fo hauing receiued perfect euidence & information of the caufe, they are to fend it ready drawen and orderly digefted vp to the *Mosko*, to the officer of the *Chetfird* whereunto that Prouince is annexed: by whom it is referred and propounded to the Emperours Counfell. But to determine in any matter criminall,or to doo executiõ vpon the partie offending,is more then their commifsion will allow them to doo.

Thirdly, if there be any publike feruice to be done within that Prouince , (as the publifhing of any Law,or common order,by way of proclamation, collecting of taxes and impofitions for the Emperour , moiftering of Souldiers,and fending them forth at the day and to the place afsigned by the Emperour or his Counfell) all thefe and fuch like perteyne to their charge.

Thefe Dukes & Dyacks are appointed to their place by the Emperour himfelfe, & are chaunged ordinarily at euery yeares end, except vpõ fome fpecial liking or fuit,the time be proroged for a yeare or two more. They are men of themfelues of no credite , nor fauour with the people, where they gouerne, being neither borne,nor brought vp among them,

---

(8–10) by whom it is referred and propounded to the Emperours Counsell *omitted*.

them , nor yet hauing inheritance of their
owne there,or els where . Onely of the Emperour they haue for that feruice an 100,
markes a yeare, he that hath moft, fome fiftie, fome but thirtie. Which maketh them
more fufpected & odious to the people, becaufe being fo bare , and comming frefh and
hungrie vpon them lightly euery yeare, they
rack & fpoile them without all regard of iuftice,or confcience.Which is eafily tollerated
by the chiefe officers of the *Chetfirds*, to the
end they may rob them againe,& haue a better bootie when they call them to account;
which comonly they doo at the end of their
feruice, making an aduātage of their iniuftice
& oppreffion ouer the poore people . There
are few of them but they come to the *Pudkey*
or whip when their time is ended , which
themfelues for the moft parte doo make account of. And therefore they furnifh themfelues with all the fpoile they can for the time
of their gouernment , that they may haue
for both turnes, afwel for the Emperour, and
Lord of the *Chetfird,*as to referue fome good
part for themfelues.

They that are appointed to gouerne a-
broad,are men of this qualitie : faue that in
the foure border townes that are of greateft
importance , are fet men of more fpeciall
valure and truft two in euery towne. Wherof

(4) markes/Rubbles or marks

of one is euer of the Emperours priuie counfell. Thefe foure border townes are *Smolenf-*
ko, Uobsko, Nouogrod, & Cazan, whereof three
lie towards the *Polonian & Sweden*, one bordereth far of vpon the *Chrim Tartar ♦* Thefe
haue larger cōmifsion then the other Dukes
of the Prouinces that I fpake of before , and
may doo execution in criminall matters ♦
Which is thought behoofull for the Com-
monwelth : for incident occafions that may
happen vpon the borders, that are far of, &
may not ftay for direction , about euery occurrent and particular matter from the Emperour and his Counfell. They are chaunged
euery yeare (except as before) and haue for
their ftipend 700. rubbels a yeare hee that
hath moft: fome haue but 400. Many of thefe
places that are of greateft importance,& almoft the whole countrie is managed at this
time, by the *Godonoes* and their clients.

The citie of *Mosko* (that is the Emperours
feat) is gouerned altogether by the Emperours Counfell. All matters there both ciuill
and criminall , are heard and determined in
the feuerall courtes , held by fome of the faid
Counfell, that refide there all the yeare long.

The Go-
uernment
of *Mosko.*

Onely for their ordinary matters (as buildings reparations, keeping of their ftreates
decent and cleane, collections, leuying of
taxes, impofitions and fuch like) are appoin-
taries,

(11-14) that are far of . . . Counsell *omitted* (20) clients/clients and favourers
(27-28) Onely . . . reparations/For their Town matters onlie (as buildings, reparations

ted two Gentlemen, & two Dyacks or Secretaries, who hold a court together for the ordering of such matters . This is called the
Zempskey house . If any townes man suf-
pect his seruant of theft or like matter , hi-
ther he may bring him to haue him examn-
ned vpon the *Pudkey*, or other torture . Befides these two Gentlemen, and Secretaries
that order the whole Citie , there are *Sta-
rusts* or Aldermen for euerie seuerall companie . The Alderman hath his *Sotskey* or
Conftable, and the Conftable hath certeine
Decetskeis or Decurions vnder him , which
haue the ouerfight of ten housholds a peece,
whereby euerie diforder is sooner fpide, and
the common seruice hath the quicker dif-
pach. The whole number of Citizens poore
and rich are reduced into companies . The
chiefe officers (as the Dyacks and Gentlemen) are appointed by the Emperour himfelfe, the *Staruft* by the Gentlemen and Dyacks, the *Sotskoy* by the *Staruft* or Alderman,
and the *Decetskoies* by the Conftables.

This manner of gouernment of their Prouinces and townes, if it were afwell fet for
the giuing of iuftice indifferently to al forts,
as it is to preuent innouations, by keeping
of the Nobilitie within order , and the commons in subiection , it might feeme in that
kinde to bee no bad, nor vnpollitique way,

F   for

(6–7) to have him . . . *Pudkey*/to have him publiquelie examined by the pudkey
(10) or Aldermen for euerie/or Alderman for the ordering of euerie   (15–17) whereby
euerie disorder . . . dispach *omitted*

for the conteyning of so large a Commonwealth, of that breadth and length as is the
kingdome of *Russia*. But the oppression
and slauerie is so open and so great, that a
man would maruell how the Nobilitie and
people shoulde suffer themselues to bee
brought vnder it, while they had any means
to auoid and repulse it: or being so strength-
ned as it is at this present, how the Emperours themselues can be content to practise
the same, with so open iniustice and oppression of their subiects, being themselues of a
Christian profession.

By this it appeareth how harde a mat-
ter it were to alter the state of the *Russe* gouernment, as now it standeth. First, because
they haue none of the Nobilitie able to
make head. As for the Lords of the foure
Chetfirds or *Tetrarchies* they are men of no
Nobilitie, but Dyacks aduanced by the Emperour, depending on his fauour, and attending onely about his owne person. And for
the Dukes that are appointed to gouern vnder them, they are but men of a titular dig-
nitie (as was saied before) of no power, authoritie, nor credit, saue that which they haue
out of the office, for the time they enioy it.
Which doth purchase the no fauour, but rather hatred of the people, for asmuch as they
see that they are set ouer the, not so much for
any

---

(1) conteyning/ordering (19–20) men of no Nobilitie *omitted*. (21) depending on
his fauour *omitted*. (22) onely about his owne person/still about his person (26)
haue/receive

any care to doo them right and iuftice as to keepe them vnder in a miferable fubiection, and to take the fliece from them, not once in the yeare (as the owner from his fheepe) but to poule and clip them all the yeare long. Befides the authority & rule which they beare, is rent and diuided into many fmall pieces, being diuers of them in euery great Shire, limited befides with a very fhort time: which giueth them no fcope to make any ftrength, nor to contriue fuch an enterprife, if happily they intended any matter of innouation. As for the common people (as may better appeare in the defcription of their ftate & qualitie afterwardes fet downe) befides their want of armour & practife of warre (which they are kept from of purpofe) they are robbed continually both of their harts & mony, (befides other means) fomtimes by pretence of fome feruice to be done for the common defence, fometimes without any fhewe at all of any necefsitie of Common-wealth or Prince. So that there is no meanes either for Nobilitie, or people to attempt any innouation, fo long as the militarie forces of the Emperour (which are the number of 8000 at the leaft in continuall pay) hold themfelues faft and fure vnto him, and to the prefent ftate. Which needes they muft doo beyng of the qualitie of Souldiours, and enioying

5
10
15
20
25
30

F 2   withall

(4) *parenthetical phrase omitted.* (5) to poule and clip them *omitted.* (6) the authority/their authority (7) small/severall (11) happily *omitted.* (12) they intended/they should intend (19) (besides other means) . . . pretence/by often exactions and soomtimes by pretence (26) 8000/80000

withal that free libertie of wronging & spoiling of the commons at their pleasure, which is permitted them of purpose, to make them haue a liking of the present state. As for the agreement of the Souldiers and commons, it is a thing not to be feared, beyng of so opposite and contrarie practise much one to the other. This desperate state of things at home, maketh the people for the most part to wishe for some forreine inuasion, which they suppose to bee the onely meanes, to rid them of the heauy yoke of this tyrannous gouernment.

Of the Emperours Counsell.

The 11. Chapter.

HE Emperours of *Russia* giue the name of coūsellour to diuers of their chiefe Nobilitie rather for honors sake, then for any vse they make of the about their matters of state. These are called *Boiarens* with-

(1–13) [and enjoying] withal . . . government/[and enioying] that licence which is permitted vnto them of purpose to make them have a liking of the present State, by wronging & spoiling of the Commons at their pleasure. As for the agreement of the souldiours & the Commons it is not to bee thought of, being so opposite and of so contrarie practize the on to the other. This maketh the people for the most part of them to wish for soom forreign invasion which they suppose to be the onlie meanes to ease them of the heavie yoke of this tyrannous government.

without any addition, and may bee called
Counfellors at large For they are feldome
or neuer called to any publique confultation. They which are of his fpeciall and priuie Counfell indeed (whom hee vfeth daily
and ordinarily for all publique matters perteining to the State) haue the addition of
Dumnoy, and are named *Dumnoy boiaren*, or
Lords of the Counfell, their office or fitting
Boarftua dumna.

  Their names at this prefent are thefe in
their order. Firft, *Knez Feoder Ioanowich*
Miethifloskey. 2. *Knez Iuan Michailowich*
Glinskoy 3. *Knez Vafilie Iuanowich Suskoy*
Scopin. (Thefe three are accounted to bee of
greater birth then wifedome taken in (as
may feeme) for that ende, rather to furnifh
the place with their honours and prefence,
then with their aduife or counfell.) 4. *Knez*
Vafilie Iuanowich Suskoy, thought to be more
wife then the other of his name. 5. *Knez*
Feoder Michailowich. 6. *Knez Micheta*
Romanowich Trowbetskoy. 7. *Knez Timophey*
Romanowich Trowbetskoy. 8. *Knez Andriew*
Gregoriwich Curakine. 9. *Knez Demetrie*
Iuanowich Foreftine. 10. *Knez Feoder Iuano-*
wich Foreftine. 11. *Bodan Iuanowich Sabaroue.*
12. *Knez Iuan Vafilowich.* 13. *Knez Feoder*
Demetriwich Sheftinoue. 14. *Knez Feoder*
Michailowich Troyconioue. 15. *Iuan Buter-*
    F 3   *lyney.*

The nůber
and names
of the Coů-
fellours of
State.

lyney. 16. *Demetric Iuanowich Godonoe.* 17. *Borrife Federowich Godonoe*, brother to the Empreffe. 18. *Stephan Vafilowich Godonoe.* 19 . *Gregorie Vafilowich Godonoe* . 20. *Iuan Vafilowich Godonoe.* 21. *Feoder Sheremitoue.* 22. *Andriew Petrowich Clefhenina.* 23. *Ignatie Petrowich Tatifloue.* 24. *Romain Michailowick Peua.* 25. *Demenfhoy Iuanowich Cheremiffen* . 26. *Romain Vafilowich Alferioue.* 27. *Andriew Shalcaloue.* 28. *Vafilie Shalcaloue.* 29. *Eleazar Wellufgin.* 30. *Drezheen Penteleoue* . 31. *Zapon Abramoue.*

Foure Secretaries.

The foure laſt of theſe are called *Dumnoy deiakey* or Lord Secretaries . Theſe are all of the Emperours priuie counſell though but fewe of them are called to any conſultation , for that all matters are aduiſed and determined vpon by *Borris Federowich Godonoe* brother to the Empreſſe with ſome fiue or ſixe more whom it pleaſeth him to call . If they come, they are rather to heare, then to giue counſel, & doo ſo demeane theſelues . The matters occurrent which are of ſtate done within the Realme, are infourmed them at their ſittings by the Lordes of the foure *Chetfirds*, or *Tetrarchies.*Whereof mention is made in the Chapter concerning the *Gouernment of their Prouinces.* Who bring in all ſuch letters as they receyue from the Dukes,

---

(7) *Tatisloue/Tatishove* (12) *Drezheen Penteleoue/Drusheen Penteleove*

Dukes, Dvacks, Captaines, and other officers of the Cities, and Caftels, perteyning to their feuerall quarter or *Chetfird*, with other aduertifements, and informe the Counfell of them.

The like is done by the chiefe officer of euery feuerall office of Record: who may come into the Counfell chamber, and informe them, as occafion incident to his office doth require. Befides matters of State, they confider of many priuate caufes, informed by way of fupplication in very great numbers. Whereof fome they intertaine and determine, as the caufe or meanes can procure fauour. Some they fend to the offices whereto they perteyne by common courfe of Lawe. Their ordinarie dayes for their fitting, are mondaies, wenfdaies, and fridayes. Their time of meeting is commonly feuen a clock in the morning. If there be any extraordinary occafion that requireth confultation on fome other day, they haue warning by the Clarke of the counfell called *Dorofey Bufhew*, who receiueth order from the *Roferad* or high Conftable of the realme, to call them together at the time appointed.

F 4   *Of*

(25) *Roserad/Roseradney Dyake*

The 1 2. Chapter.

The offices of receipt.

OR the receyuing of cuſtomes, and other rentes belonging to the Crowne, there are appoynted diuers vnder officers, which deliuer ouer the ſame into the head treaſurie. The firſt is the office of *Dwoertſoua* or Steward of the houſholde. The ſecond is the office of the *Chetfirds*: which I comprehend ynder one, though it bee diuided into foure ſeuerall partes, as was ſayd before. The third is called *Bulſha prechode*, or the great Income.

The Steward receiuer of the crowne lãd rentes.

As touching the firſt, which is the office of the Steward, it receyueth all the rents of the Emperours inheritance, or Crowne lande, whiche they call *Vochin*. The *Vochin* or Crowne lande conteyneth in it 36. townes with the territories or hundreds belonging vnto them Whereof the chiefe that yeeld the greateſt rents are theſe : *Alexandriſca, Corelska, Otfer, Slobodey, Danielſka, Moiſalskoy, Chara, Sametska, Strararouſe, Branſoue,*

---

(29) *Corelska/Coselska* (29) *Slobodey/Sloboday* (30) *Chara, Sametska/Charasametska*

Branſoue, &c. The inhabitants or tenants of theſe and the other townes, pay ſome rent money, ſome other rent dueties (called *O-brokey*) as certeine *(hetfirds* , or meaſures of graine, wheate, rye, barley, oates, &c. or of other victuall , as Oxen, Sheepe , Swannes, Geeſe, Hares, Hennes, wild fowle, Fiſh, Hay, Wood, Honie, &c. Some are bound to ſowe for the Emperours prouiſion certaine Akers of ground, and to make the corne ready for his vſe : hauing for it an allowance of cer-taine akers of ground for their owne proper vſe.

This prouiſion for the houſhold, ſpecially of graine ſerued in by the Tenants, is a great deale more then is ſpent in his houſe , or in other allowance ſerued out in liuerie , or for the Emperours honour, called *Schalouaney:* for which vſe there is beſtowed very much both in graine, and other victuall. This ſur-plus of prouiſion is ſold by the Steward to the beſt hand , and runneth into the Empe-rours treaſurie.

In the time of *Iuan Vaſilowich* , father to this Emperour (who kept a more Princely & bountiful houſe then the Emperour now doth) this ouerplus of graine, and other in-comes into the Stewardes office, yeelded to his treaſurie not paſt 60. thouſand rubbels yeerely, but riſeth now by good husbanding of of the Steward *Gregory Vasilowich Godonoe*, to 230.thoufand rubbels a yere. And this by the meanes of the Empreffe, and her kinred, fpecially (*Borris Fedorowich Godonoe*) that account it al their owne that runneth into the Emperors treafure. Much of this furplufage that rifeth out of the rent prouifion, is emploied to the paimet of the wages of his houfhold officers, which are very many attending at home, and purueying abroad.

The office of *Chetfird*. The fecond office of receipt called the *Chetfirds*, (being deuided into foure feuerall partes, as before was fayde) hath foure head officers: which befides the ordering and gouernment of the fhires conteyned within their feuerall *Chedfirds*, haue this alfo

Tagla and Podat. as a part of their office, to receiue the *Tagla* and *Podat* belonging to the Emperour, that rifeth out of the foure *Chetfirds* or Quarters. The *Tagla* is a yeerely rent or impofition rayfed vpon euery *Wite* or meafure of graine, that groweth within the land, gathered by fworne men, and brought into the office. The *Wite* conteyneth fixtie *Chetfirds*. Euery *Chetfird* is three bufhelles Englifh, or little leffe. The *Podat* is an ordinarie rent of money impofed vpon euerie foake, or Hundred within the whole Realme.

This *Tagla* and *Podat* bring in yeerely to

to the Offices of the *Chetfirdes* a greate
fumme of money : as may appeare by the
particulars heere fet downe . The towne
and Prouince of *Vobsko* pay yeerely for
Tagla & *Podat* about 18000. rubbels.*Nouo-*
grod 35000.rubbels.*Torſhocke* & *Otſer* 8000.
rubbels. *Razan* 30000. rubbels. *Morum*
12000.rubbels. *Colmigroe* and *Duyna* 8000.
rubbels.*Vologda* 12000.rubbels.*Cazan* 18000
rubb.*Vſting* 30000. rubbels. *Roſtoue* 50000.
The citie of *Moſko* 40000.rubbels. *Sibier-*
skoy 20000. rubbels. *Caſtrome* 12000. rubbels . The totall amounteth to 400000.
rubbels,or marks a yeere, which is brought
in yeerely the firſt day of September, that
is reckoned by them the firſt day of the
yeere.

The thirde (that is called the *Bulſha Pre-* The office
chod, or great Income) receyueth all the of *Bulcha*
cuſtomes that are gathered out of all the *Preebod* or
great in-
principall townes and Cities within the come.
whole Realme . Beſides the fees and o-
ther dueties which riſe out of diuers fmaller Offices, which are all brought into this
office of *Bulſha Prechod* . The townes of
moſte trade that doe yeelde greateſt cuftome , are theſe heere fette downe . *Mo-*
sko, *Smolensko* , *Vobsko* , *Nouogrod Velica*,
Strararouſe , *Torſhocke* , *Otſer*, *Yaruslaue*, *Ca-*
ſtrome, *Neſna Nouogrod*, *Cazan*,*Vologda*.This
cuſtome

custome out of the great townes is therefore more certaine, and easie to be reckoned, because it is set and rated precisely what they shal pay for the custome of the yeere Which needes must bee paide into the saide office, though they receiue not so much. If it fal out to be more, it runneth al into the Emperours aduantage.

The Emperours custome.

The custome at *Mosko* for euerie yeere, is 12000. rubbels. The custome of *Smolensko*, 8000. *Vobsko* 12000. rubbels. *Nouogrod velica* 6000. rubbels. *Stararouse* by salt and other commodities 18000. rubbels. *Torshock* 800. rubbels. *Otfer* 700. rubbels. *Yarusflaue* 1200 rubbels. *Castrome* 1800. rubbels. *Nesna Nouogrod* 7000. rubbels. *Cazan* 11000. rubbels. *Vologda* 2000. rubbels. The custome of the rest that are townes of trade is sometimes more, sometimes lesse, as their traffike, and dealings with commodities too and fro, falleth out for the yeere.

The whole receipt of the *Bulsha Prechod* or great income.

This may bee saide for certaine, that the three tables of receipts belonging to this office of *Bulsha Prechod*, when they receiue left, account for thus much, vz. The first table 160000. rubbels. The second table 90000. rubbels. The third 70000. rubbels. So that there commeth into the office of *Bulsha Prechod*, at the least reckoning (as appeareth by their bookes of customs) out of these and other

ther

(25) lest/least   (28–29) *Bulsha Prechod/Bulsha Prechod*, for coustom only

ther townes, and maketh the fumme of
340000. rubbles a yeere. Befides this cuftome out of the townes of trade, there is
receiued by this office of *Bulſha Prechod,*the
yeerely rent of the common Bathftoaues, &   5
Cabacks or drinking houfes, which pertein
to the Emperour, Which (though it be vn-
certaine for the iuft fumme, yet becaufe it
is certaine and an ordinary matter, that the
Ruſſe wil bath himfelfe afwel within as with-   10
out) yeeldeth a large rent to the Emperours
treafurie.

There is befides, a certeine mulct or pe-   Rents out
naltie that groweth to the Emperour out of ofrhe iudi-
euery iudgement,or fentence that paffeth in cial offices   15
any of his courts of Record in all ciuill mat-
ters.This penaltie,or mulct is 20,*Dingoes* or
pence vpon euery rubble or marke, and fo
ten in the hundred, Which is paide by the
partie that is conuict by lawe. Hee hath be-   20
fides for euery name conteyned in the writs
that paffe out of thefe courts,fiue *Alteens.*
An *Alteen* is fiue pence fterling, or there a-
bouts, This is made good out of the office,
whence the writ is taken foorth. Thence it   25
goeth to the office that keepeth the leffer
feale, where it payeth as much more to the
Emperours vfe. This rifeth commonly to
3000. rubbels a yeere, or thereabouts. Farther alfo out of the office of *Roiſbonia,*where   30
all

(16–17) ciuill matters/civill matters of contract   (23) fiue/iiij   (26) office that
keepeth/office of *Pechatney* that keepeth   (30) *Roisbonia*/*Rosboyna*

all fellonies are tried, is receiued for the Emperour the halfe part of fellons goodes, the other halfe goeth the one part to the informer, the other to the officers.

All this is brought into the office of *Bulsha Prechod*, or great income. Besides the ouerplus or remainder that is saued out of the land rents, allotted to diuers other offices: as namely to the office called *Roserade*, which hath landes and rentes afsigned vnto it to pay the yeerely salaries of the souldiers, or horsemen, that are kept still in pay. Which in time of peace when they rest at home not employed in anie seruice, is commonly cut off and payde them by halfes, sometimes not the halfe: so that the remainder out of the *Roserade* Office that is layde into the Emperours treasurie, commeth for the most part euerie yeere to 250000. rubbels.

In like sort (though not so much) is brought in the surplus out of the *Strelletskey* offices which hath proper lands for the payment of the *Strelsey* men or gunners, aswell those at *Mosko*, that are of the Emperors gard (12000. in ordinary) as on the borders, and other garrison townes and castels. Likewise out of the office of *Prechase, Shisiuoy Nemshoy* which hath set allowance of landes to mainteine the forreyne mercenarie

---

(5–6) All this is brought into the office of *Bulsha Prechod*, or great income *omitted*. (11) souldiers/*Boiaren* Souldiours   (21–23) In like sort . . . offices/The like though not so much is brought into the *Bulsha Prechod* owt of the *Strelletskoy* Office   (28–29) *Prechase, Shisiuoy Nemshoy* omitted; [blank space left presumably for words to be inserted].

rie fouldiers., as *Poles*, *Sweadens*, *Doutches*, Scots,*&c.* So out of the office of *Pufharskoy,* (which hath lands and rents allowed for the prouifion of munition ,*great Ordinance,pow-* *der*, *Shot*, *Salpeeter*, *Brimftone*, *Ledde*, and 5 fuch like) there is left fomewhat at the yeres ende, that runneth into the treafurie. All thefe bring into the office of *Bulfha Pre-* *chod* that which remaineth in their hand at the yeeres end. Whence it is deliuered into 10 the Emperours treafurie. So that the whole fumme that groweth to this office of *Bul-* *fha Prechod,* or the great income (as appeareth by the bookes of the faid office)amounteth to 80000, rubbels a yeere, or therea- 15 bouts.

All thefe offices,to wit, the office of the The EmpeSteward, the foure *(hetfirds*, and the *Bul-* rours trea-
fha Prechod deliuer in their receiptes to the fure houfe within his head treafurie,that lyeth within the Empe- caftle of 20 rours houfe or caftle at the *Mosko*. Where *Mosko.* lye all his moneyes, iewels, crownes, fcepters, plate,and fuch like , the chefts,hutches, and bagges beyng figned by the Emperours themfelues with their owne feale. Though 25 at this time the L. *Borris Federowich Godonoe* his feale and ouerfight fupplieth for the Emperor,as in al other things. The vnder officer at this time is one *Stepan Vafilowich Godo-* *noe.* Coofin germane to the fayde *Borris,* 30 who

who hath two Clearkes allowed to serue vnder him in the office.

The summe of the Emperours rét money.	The súme that groweth to the Emperoures treasurie in money onely, for euerie yeere.	1 *Out of the Stewards office aboue the expense of his house* 23000. *rubbels.* 2 *Out of the foure Chetfirds for soake & head money* 400000 *rubbels.* 3 *Out of the* Bulsha Precod *Office, or great incoome, for custome and other rents.* 800000. *rubbels.*	Summe 1430000 rubbles cleere, besides all charges for his house, & ordinary saleries of his souldiers otherwise discharged.

But besides this reuenue that is paid all in money to the Emperours treasurie, he receiueth yeerely in furres, and other dueties to a great value out of *Siberia, Pechora, Permia,* and other places, which are solde or bartred away for other forreine commodities to the *Turkish Persian, Armenian, Georgian* and *Bougharian* Marchants that trade within his coũtries, besides others of Christendome, What it maketh in the whole (though the value can not be set downe precisely, as being a thing casual as the commodity may be got) it may

be

be geſſed by that which was gathered the
laſt yeere out of *Siberia* for the Emperours
cuſtome, vz. 466. timber of Sables, fiue timber of Martrones, 180. blacke Foxes, beſides
other commodities.

To theſe may bee added their ſeazures,
and confiſcations vpon ſuch as are in diſpleaſure, which riſeth to a great ſumme Beſides other their extraordinary impoſitions,
and exactions done vpon their officers, Monaſteries, &c. not for any apparant necefsity
or vſe of the Prince, or common wealth, but
of will and cuſtome : yet with ſome pretence
of a *Scythian*, that is, groſſe and barbarous
pollicie (as may appeare) by theſe fewe *So-*
phiſmata, or counterfeit pollicies, put in practiſe by the Emperours of *Ruſſia*, all tending
to this end to robbe their people, and to in-
rich their treaſurie. To this purpoſe this by-
word was vſed by the late Emperour *Iuan*
Vaſilowich: That his people were like to his beard.
The oftner ſhauen, the thicker it would grow. Or
like ſheepe that muſt needes be ſhorne once
a yeere at the leaſt: to keepe them
from being ouerladen with their
wooll.

G   Meanes

Meanes vſed to draw the wealth
of the land into the Emperours
Treaſurie.

5

TO preuent no extortions exactions, or briberies whatſoeuer, done vpon the cōmons by their Dukes, Diacks, or other officers in their Prouinces: but to ſuffer them to go on till their time bee expired, and to ſucke themſelues ful. Then to cal them to the *Praueuſh*(or whippe)for their behauiour, and to beat out of them all, or the moſt part of the bootie, (as the honie from the Bee) which they haue wrung from the commons, and to turne it into the Emperours treaſurie, but neuer any thing backe againe to the right owners, how great or euident ſoeuer the iniurie be. To this end the needy Dukes, & Diacks, that are ſent into their prouinces, ſerue the turne very well, being chaunged ſo often (to wit) once a yeere : where in reſpect of their owne, and the qualitie of the people (as before was ſaid) they might be continued for ſome longer time, without all feare of innouation. For comming ſtill freſh vpon the commons, they ſucke more egerly : like *Tiberius* the Emperours flies, that came newe ſtill vpon all olde ſore. To whome hee was

wont

wont to compare his *Pretors*, and other pro-
uinciall officers.

2

TO make of thefe officers (that haue robbed their people) fometimes a publike
example, if any be more notorious then the
reſt: that the Emperour may feem to miſlike
the oppreſsions done to his people, & tranſ-
ferre the fault to his ill officers.

As among diuers other, was done by the
late Emperour *Iuan Vaſilowich* to a Diack in
one of his Prouinces: that (befides many o-
ther extortions, and briberies) had taken a
goofe ready dreſt full of money. The man
was brought to the market place in *Moſko.* The Emperour himſelfe prefent made an
Oration. Thefe good people are they that
would eate you vp like bread, &c. Then aſ-
ked hee his *Polachies* or executioners, who
could cut vp a goofe, and commaunded one
of them firſt to cut off his legges about the
middes of the ſhinne. then his armes aboue
his elbowes (asking him ſtill if goofe fleſhe
were good meate) in the ende to choppe off
his head : that he might haue the right faſhion of a goofe readie dreſſed. This might
feeme to haue beene a tollerable piece of iuſtice (as iuſtice goeth in *Ruſſia*) except his
fubtill end to couer his owne oppreſſions.

G 2 3 To

5

10

15

20

25

30

(4–5) (that haue robbed their people)/(that have robbed their people and are spoiled
again by the Emperour him self) (11–12) to a Diack . . . Prouinces/to one *Ivan
Michaelowich Visekovatl*

3

TO make an open ſhew of want, when a-
nie great taxe, or impoſition is towards.
As was done by this Emperour *Theodore Iu-*
anowich, by the aduiſe of ſome about him
at the beginning of his reigne : when being left very rich (as was thought) by his father, he ſold moſt of his plate, and ſtamped
ſome into coyne : that hee might ſeeme to
want money. Whereupon preſently out
came a taxation.

4

TO ſuffer their ſubiects to giue freely to
the Monaſteries (which for their ſuperſtition very many doe, ſpecially in their laſt
wils) & to lay vp their money and ſubſtance
in them, to keepe it more ſate. Which all is
permitted thē without any reſtraint, or prouiſo, as was & is in ſome countries of chriſtē-
dome. Whereby their Monaſteries grow to
exceeding great wealth. This they do to haue
the money of the Realme better ſtored together, and more ready for their hand, when
they liſt to take it. Which manie times is
done without anie noyſe: the Fryers beeyng
content rather to part from ſomewhat (as
the encreaſe groweth) then to looſe all at
once. Which they were made to doubt of in
the other Emperours dayes.

To this end *Iuan Vaſilowich* late Emperour
vſed

---

vſed a very ſtrange practiſe, that few Princes would haue done in their greateſt extremities. He reſigned his kingdome to one *Veliea Knez Simeon* , the Emperours ſonne of *Cazan:* as though hee meant to draw himſelfe from al publike doings to a quiet priuat life. Towards the end of the yeere , hee cauſed this newe King to call in all Charters graunted to Biſhoprickes and Monaſteries, which they had enioyed manie hundred yeeres before. Which were all cancelled . This done (as in diſlike of the fact and of the miſgouernment of the newe King) hee reſumed his ſcepter, and ſo was content (as in fauour to the Church and religious men) that they ſhould renew their charters, & take them of himſelfe: reſeruing and annexing to the Crowne ſo much of their lands, as himſelfe thought good.

By this practiſe hee wrung from the Biſhoprickes, and Monaſteries (beſides the landes which he annexed to the Crowne) an huge maſſe of money. From ſome 40, from ſome 50, from ſome an hundred thouſande rubbels ♦ And this aſwell for the increaſe of his treaſurie , as to abate the ill opinion of his harde gouernment, by a ſhewe of woorſe in an other man ♦ Wherein his ſtrange ſpirite is to bee noted : that beyng hated of his ſubiectes, (as himſelfe knew wel

G 3   inough)

(6) from al publike doings/quite from the troubles of his kindoom (13–14) resumed his scepter/retourned into his seat and resumed his Kingdoom (28) woorse . . . man/woorse government in an other Emperour

inough) yet would venture such a practise,to
set an other in his saddle, that might haue
ridde away with his horse, while himselfe
walked by on foote.

5

TO sende their messengers into the Prouinces,or shires where the special commodities of their countrey grow , as surres,
waxe,hony,&c.There to forestall & ingrosse
somtime one whole commodity, sometime
two,or more, taking the at smal prices what
theselues list,& selling them againe at an ex-
cessiue rate to their own marchants, and to
marchants strangers. If they refuse to buy
them,then to force them vnto it.

The like is done when any commoditie
eyther natiue,or forreine (as cloth of golde,
broade cloth,&c.)thus engrossed by the Emperour,and receiued into his treasurie, happeneth to decay,or marre by long lying , or
some other casualtie. Which is forced vpon
the Marchants,to be bought by them at the
Emperours price, whether they will or no.
This last yeere of 1 5 8 9. was engrossed all
the waxe of the countrey:so that none might
deale with that commoditie, but the Emperour onely.

6

TO take vp & engrosse in like sort sometime forreine commodities (as silkes,
cloth,

cloth, ledde, pearle, &c. brought into his realm by *Turkish* marchants, *Armenians,Bougharians,Poles,English,*and other. And then to force his marchants to buy them of his officers at his owne price.

7

TO make a Monopoly for the time of such comodities as are paid him for rēt, or custom,& to inhanse the price of thē,as surres, corn,wood,&c. What time none must sell of the same kind of cōmodity,til the Emperors be all sold.By this means hee maketh of his rent,corn,& other prouisiō of victual (as before was said)about 200000. rubb, or marks a yeere. Of his rent wood, hay, &c,300 00, rubbels,or thereabouts.

8

IN euery great towne of his Realme he hath a *Caback* or drinking house,where is sold *aquavita*(which they cal *Russe wine)mead,beere, &c*. Out of these hee receiueth rent that amounteth to a great summe of money.Some yeeld 800,some 900,some a 1000 some 2000 or 3000. rubbels a yere.Wherein besides the base,and dishonourable meanes to encrease his treasurie , many foule faultes are committed . The poore labouring man , and artificer , manie times spendeth all from his wife and children.Some vse to lay in twentie,thirtie,fourtie rubbels, or more into the

Caback,

Caback, and vowe themselues to the pot, till all that be spent. And this (as he will say) for the honour of *Hospodare*, or the Emperour. You shall haue manie there that haue drunk all away to the verie skinne, and so walk naked (whom they call *Naga.*) While they are in the *Caback*, none may call them foorth whatsoeuer cause there be, becaufe he hindereth the Emperours reuenue.

9

TO cause some of his *Boiarens*, or *Nobles* of his court, (whomhe vseth vpon trust) that haue houses in the *Mosko*, to faine themselues robbed. Then to send for the *Zemskey* men, or Aldermen of the citie, and to commaund them to finde out the robberie. In default of not finding it, to praue or seasse the citie for their misgouernment in 8000. 9000. or 10000. rubbels at a time. This is many times practised.

10

IN these exactions to shew their soueraigntie, sometime they vse very plaine, and yet strange cauillations. As was that of *Iuan Vasiliowich*, father to this Emperour, after this sort. He sent into *Permia* for certaine loads of *Cedar wood*, whereof hee knew that none grew in that Countrey. The inhabitants returned answere they could find none there: Whereupon hee seassed their Countrey in 12000.

12000.rubbels, as if they côcealed the commoditie of purpofe. Againe he fent to the
citie of *Mosko* to prouide for him a *Colpack*,
or meafure full of liue fleas for a medicine.
They returned anfwere that the thing was
impofsible. And if they could get them, yet
they could not meafure them, for leaping
out. Whereupon he praued, or beat out of
their fhinnes 7000.rubbels for a mulct.

By like cauillation hee extorted from his
Nobilitie 30000.rubbels, becaufe he miffed
of his game, when he went a hunting for the
Hare: as if their hunting and murdering of
hares had bin the caufe of it. Which the Nobilitie (as the manner is) praued prefently
againe vpon the *Mouficks*, or common people of the Countrie. This may feeme a
ftraunge kinde of extortion, by fuch pleafant cauils to fliefe his poore fubiectes in
good fadneffe : but that it agreeth with the
qualitie of thofe Emperours, and the miferable fubiection of that poore Countrie.
Thefe, and fuch like meanes are practi-
fed by the Emperours of Ruffia,
to encreafe their Trea-
furie.

Of

Of the ſtate of the Communaltie, or
vulgar ſorte of people in the coun-
trie of Ruſſia.

The 13.Chapter.

THE condition of the com-
mons, and vulgar ſort of people may partly be vnderſtood
by that which already hath
bin ſaid concerning the mã-
ner of their gouernment, &
the ſtate of the Nobilitie, with the ordering
of their Prouinces, and chiefe townes of the
land. And firſt touching their libertie how
it ſtandeth with them, it may appeare by
this: that they are reckoned in no degree at
all, nor haue any ſuffrage nor place in their
Zabore, or high court of Parliament, where
their lawes and publique orders are concluded vpon. Which commonly tend to the oppreſsion of the commons. For the other two
degrees vz: of the Nobilitie, and Cleargie, whiche haue a vote in the Parliaments
(though farre from that libertie that ought
to bee in common conſultations for the publique benefite, according to the meaſure
and proportion of their degrees) are well
contented that the whole burden ſhall light
vpon the commons, ſo they may eaſe their
owne

*The ſeruile
and miſera-
ble eſtate of
the Ruſſe
people.*

owne shoulders by laying all vpon them. A-
gaine into what seruile condition their libertie is brought, not onely to the Prince, but to
the Nobles, and Gentlemen of the Countrie
(who themselues also are but seruile, specially of late yeares) it may farther appeare by
their owne acknowledgments in their sup-
plications, and other writings to any of the
Nobles or chiefe officers of the Emperours.
Wherein they name and subscribe themselues *Kolophey*, that is, their villaines, or
bondslaues: as they of the Nobilitie doo vnto the Emperour. This may truely be saide
of them, that there is no seruant nor bondslaue more awed by his Maister, nor kept
downe in a more seruile subiection, then the
poore people are, & that vniuersally, not only
by the Emperour, but by his Nobilitie, chief
officers, and souldiers. So that when a poore
Mousick meeteth with any of them vpon the
high way, he must turne himselfe about, as
not daring to looke him on the face, and fall
down with knocking of his head to the very
ground, as he doth vnto his Idoll.

    Secondly concerning the landes, goods,
and other possessions of the commons, they
answere the name and lie common indeed
without any fense againſt the rapine, and
spoile, not onely of the higheſt, but of his
Nobilitie, officers, and souldiers. Besides
the

the taxes, cuſtomes, ſeazures, and other publique exactions done vpon them by the
Emperour, they are ſo racked and pulled by
the Nobles, officers, and meſſengers ſent a-
broad by the Emperour in his publique affaires, ſpecially in the *Yammes* (as they call
them)and thorough faire townes, that you
ſhall haue many villages and townes of halfe
a mile, and a mile long,ſtande all vnhabited:
the people being fled all into other places
by reaſon of the extreame vſage, and exactions done vponthem. So that in the way towards *Mosko*, betwixt *Vologda* and *Yaruſl i-
neley*(which is two nineties after their reckoning,litle more then an hundreth miles Engliſh) there are in ſigt fiftie *Darienne*s or villages at the leaſt, ſome halfe a mile, ſome a
mile long(that ſtand vacant)& deſolate with
out any inhabitant. The like is in all other
places of the realme (as is ſaid by thoſe that
haue better trauelled the countrie then my
ſelfe had time, or occaſion to doo.

The great oppreſsion ouer the poore
Commons, maketh thē to haue no courage
in following their trades : for that the more
they haue,the more daunger they are in, not
onely of their goods, but of their liues alſo.
And if they haue any thing,they conceale it
all they can,ſomtimes conueying it into Monaſteries, ſometimes hiding it vnder the
ground

grcund, and in woods, as men are woont to
doo where they are in feare of forreine inuafion. In fo much that many times you fhall
fee them afraid to be knowen to any *Boiuren*
or Gentleman of fuch commodities as they
haue to fell. I haue feene them fometimes
whenthey haue layed open their commodities for a liking (as their principall furres &
fuch like) to looke ftill behind them, and towards euery doore:as men in fome feare,that
looked to be fet vpon,& furprifed by fome
enimie, Whereof asking the caufe,I found it
to be this,that they haue doubted leaft fome
Noblemã or *Sinaboiarskey* of the Emperour
had bene in côpanie, & fo layed a traine for
thê to pray vpon their cômodities perforce.
     This maketh the people (though other-
wife hardened to beare any toile) to giue
them elues much to idlenes and drinking:
as pafsing for no more, then from hand to
mouth. And hereof it commeth that the cômodities of *Ruffia* (as was faid before) as *wax,
tallow, hydes, flaxe, hempe, &c.*)grow and goe
abroad in farre leffe plentie then they were
woont to doo: becaufe the people being oppreffed and fpoiled of their gettings,are dif-
couraged from their laboures. Yet this one
thing is much to be noted,that in all this opprefsion there were three brethren Marchants of late that traded together with one
                                   ftocke

ftocke in common, that were found to bee
woorth 300000. rubbels in money, befides
landes , cattels , and other commodities.
Which may partly be imputed to their dwellings far of from the eye of the Court, vz, in
Wichida, a 1000. miles from *Mosko*, & more.
The fame are faid by thofe that knew them
to haue fet on worke all the yeare long ten
thoufand men in making of falt, carriages by
cart, & boat, hewing of wood, and fuch like:
befides 5000 bondflaues at the leaft, to inhabite and till their land.

They had alfo their phyfitions, furgeons,
apothecaries, and all manner of artificers of
Doutches and others, belonging vnto them.
They are faid to haue paied to the Emperour
for cuftome to the fum of 23000. rubbles a
yeare (for which caufe they were fuffered to
enioy their trade) befides the mainteining
of certeine garrifons on the borders of *Siberia*, which were neare vnto the. Wherin the
Emperour was content to vfe their purfe, till
fuch time as they had got ground in *Siberia*,
and made it habitable, by burning, and cutting downe woods from *Wichida* to *Perm* ,
aboue a 1000 verfe and then tooke it all a-
way from them perforce.

But this in the end beyng enuied, and
difdained, as a matter not ftanding with
their pollicie to haue any fo great, fpecially

(4–6) Which may . . . & more/*omitted*.   (18–19) *Parenthetical phrase omitted.*

ally a *Mousick*, the Emperour began first to
to pull frō them by pieces, sometimes 20000
rubbels at a time, sometime more: till in the
end their sonnes that now are, are well eased of their stocke, and haue but small parte   5
of their fathers substance : the rest being
drawen all into the Emperours treasurie.
Their names were *Iacone, Gregorie,* & *Simon*
the sonnes of *Onyka.*

For the qualitie of their people other- The tyran-   10
wise, though there seemeth to be in them ny and op-
some aptnesse to receyue any art (as appea- uer their
reth by the naturall wittes in the men, and very minds
very children) yet they excell in no kinde of and wits.
common arte, much lesse in any learning,   15
or litterall kinde of knowledge : which they
are kept from of purpose, as they are also
from all militarie practise : that they may be
fitter for the seruile condition, wherein now
they are, and haue neyther reason, nor va-   20
lure to attempt innouation. For this purpose also they are kept from traueling, that
they may learne nothing, nor see the fashions of other Countries abroad . You
shall seldome see a *Russe* a traueller, ex-   25
cept he be with some Ambassadour, or that
he make a scape out of his Countrie. Which
hardly he can doo, by reason of the borders
that are watched so narrowly, and the punishment for any such attempt, which is   30
death

death if he be taken, and all his goods con-
fifcate. Onely they learne to write, and to
read, and that very few of them. Neither doo
they fuffer any ftraunger willingly to come
into their realme out of any ciuill Countrie,
for the fame caufe, farther then necefsitie of
vttering their commodities, and taking in of
forreine doth enforce them to doo.

The ielou-
fie of the
Emperour
concerning
his ftate.
And therefore this yeare 1589. they con-
fulted about the remouing of all Marchants
ftraungers to the border townes, to abide
and haue their refidencie there, and to bee
more wary in admitting other ftraungers
hereafter into the Inland parts of the realm,
for feare of infection with better manners
and qualities, then they haue of their owne.
For the fame purpofe alfo they are kept
within the boundes of their degree by the
lawes of their countrie : fo that the fonne of
a *Moufick*, artificer, or husbandman, is euer
a *Moufick* artificer, &c : and hath no means
to afpire any higher: except hauing learned
to write and read, he attaine to the preferment of a Prieft, or Dyack. Their language is
all one with the *Slauonian*, which is thought
to haue bene deriued from the *Ruffe* tongue,
rather then the *Ruffe* from the *Slauonian*. For
the people called *Sclaui*, are knowen to haue
had their beginning out of *Sarmatia*, and to
haue termed themfelues of their conqueft
Sclauos

(24) Their language . . . [to end of paragraph on p. 49] *omitted.*

Sclauos, (that is) famous or glorious, of the word *Sclaua*, which in the *Ruſſe* & *Slauonian* tongue, ſignifieth as much as *Glory*, or *Fame.* Though afterwards being ſubdued and trod vpon by diuers nations, the *Italians* their neighbours haue turned the worde to a contrary ſignification, and terme euery ſeruant or peaſant by the name of *Sclaue*, as did the *Romanes* by the *Getes* & *Syrians*, for the ſame reaſon. The *Ruſſe* character or letter is no other then the *Greeke*, ſomewhat diſtorted.

Concerning their trades, diet, apparell, and ſuch like, it is to be noted in a ſeuerall chapter of their priuate behauiour. This order that bindeth euery man to keepe his rancke, and ſeuerall degree, wherin his forefathers liued before him, is more meet to keepe the ſubiects in a ſeruile ſubiection and ſo apt for this and like Common-wealths, then to aduaunce any vertue, or to breed any rare or excellent qualitie in Nobilitie or Commons : as hauing no farther rewarde nor preferment, whereunto they may bend their endeuours, and imploy themſelues to aduaunce their eſtate but rather procuring more danger to themſelues, the more they excell in any noble or principall qualitie.

H   Of

The 14. Chapter.

Courts of ciuill iustice three.

Heir courts of ciuil iustice for matters of contract, & other of like sort, are of three kinds, the one beyng subiect vnto the other by way of appeale. The lowest Court (that seemeth to be appointed for some ease to the subiects) is the office of the *Gubnoy Starust*, that signifieth an Alderman, & of the *Sotskoy Starust*, or Bailief of the soake or hundred, wherof I spake before in the ordering of the Prouinces. These may ende matters among their neighbours within their soke, or seuerall hudred, where they are appointed vnder the Dukes & Diacks of the Prouinces, to whom the parties may remoue their matter, if they cannot be agreed by the said *Gubnoy*, or *Sotskoj Starust*.

The Dukes and Diacks Court.

The second is kept in the head townes of euery Prouince or Shire, by the said Dukes and Diacks, that are deputies to the foure

Lords

Lords of the *Chetfirds* (as before was fayd)
From these courts they may appeale,and remoue their suites to the chiefe Court, that is
kept at the *Mosko,*where are resident the officers of the foure *Chetfirds ,* These are the
chiefe Iustices or Iudges,euery of them in all
ciuill matters that grow within their seuerall
Chetfird or quarter , and may be either com-
menced originally before them,or prosequu-
ted out of the inferiour Courts of the Shires
by way of appeale.

The high
Court of
Mosko.

5

10

Their commencing, and proceeding in
ciuill actions is on this manner . First , the
plaintife putteth vp his supplication,where-
in hee declareth the effect of his cause , or
wrong done vnto him. Whereupon is granted vnto him a *Wepis* , or warrant, which
hee deliuereth to the *Præstane* , or Sergeant,
to doo the arrest vpon the partie whom hee
meaneth to implead . Who vpon the arrest , is to put in sureties to answere the day
appointed , or els standeth at the Sergeants
deuotion , to be kept safe by such meanes as
he thinketh good.

Their mā-
ner of pro-
cedcing in
Ciuill mat-
ters.

15

20

The Sergeants are many , and excell for
their hard and cruell dealing towards their
prysoners , commonly they clappe irons
vpon them, as many as they can beare, to
wring out of them some larger fees, Though
it bee but for sixe pence, you shall see them

25

30

H 2   goe

---

(1) (as before was sayd)/(as beefore was saied) yet at the Emperours appointment
(4) *Mosko*, where arc resident/*Mosko*, where is the head & cheef Court, whear are
resident (29) some larger fees/a better bribe

goe with chaynes on their legges, armes, and necke. When they come before the Iudge, the plaintife beginneth to declare his matter after the content of his supplication. As for Attourneis, Counsellours, Procuratours & Aduocates to plead their cause for them, they haue no such order, but euery man is to tell his owne tale, and plead for himselfe so well as he can.

If they haue any witnesse, or other euidence, they produce it before the Iudge. If

Ending of controuersies by kissing the Crosse.

they haue none, or if the truth of the cause cannot so well bee decerned by the plea, or euidence on both partes: then the Iudge asketh eyther partie (which hee thinketh good plaintife or defendant) whether hee will *kisse the Crosse*, vpon that which he auoucheth, or denieth. Hee that taketh tho Crosse (being so offered by the Iudge) is accounted cleare, and carrieth away the matter. This ceremonie is not done within the Court or office, but the partie is carried to the Church by an officer, and there the ceremonie is done: the mony in the meane while hanging vpon a naile, or els lying at the idols feete, ready to be deliuered to the partie, as soone as he hath kissed the Crosse before the said Idoll.

This kissing of the Crosse (called *(reustina chelouania)* is as their corporall oath

and

and accounted with them a very holy thing, which no man will dare to violate, or prophane with a falſe allegation. If both parties offer to kiſſe the Croſſe in a contradictorie matter, thcn they drawe lottes. The better lotte is ſuppoſed to haue the right, and beareth away the matter. So the partie conuicted is adiudged to pay the debt or penaltie whatſoeuer, and withall to pay the Emperours fees, which is twentie pence vpon euery marke, as before hath bene noted.

Iudgement by lotte.

When the matter is thus ended, the partie conuicted is deliuered to the Sergeant, who hath a writte for his warrant out of the office, to carry him to the *Praueuſh* or Righter of Iuſtice, if preſently hee pay not the monie, or content not the partie. This *Praueuſh* or Righter, is a place neare to the office where ſuch as haue ſentence paſſed againſt them, and refuſe to pay that which is adiudged, are beaten with great cudgels on the ſhinnes, and calues of their legges. Euery forenoone from eight to eleuen, they are ſet on the *Praueuſh*, and beate in this ſort till the monie be payd. The afternoone and night time, they are kepte in chaines by the Sergeant: except they put in ſufficient ſuerties for their apparance at the *Praueuſh* at the hower appointed. You ſhall ſee for-

H 3   tie

tie or fiftie ſtand together on the *Prаиеиſh* all on a rowe, and their ſhinnes thus becud-gelled, and bebaſted euery morning with a piteous crie. If after a yeares ſtanding on the *Prаиеиſh*, the partie will not, or lacke wherewithall to ſatisfie his creditour, it is lawfull for him to ſell his wife, and children, eyther out right, or for a certaine terme of yeares. And if the price of them doo not a-mount to the full payment, the creditour may take them to bee his bondſlaues, for yeares or for euer, according as the value of the debt requireth.

Such kinde of ſuites as lacke direct euidence, or ſtande vpon coniectures and circumſtances to bee waighed by the Iudge, drawe of great length, and yeeld great aduantage to the Iudge, and officers. If the ſuite be vpon a bond, or bill, they haue for the moſte parte good and ſpeedy iuſtice. Their bonds, or billes are drawen in a very plaine ſorte, after this tenour. *I Iuan Vaſileo haue borrowed of Alphonaſſe Dementio, the ſumme of one hundred rubbles of going money of Mosko, from the Kreſhenеa (or hallowing of the water) vntill the Saburney yoſcreſhenеa (or Counſell Sunday) without intereſt And if this money reſt vnpayed after that day, then hee ſhall giue intereſt vpon the ſayd money, after the common rate, as it goeth among the*

The forme of *Ruſſe* bils or bonds.

---

(19) or bill/or bill of his hand (25) [In the manuscript the word *Kreshenea* is marked with the symbol (a), which refers to a marginal note: "*This is about Twelftyde when they hallow all their waters.*"] (26) [The word *Sabourney* is marked with the symbol (b), which refers to the marginal note: "*which is midlent sonday, when the Appostles mett all together (as sayeth their tradition).*"]

the people, *vz.* for euerie fiue the fixt rubbell.
Vpon this there are witnesses, *Micheta Sydro-*
ueskoy,&c: Subscribed. This bill haue I written
Gabriell Iacouelesni, in the yeare 7 0 9 6. The
witnesses, and debter (if he can write) en-   5
dorse their names on the backe side of the
bill . Other signing, or sealing haue they
none.

When any is taken for a matter of crime   Proceeding
(as treason, murder, thefte, and such like) in criminall   10
hee is first brought to the Duke, and Diack,   matters.
that are for the Prouince where the partie
is attached, by whom hee is examined . The
manner of examination in such cases, is all
by torture, as scourging with whips made   15
of sinowes, or whitleather (called the *Pud-*
key) as bigge as a mans finger , which giueth a sore lash, and entreth into the flesh,
or by tying to a spit and rosting at the fire,
sometimes by breaking and wresting one   20
of their ribbes with a payre of hote tongues,
or cutting their flesh vnder the nayles , and
such like.

The examination thus taken withall the
proofes, and euidences that can bee alleadg-   25
ged against the partie, it is sent vp to the
Mosko to the Lord of the *Chetfird* or Fourth-
parte, vnder whom the Prouince is, and by
him is presented to the Counsell table, to
bee read and sentenced there, where onely   30
H 4   iudge-

---

(4) *Iacouelesni/Jacoveliovesyn* (30) sentenced there/sentenced by the Emperours
Counsell

iudgement is giuen in matter of life & death, and that by euidence vpon information, though they neuer sawe nor heard the partie, who is kept still in pryson where the fact

5   was committed, and neuer sent vp to the place where he is tried. If they find the partie guiltie, they giue sentence of death according to the qualitie of the fact: which is sent downe by the Lord of the *Chetfird*, to the

10   Duke and Diack to bee put in execution. The prisoner is carried to the place of execution with his handes bounde, and a waxe candle burning helde betwixt his fingers.

      Their capitall punishmentes are hang-

15   ing, hedding, knocking on the head, drowning, putting vnder the yse, setting on a stake, and such like. But for the most part the prisoners that are condemned in Sommer, are kept for the winter, to be knockt

20   in the head, and put vnder the yse. This is to bee vnderstood of common persons. For theft, and murder, if they be committed vpon a poore *Mousick* by one of Nobilitie are not lightly punished, nor yet is hee cal-

25   led to any account for it. Their reason is, becaufe they are accounted their *Kolophey*, or bondslaues. If by some *Sinaboiarskey*, or Gentleman fouldier, a murder or theft bee committed, peraduenture he shal be im-

30   prisoned at the Emperours pleasure. If the
                manner

(5–6) and neuer sent vp to the place where he is tried *omitted*. (8–10) which is sent downe by the Lord of the *Chetfird*, to the Duke and Diack to bee put in execution *omitted*. (17) *After the words* and such like *the following passage is inserted*: This Sentence is delivered by the Counsell to the Lord of the *Chetfird*, and by him sent to the Duke and Diake of the Shire, whear the fact was committed, to execute the partie condemned according to the tenour of the Sentence. (17–20) But for the most part . . . under the yse *omitted*.

manner of the fact be verie notorious, he is
whipped perchance , and this is commonly
all the punishment that is inflicted vpon
them.

If a man kill his owne seruant,little,or no-   5
thing is said vnto him,for the same reason:
because hee is accounted to be his *Kolophey*,
or bondslaue, and so to haue right ouer his
verie head. The most is some small mulct to
the Emperour,if the partie be rich:& so the   10
quarell is made rather against the purse,then
against the iniustice . They haue no written
law ,saue onely a smal booke that conteineth
the time,and manner of their sitting , order
in proceeding,and such other iudicial forms   15
and circumstances,but nothing to direct the
to giue sentence vpon right or wrong.Their
onely lawe is their *Speaking Law*, that is, the
pleasure of the Prince,and of his Magistrates
and officers. Which sheweth the miserable   20
condition of this poore people,that are forced to haue them for their law,and direction
of iustice, against whose iniustice,and extreame oppresion,they had neede
to be armed with many good,   25
and strong lawes.

Their

(1) verie *omitted*. (3) all the punishment/the greatest punishment (10–12) the
Emperour . . . iniustice/the Emperours treasurie if the partie bee rich and so they
list to make a quarrell more to his purse then to him (20) and officers/and Officers
that are sett under him (23–24) extreame *omitted*. (26) and strong *omitted*.

The 15. Chapter.

He souldiers of *Russia* are called *Sinaboiarskey*, or the sons of Gentlemen: because they are all of that degree, by vertue of their millitary profession. For euery souldier in *Russia* is a gentleman, and none are gentlemen, but only the souldiers, that take it by discent from their anceſtors: so that the sonne of a gentleman (which is borne a souldier) is euer a gentlemā, & a souldier withal, & professeth nothing els but militarie matters. Whē they are of yeeres able to beare armes, they come to the office of *Roserade*, or great Conſtable, and there present themselues : who entreth their names, and allotteth them certeine lands to maintein their charges, for the moſt part the same that their fathers enioyed. For the lands afsigned to mainteine the army, are euer certein, annexed to this office without improuing, or detracting one foot. But that if the Emperour haue sufficient in wages, the roomes being full so farre as the lande doeth extend already, they are manie times

Souldiers by birth & inheritāce.

(10–14) by vertue . . . only the souldiers *omitted*. (22–30) allotteth them . . . extend already/allotteth them a certain stipend, with lands to maintain their charges. But if the Emperour have manie and sufficient in wages allreadie times deferred, and haue nothing allowed them, except fome one portiō of the land be deuided into two. Which is a caufe of great diforder within that countrie: when a fouldi-er that hath many children, fhal haue fome-times but one intertained in the Emperours pay. So that the reft hauing nothing, are for-ced to liue by vniuft and wicked fhiftes, that tend to the hurt & opprefsion of the *Mou-fick*, or common fort of people. This incon-uenience groweth by mainteining his forces in a continual fuccefsion. The whole num-ber of his fouldiers in continual pay, is this. Firft, he hath of **His** *Dworaney*, that is, Penfio-ners, or Gard of his perfon, to the number of 15000. horfemen, with their captaines, and other officers, that are alwaies in a readines.

Of thefe 15000. horfemen, there are three forts or degrees, which differ afwell in efti-mation, as in wages, one degree from ano-ther. The firft fort of them is, called *Dwora-ney Bulfhey*, or the company of head Penfio-ners, that haue, fome an hundred, fome four-fcore rubbels a yeere, and none vnder 70. The fecond fort are called *Seredney Dwora-ney*, or the middle ranke of Penfioners. Thefe haue fixty, or fiftie rubbels by the yere, none vnder fourtie. The third and loweft fort, are the *Dyta Boiarfkey*, that is, the lowe Penfio-ners. Their falarie is thirty rubbels a yere for

5

10

15

Degrees of horfemen.

20

1. *Prætoria-nior* fuch as attend the Emperours. perfon, 15000.

25

him

30

(1–5) and haue nothing . . . many children/and have little allowed them, which is a cawse of great disorder within that Countrey, whenas a souldier that hath manie children (10–17) This inconuenience . . . readines/The Emperour hath of them in continuall pay to the number of 15000 horsemen with their Captains and other officers that are allwaies in a readiness (27) sixty, or fiftie rubbels/60.50 & 40. Rubbells

him that hath moſt, ſome haue but fiue and twentie, ſome twentie, none vnder twelue. Whereof the halfe part is paid them at the *Mosko*, the other halfe in the field by the generall, when they haue anie warres, and are imployed in ſeruice. When they receiue their whole pay, it amounteth ʲto 55000. rubbels by the yeere.

And this is their wages, beſides lands allotted to euery one of them, both to the greater and the leſſe, according to their degrees. Whereof he that hath leaſt, hath to yeeld him twentie rubbels, or marks by the yeere. Beſides theſe 15000. horſemen, that are of better choyce (as being the Emperors own gard when himſelf goeth to the warres, not vnlike the Romane ſouldiers called *Prætoriani*) are a 110. men of ſpecial account for their Nobilitie, and truſt, which are choſen by the Emperour, and haue their names regiſtred, that find among them for the Emperours warres, to the number of 65000. horſmen, with all neceſſaries meet for the warres after the *Ruſſe* manner.

Two other troupes to the number of 65000.

To this end they haue yeerely allowance made by the Emperour for themſelues, and their companies, to the ſumme of 40000. rubbels. And theſe 65000 are to repaire to the field euery yeere on the borders towards the *Chrim Tartar*, (except they bee appoynted

ted for fome other feruice) whether there be
warres with the *Tartars*, or not. This might
feeme peraduenture fomwhat dangerous for
fome ftate, to haue fo great forces vnder the
command of Noblemen to affemble euerie
yeere to one certeine place. But the matter is
fo vfed, as that no danger can grow to the
Emperour, or his ftate by this meanes. 1. Becaufe thefe noblemen are manie, to wit, an
110. in all, and changed by the Emperor fo
oft as he thinketh good, 2. Becaufe they haue
their liuings of the Emperour, being otherwife but of very fmall reuenue, and receiue
this yeerely pay of 40000. rubbels, when it
is prefently to be paide foorth againe to the
fouldiers that are vnder them. 3. Becaufe for
the moft part they are about the Emperours
perfon being of his Councel, either fpeciall,
or at large. 4. They are rather as payma-
fters, then Captaines to their companies,
themfelues not going forth ordinarily to the
warres, faue when fome of them are appointed by fpeciall order from the Emperour
himfelfe. So the whole number of horfemen **Horfemen**
that are euer in a readineffe, and in continu- **in cótinuall**
all pay, are 80000, a few more or leffe. **pay 80000.**

If hee haue neede of a greater number
(which feldome falleth out) then he inter-
teineth of thofe *Sinaboiarskey*, that are out of
pay fo many as hee needeth: and if yet hee
want

5

10

15

20

25

30

(11) 2. Because . . . their liuings/2. bycawse these 110 are of the Emperours Counsell
and have their livings (27–28) greater number (which seldome falleth out)/greater
number then hee hath in ordinarie pay (which seldoom falleth owt)

want of his number, he giueth charge to his Noblemen, that hold lands of him, to bring into the fielde euery man a proportionable number of his feruaunts (called *Kolophey*, fuch as till his lands) with their furniture, according to the iuft number that he intendeth to make. Which the feruice being done, prefently lay in their weapons, and returne to their feruile occupations againe.

Footmen in continuall pay 12000. Of footmen that are in continuall pay, he hath to the number of 12000. all Gunners, called *Strelfey*. Whereof 5000. are to attend about the Citie of *Mosko*, or any other place where the Emperour fhall abide, and 2000. (which are called *Stremaney, Strefley,* or Gunners at the ftirrop) about his owne perfon at the verie Court or houfe where himfelfe lodgeth. The reft are placed in his garrifon Townes, till there be occafion to haue them in the fielde, and receiue for their falarie or ftipend euery man feuen rubbels a yeere, befides twelue meafures, a piece of Rye, and Oates. Of mercenarie Souldiers, that are ftrangers (whom they **Strangers mercenaries in pay 4300.** call *Nimfchoy*) they haue at this time 4300. of *Polonians*: of *Chirchaffes* (that are vnder the *Polonians*) about 4. thoufand, whereof 3500. are abroad in his garrifons: of *Doutches* and *Scots* about 150: of *Greekes, Turks, Danes*

---

(16) *Stremaney, Stresley/Stremaney strelsey* (25–26) *parenthetical phrase omitted.*
(26) 4300/abowt 4300

Danes and *Sweadens*, all in one band, an 100. or thereabouts. But thefe they vfe onely vp-on the *Tartar* fide, and againſt the *Siberi-ans*: as they doe the *Tartar* fouldiers (whom they hire fometimes but onely for the pre-fent) on the other fide againſt the *Polonian* and *Sweaden:* thinking it beſt pollicie fo to vfe their feruice vpon the contrary bor-der.

The chiefe Captaines or leaders of thefe forces, according to their names, and de-grees, are thefe which follow. Firſt, the *Voy-auodey Bulſhaia*, that is, the *Great Captaine*, or *Lieftenant* generall vnder the Emperour. This commonly is one of the foure hou-fes of the chiefe Nobilitie of the lande: but fo chofen otherwife, as that hee is of fmall valure, or practife in martiall mat-ters, beeyng thought to ferue that turne fo much the better, if hee bring no other partes with him faue the countenance of his Nobilitie, to bee liked of by the fouldiers for that, and nothing els. For in this poynt they are very warie, that thefe two (to wit) no-bilitie, and power meet not both in one, fpe-cially if they fee wifedome with all, or apt-neſſe for pollicie.

Their great *Voiauod* or Generall at this prefent in their warres, is commonly one of thefe foure: *Knez Feoder Iuanowich Methiſ-loskey*

[margin notes]
5

The chiefe captaines ot leaders.

10

1. The *Voi-auod* or Ge-nerall.

15

20

25

30

(24–25) nobility . . . both/Nobilitie and greatnes of power and authoritie meet not both

Joskey. Knez *Iuan Michailowich* Glinskoy, *Cherechaskoy,*and *Trowbetskoy,*all of great Nobilitie,but of very fimple qualitie otherwife: though in *Glinskoy* (as they fay) there is fomewhat more then in the reft. To make

2.Liefetenant generall.

vp this defect in the *Voiauod* or Generall, there is fome other ioyned with him as *Lieftenant Generall,*of farre leffe nobilitie, but of more valure and experience in the warres then he, who ordereth all things that the other countenanceth. At this time their principall man,and moft vfed in their warres, is one *Knez Demetrie IuanoWich Foreftine ,* an auncient and expert captaine, and one that hath done great feruice (as they fay) againft

3.Marfhals of the field foure.

the *Tartar,*and *Polonian.*Next vnder the *Voiauod* and his *Lieftenant generall* are foure other that haue the marfhalling of the whole army,deuided among them,and may be called the marfhals of the field.

Euery man hath his quarter , or fourth part vnder him. Whereof the firft is called the *Praua Polskoy,*or right wing. The fecond is the *Leuoy Polskoy,* or left wing. The third is *Rufnoy* Polskoy,or the broken bad. becaufe out of this there are chofen to fend abroad vpon any fodaine exploit, or to make a re-

Foure marfhals deputies 8.

fcue,or fupply,as occafion doth require.The fourth *Storefhouoy Polskoy* , or the warding bande. Euery one of thefe foure Marfhals haue

haue two other vnder them (eight in all) that twife euery weeke at the leaft muft mufter and traine their feueral wings or bands, and hold and giue iuftice for all faultes, and diforders committed in the campe.

And thefe eight are commonly chofen out of the 110. (which I fpake of before) that receiue and deliuer the pay to the fouldiers. Vnder thefe eight are diuers other Captains, as the *Gul anoy*, Captaines of thoufands fiue hundreds and 100. The *Petyde Setskoy* or Captaines of fifties, and the *Decetskies* or Captaines of tennes.

Befides the *Voiauoda* or Generall of the Armie (fpoken of before) they haue two other that beare the name of *Voiauoda*: whereof one is the Mafter of the great Ordinance (called *Naradna voiauoda*) who hath diuers vnder Officers, neceffarie for that feruice. The other is called the *Voiauoda gulanoy*, or the walking Captaine, that hath allowed him 1000. good horfemen of principall choyfe, to range and fpie abroad, and hath the charge of the running Caftle, which we are to fpeake of in the Chapter folowing. All thefe Captaines, and men of charge muft once euery day refort to the *Bulfba voiauoda*, or Generall of the Armie, to know his pleafure, & to informe him, if there be any requifite matter perteining to their office.

Of

Fiue Coronels vnder Captaines.

Sixe Mafters of the Artillerie.

The walking Captaine.

5

10

15

20

25

30

(10–13) as the . . . Captaines of tennes/as the *Gollovey* or Captaines of thowsands or five hundreds the *pedtyde Setskey*, or Captains of fiveties, & the *Decetskoy*s, or Captaines of tenns

Of their muſtering, and leuying of for-
ces , manner of armour, and
prouiſion of victuall for
the warres.

The 16. Chapter.

WHen warres are towards (which they fayle not of lightly euery yeere with the *Tartar*, and ma- nie times with the *Polonian* and *Sweden*(thefoure Lordes of the

Their order for muſte- ring.

Chetfirds fende foorth their fummons in the Emperours name, to all the Dukes and Dy- acks of the Prouinces , to bee proclaymed in the head Townes of euery Shire: that all the *Sinaboiarskey,* or fonnes of gentlemen make their repaire to fuch a border where the feruice is to be done , at fuch a place, and by fuch a day, and there prefent them felues to fuch, and fuch Captaines. When they come to the place afigned them in the

the ſummons or proclamation, their names are taken by certaine Officers that haue Cōmiſsion for that pourpoſe from the *Roſerade*, or high Conſtable, as Clarkes of the Bandes.

If any make default and faile at the day, hee is mulⱥted, and puniſhed very ſeuerely. As for the Generall and other chiefe Captaines, they are ſent thither from the Emperours owne hande, with ſuch Commiſsion and charge as hee thinketh behoofull for the preſent ſeruice. When the ſouldiers are aſſembled, they are reduced into their Bands, and companies, vnder their ſeuerall Captaines of tennes, fifties, hundreds, thouſands, &c. and theſe Bands into foure *Polſkeis*, or Legions (but of farre greater numbers then the Romaine Legions were) vnder their foure great Leaders, which alſo haue the authoritie of Marſhals of the fielde (as was ſayd before.)

Concerning their armour they are but ſlightly appointed. The common horſeman hath nothing els but his bow in his caſe vnder his right arme, and his quiuer & ſword hanging on the left ſide : except ſome fewe that beare a caſe of dagges, or a Iauelin, or ſhort ſtaffe along their horſe ſide. The vnder captains wil haue cōmonly ſome piece of armour beſides, as a ſhirt of male, or ſuch like.

The horſe mans furniture.

I 2   The

5

10

15

20

25

30

(4) as Clarkes/and are Clarks

The Generall with the other chiefe Captaines and men of Nobilitie , will haue their
horſe very richly furniſhed , their Saddles of
cloth of golde,their Bridles faire boſſed and
taſſelled with golde , and ſilke frindge,be-
ſtudded with Pearle and precious ſtones,
themſelues in very faire armour,which they
call *Bullatnoy* , made of faire ſhining ſteele,
yet couered commonly with cloth of golde,
and edged rounde with armin furre , his
ſteele helmet on his head of a very great
price,his ſword bow and arrowes at his ſide,
his ſpeare in his hande , with an other faire
helmet, and his *Sheſtapera*, or horſemans
ſcepter carried before him. Their ſwordes,
bowes,and arrowes are of the Turkiſh faſhion. They practiſe like the *Tartar* to ſhoote
forwards and backwards , as they flie and
retire.

**The foote-
mans fur-
niture.**
The *Strelſey* or footeman hath nothing
but his piece in his hande, his ſtriking hat-
chet at his backe, and his ſworde by his ſide.
The ſtocke of his piece is not made calie-
uer wiſe, but with a plaine and ſtraite ſtocke
(ſomewhat like a fowling piece) the barrel
is rudely and vnartificially made , very hea-
uie, yet ſhooteth but a very ſmall bullet. As
**Prouiſion
of victuall.**
for their prouiſion of victuall, the Emperour alloweth none, either for Captaine,
or ſouldiour , neither prouideth any for
them

them except peraduenture some corne for
their money. Euery man is to bring sufficient for him selfe, to serue his turne for
foure moneths , and if neede require to
giue order for more to bee brought vnto
him to the Campe from his tenant that
tilleth his land, or some other place. One
great helpe they haue, that for lodging and
diet euery *Russe* is prepared to bee a soul-
diour beforehand. Though the chiefe Captaines and other of account carry tents with
them after the fashion of ours , with some
better prouision of victuall then the rest.
They bring with them commonly into the
Campe for victuall a kinde of dryed bread,
(which they call *Sucharie*) with some store
of meale, which they temper with water,
and so make it into a ball, or small lumpe of
dowe, called *Tollockno*. And this they eate raw
in steade of bread. Their meate is bacon, or
some other flesh or fish dryed, after the
Dutch manner. If the *Russe* souldier were as
hardy to execute an enterprise, as he is hard
to beare out toyle and trauaile, or were o-
therwise as apt & wel trained for the warres,
as he is indifferent for his lodging and dyet, hee would farre exceede the souldiours
of our partes. Whereas now he is farre meaner of courage and execution in any warlike seruice. Which commeth partly of his

I 3   seruile

5

10

15

20

25

30

(9–11) euery *Russe* . . . chiefe Captaines/everie Russ is a souldier. Their ordinarie
lodging upon benches at home (when they are best interteined) prepareth them well
to camp on the grownd, and their hard fare at home, to live hardlie in the field, though
the chief Captaines

ſeruile condition , that will not ſuffer any great courage or valure to growe in him. Partly for lacke of due honour andreward, which he hath no great hope of, whatſoeuer ſeruice or execution he doe.

Of their marching , charging , and other Martiall diſcipline.

The 17. Chapter.

HE Ruſſe tru-ſteth rather to his number, thē to the valure of his ſouldiers, or good ordering of his forces. Their marching or leading is without all or-der, ſaue that the foure *Polſkey* or Legions, (whereinto their armie is deuided) keepe themſelues ſeueral vnder their enſignes, and ſo thruſt all on together in a hurrey, as they are directd by their Generall. Their Enſigne is the image of Saint George. The *Bulſba Dworaney* or chiefe horſemen , haue euery Horſemens man a ſmall drumme of braſſe at his ſaddle drummes. bowe, which hee ſtriketh when hee giueth the

(2–5) to growe . . . he doe/to grow in him, though otherwiſe hee bee of a verie ſtrong and fleſhie bodye apt to bear owt anie labour

the charge, or onfet.

They haue drummes befides of a huge bigneffe, which they carry with them vpon a board laydeon foure horfes, that are fparred together with chaines, euery drumme hauing eight ftrikers, or drummers, befides trumpets and fhawmes, which they founde after a wilde manner, much different from ours. When they giue any charge, or make any inuafion, they make a great hallowe or fhoute altogether, as loude as they can, which with the found of their trumpets, fhawmes, and drummes, maketh a confufed and horrible noyfe. So they fet on firft difcharging their arrowes, then dealing with their fwordes, which they vfe in a brauerie to fhake, and brandifh ouer their heads, before they come to ftrokes.

Their footemen (becaufe otherwife they want order in leading) are commonly placed in fome ambufh or place of aduantage, where they may moft annoy the enemie, with leaft hurt to themfelues. If it bee a fet battell, or if any great inuafion be made vpon the *Ruffe* borders by the *Tartar*, they are fet within the *running* or *mouing Caftle* (called *Beza*, or *Gulay gorod*) which is caried about with them by the *Voiauoda gulauoy* (or the *walking General*) whom I fpake of before. This walking or moouing Caftle is fo framed,

I 4 med,

The horfemans maner of charging.

5

10

15

The footemans charge.

20

25

The walking Caftle

30

(16) in a brauerie *omitted.*

med, that it may bee fet vp in length (as
occafion doeth require) the fpace of one,
two, three, foure, fiue, fixe, or feuen miles:
for fo long it will reach. It is nothing els but
a double wall of wood to defende them on
both fides behinde and before, with a fpace
of three yardes or thereabouts betwixt the
two fides: fo that they may ftande within it,
and haue roome ynough to charge and dif-
charge their pieces, and to vfe their other
weapons. It is clofed at both endes, and
made with loope holes on either fide, to
lay out the nofe of their piece, or to pufh
foorth any other weapon. It is carried with
the Armie wherefoeuer it goeth, being taken into pieces, and fo layed on cartes fparred together, and drawen by horfe that are
not feene, by reafon that they are couered
with their carriage as with a fhelfe or pent-
houfe. When it is brought to the place where
it is to be vfed(which is deuifed & chofen out
before by the *walking voiauod*) it is planted
fo much as the prefent vfe requireth, fometime a mile long, fometimes two, fometimes
three, or more: Which is foone done without
the helpe of any Carpenter, or inftrument:
becaufe the timber is fo framed to clafpe
together one piece within an other: as is eafily vnderftood by thofe that know the maner of the *Ruffe* building.

In

In this Castle standeth their shotte well
fenced for aduantage, specially against the
Tartar, that bringeth no ordinance, nor o-
ther weapon into the field with him, saue his
swoord, and bow and arrowes. They haue
also within it diuers field pieces, which they
vse as occasion doth require. Of pieces for
the field they carry no great store, when they
warre against the *Tartar* : but when they
deale with the *Polonian* (of whose forces they
make more account) they goe better furnished with al kind of munition, and other necessarie prouisions. It is thought that no
Prince of Christendome hath better stoare
of munition, then the *Russe* Emperour. And
it may partly appeare by the Artillerie house
at *Mosko*, where are of all sortes of great
ordinance, all brasse pieces, very faire, to an
exceeding great number.

The *Russe* souldier is thought to be better at his defence within some castle, or town,
then hee is abroad at a set pitched field.
Which is euer noted in the practise of his
warres, and namely at the siege of *Vobsko*, a-
bout eight yeares since : where hee repulsed
the *Polonian* king *Stepan Batore*, with his
whole armie of 100000, men, and forced
him in the ende to giue ouer his siege, with
the losse of many of his best Captaines and
souldiers. But in a set field the *Russe* is noted
. to

5

10

15

20

25

30

(13) prouisions/provision both for the feild & for battry   (18) very faire *omitted*.
(22) set pitched field/sett or pitched field

to haue euer the worfe of the *Polonian*, and *Sweden.*

If any behaue himfelfe more valiantly then the reft, or doo any fpeciall piece of feruice, the Emperour fendeth him a piece of golde, ftamped with the Image of Saint George on horfebacke. Which they hang on their fleeues, and fet in their caps. And this is accounted the greateft honour they can receiue, for any feruice they doo.

Reward for valure.

Of their Colonies, and mainteyning of their conquefts, or purcha-fes by force.

The 18. Chapter.

HE *Ruffe* Emperours of late yeres haue verie muche enlarged their dominions, and territories. Their firft conqueft after the Dukedom of *Mosko* (for before that time they were but Dukes of *Volodomer*, as before was fayd) was

(25–26) Their first conquest . . . [to end of paragraph on p. 62v] *omitted.*

was the Citie, and Dukedome of *Nouograd*
on the Weſt, and Northweſt ſide:which was
no ſmall enlargement of their dominion , &
ſtrengthning to them for the winning of the
reſt . This was done by *Iuan* great grandfa- 5
ther to *Theodore* now Emperour, about the
yeare 1480.The ſame began likewiſe to en-
croach vpon the countries of *Lituania,* and
Liuonia, but the conqueſt onely intended,&
attempted by him vpon ſome parte of thoſe 10
countries,was purſued and performed by his
ſonne *Baſileus* , who firſt wan the citie and
dukedome of *Plesko* , afterwards the citie &
dukedome of *Smolensko,* & many other faire
towns, with a large territorie belonging vn- 15
to thē about the yeare 1514.Theſe victories
againſt the *Lettoes* or *Lituanians* in the time
of *Alexander* their Duke, he atchiued rather
by aduantage of ciuill diſſentions, and trea-
ſons among themſelues, then by any great 20
policie,or force of his owne . But all this was
loſt againe by his ſonne *Iuan Vaſilowich* , a-
bout eight or nine yeares paſt, vpon com-
poſitiō with the Polonian king *Stepan Batore :*
whereunto hee was forced by the aduanta- 25
ges which the *Pole* had then of him , by reaſon of the foile he had giuen him before,and
the diſquietnes of his owne ſtate at home.
Onely the *Ruſſe* Emperour, at this time hath
left him on that ſide his countrie,the cities of 30
       Smolensko,

Entire page omitted.

Of their Colonies.

Smolensko, Vitobsko, Cheringo and *Beala gorod* in *Lituania.* In *Liuonia,* not a towne, nor one foote of ground.

Lituania.

When *Basileus* firſt conquered thoſe countries, he ſuffered the natiues to keepe their poſſeſsions, and to inhabite all their townes, onely paying him a tribute, vnder the gouernment of his *Ruſſe* Captaines, But by their conſpiracies and attempts not long after, he was taught to deale more ſurely with them. And ſo comming vpon them the ſecond time, hee killed and carried away with him, three partes of foure, which hee gaue or ſolde to the *Tartars* that ſerued him in thoſe warres, and in ſteede of them placed there his *Ruſſes*, ſo many as might ouermatch the reſt, with certaine garriſons of ſtrength beſides. Wherein notwithſtanding this ouerſight was committed, for that (taking away with him the vpland, or countrie people (that ſhould haue tilled the ground, and might eaſily haue bene kept in order without any daunger, by other good pollicies) he was driuen afterwards many yeares together, to vittaile the countrie (ſpecially the great townes) out of his owne countrie of *Ruſſia,* the ſoile lying there in the meane while waſt, and vntilled.

Narue.

The like fell out at the port of *Narue* in *Liefland,* where his ſonne *Iuan Vaſilowich* deuiſed

(1–3) *Smolensko* . . . ground *omitted.* (4–28) *The following two paragraphs in the manuscript follow variant of line 1, p. 63v.* (4–5) When Basileus . . . he suffered/ When hee [Ivan Vasilevich] first wan that Countrey hee suffred (13) three partes of foure/three parts of the people with him (14–15) that serued him in those warres *omitted.* (16–17) ouermatch/over maister (30) *Liefland* . . . deuised/ Liefland, whear hee [Ivan Vasilevich] divised

uifed to build a towne, and a caftle on the o-
ther fide the riuer (called *Iuangorod*) to keepe
the towne, and countrie in fubiection. The
Caftle he caufed to be fo built, and fortified,
that it was thought to be inuincible. And 5
when it was finifhed, for reward to the Ar-
chitect (that was a *Polonian*) he put out both
his eyes, to make him vnable to build the
like againe. But hauing left the natiues all
within their owne countrie, without abating 10
their number or ftrength, the towne and caftle not long after was betrayed, and furren-
dred againe to the king of *Sweden.*

On the Southeſt fide, they haue got the
kingdomes of *Cazan,* and *Aſtracan.* Theſe 15
were wonne from the *Tartar*, by the late
Emperour *Iuan Uaſilowich*, father to the
Emperour that now is: the one about 35,
the other about 33. yeares agoe, Northward
out of the countrie of *Siberia*, he hath layed 20
vnto his realme, a great breadth and length
of ground, from *Wichida* to the riuer of *Obba*, about a 1000. miles fpace: fo that hee is
bold to write himfelfe now, *The great Commaunder of Siberia.*

The countries likewife of *Permia*, and *Pe-* 25
chora, are a diuers people and language from
the *Ruſſe*, ouercome not long fince, and that
rather by threatning, and fhaking of the
fword, then by any actuall force: as being a 30
weake

---

(2) (called *Iuangorod*) *omitted.* (14 through p. 63v, lines 1–2) *In the manuscript,
this and the following paragraph follow the opening sentence of the chapter (here p.
61v, lines 20–25).* (19) Northward/Northeastward

weake and naked people, without meanes to
refift.

Meanes of holding his chiefe townes. That which the *Ruſſe* hath in his preſent poſſeſsion, hee keepeth on this ſorte.
In his foure chiefe border townes of *Vobſ-
ko, Smolensko*, *Aſtracan*, and *Cazan*, he hath
certeine of his Counſell not of greateſt nobilitie, but of greateſt truſt, which haue more
authoritie within their precinĉts (for the
countenauncing and ſtrengthning of their
gouernment there) then the other Dukes that
are ſet to gouerne in other places, as was noted before, in the manner of ordering their
Prouinces. Theſe hee chaungeth ſometime
euery yeare, ſometime euery ſecond or third
yeare, but exceedeth not that time, except vpon very ſpeciall truſt, and good liking of the
partie, and his ſeruice: leaſt by enlarging of
their time, they might grow into ſome fami-
liaritie with the enimie (as ſome haue done)
being ſo farre out of ſight.

The townes beſides are very ſtrongly
fenced with trenches, caſtels, and ſtore of munition, and haue garriſons within them, to
the nũber of two or three thouſand a piece.
They are ſtoared with vittaile if any ſiege
ſhould come vpon them, for the ſpace of two
or three yeares before hande. The foure Caſtels of *Smolensko, Vobsko, Cazan* and *Aſtracan*, he hath made very ſtrong to beare out
any

(1) people / people. But the principall part of all his conquests was that which hee had in
Lituania and *Livonia* whear hee had manie goodlie Townes to the number of 36 or
thearabowts with a large territorie belonging to everie on. which he gott rather by
the advantage of civill dissentions and secreat treasons then among them selves, then by
anie force of armes. And so lost them again abowt. 7. yeares since by a dishonourable
composicion, whereunto he was forced by the great advantages that the Pole had
then of him, by meanes of the foiles he had given him before; and the disquiet of

any fiege: fo that it is thought that thofe townes are impregnable.

As for the countries of *Pechora* and *Per-* mia, and that part of *Siberia*, which he hath now vnder him, they are kept by as eafie the coun. meanes, as they were firft got. vz. rather by fhewing, then by vfing of armes. Firft, hee hath ftoared the Countrie with as manie *Ruffes* as there are natiues, and hath there fome fewe fouldiers in garrifon, inough to to keepe them vnder. Secondly, his officers and Magiftrates there, are of his owne *Ruffe* people, and hee chaungeth them very often, vz. euery yeare twife or thrife: notwith-ftanding there bee no great feare of any in-nouation. Thirdly, he deuideth them into many fmall gouernments like a ftaffe broke in many fmall pieces: fo that they haue no ftrength beyng feuered, which was but li-tle neyther when they were all in one. Fourthly, hee prouideth that the people of the Countrie haue neither armour, nor mo-nie, beyng taxed and pilled fo often as hee thinketh good: without any means to fhake of that yoke, or to relieue themfelues.

In *Siberia*(where he goeth on in purfu-ing his conqueft) he hath diuers caftles and garrifons, to the nūber of fix thoufand foul-diers of *Ruffes*, and *Polonians*, and fendeth many new fupplies thither, to plant and to inhabite,

Meanes of holding the coun-tries of Pe-chora, Per-mia, and Si-beria.

5

10

15

20

25

30

his own state at home. Onlie hee hath left of that side his Countrey the Cities of *Smolen-sko, Vitobshey, Chernigo Beaelagorod* in *Lituania*, in Livonia not a Town nor on foot of grownd. (3) *In the manuscript this paragraph follows line 13 on p. 63.*

p. 64

(7) by vsing of armes/by vsing of armes, the people being of a naked and allmost of a savage kinde, withowt anie use of armour or of civill government of them selves. (14) vz. euery yeare twise or thrise *omitted.* (16–20) Thirdly . . . all in one

inhabite, as he winneth ground. At this time befides he hath gotten the kings brother of *Siberia*, allured by certeine of his Captaines, to leaue his owne countrie by offers of great intertainement, and pleafanter life with the *Ruffe* Emperour, then he had in *Siberia*. He was brought in this lafte yeare, and is now with the Emperour at *Mosko* well intertey-ned.

This may be fayd of the *Ruffe* practize, wherefoeuer he ruleth, either by right of in-heritance, or by conqueft. Firft, he berie-ueth the countrie of armour & other means of defence, which he permitteth to none, but to his *Botarskeis* onely. Secondly, he robbeth them continually of their monie, and com-modities, and leaueth them bare with no-thing but their bodies, and liues, within cer-teine yeares compaffe. Thirdly, he renteth and deuideth his territories into many fmall pieces by feuerall gouernments: fo that none hath much vnder him to make any ftrength, though he had other oportunities. Fourth-ly, he gouerneth his Countries by men of fmall reputation, & no power of themfelues, and ftraungers in thofe places where their gouernment lieth. Fiftly, he chaungeth his gouernours once a yeare ordinarily, that there grow no great liking nor intiernefle betwixt the people and them, nor acquain-tance

tance with the enemy if they lie towards the borders. Sixtly, he appointeth in one and the fame place aduerfarie gouernours, the one to bee as Controller of the other, as the Dukes and Diacks : where (by meanes of their enuies and emulations) there is leffe hurt to bee feared by their agreement, and himfelfe is better infourmed what is done amiffe. Seuenthly, he fendeth many times into euery Prouince fecrete meffen-gers of fpeciall truft about him, as intelligen-ces, to prie and harken out what is doing, and what is a miffe there. And this is ordi-nary, though it be fodaine, and vnknowen what time they will come.

Of the Tartars, and other borderers to the Countrie of Ruſſia, with whome they haue moſt to doo in warre, and peace.

The 19. Chapter.

Heir neighbours with whom they haue greateft dealings & intercourfe, both in peace & warre, are firft the *Tartar* : Secondly the *Polonian* whom the *Ruſſe* calleth *Laches*, no-ting the firft author or founder of the Na-tion,

The *Poloni-ans* called *Laches by* the *Ruſſe*

K

(1–15) if they lie towards the borders . . . what time they will come *omitted*. (27–30) & warre . . . Nation/& warrs are the *Polonians* and *Sweadens* and *Tartars*. [*From here to line 6 on p. 65v omitted.*]

tion, who was called *Laches* or *Leches*. wher-
vnto is added *Po*, which fignifieth *People*, &
fo is made *Polaches*, that is, the *People or pofteritie of Laches*: which the *Latines* after their
manner of writing call *Polanos*. The third
are the *Swedens*. The *Polonians* and *Swedens*
are better knowen to thefe partes of *Europe*
then are the *Tartars*, that are farther of
from vs (as being of *Afia*) and diuided into many tribes, different both in name, and
gouernment one from another, The greateſt
and mightieſt of them is the *Chrim Tartar*,
(whom fome call the *Great Cham*) that lieth
South, and Southeaſtward from *Ruſſia*, and
doth moſt annoy the Countrie by often in-
uaſions, commonly once euery yeare, fometimes entring very farre within the inland
parts. In the yeare 1571. he came as farre as
the citie of *Mosko*, with an armie of 200000.
men, without any battaile, or refiſtance at
all, for that the *Ruſſe* Emperour (then *Iuan
Vafilowich*) leading foorth his armie to encounter with him, marched a wrong way:
but as it was thought of very purpofe, as not
daring to aduenture the fielde, by reafon
that hee doubted his nobilitie, and chiefe
Captaines, of a meaning to betray him to
the *Tartar*.

The citie he tooke not, but fired the Sub-
burbs, which by reafon of the buildinges
(which

The *Chrim
Tartar*.

(which is all of wood without any ftone, brick,or lime,fauc certein out roomes)kind-led fo quickly,and went on with fuch rage,as that it côfumed the greateft part of the citie almoft within the fpace of foure houres, be-ing of 30.miles or more of compaffe. Then might you haue feene a lamétable fpectacle: befides the huge & mighty flame of the citie all on light fire, the people burning in their houfes and ftreates, but moft of all of fuch as laboured to paffe out of the gates far-theft from the enemie, where meeting toge-ther in a mightie throng, and fo prefsing e-uery man to preuent another,wedged them-felues fo faft within the gate, and ftreates neare vnto it,as that three ranks walked one vpon the others head, the vppermoft trea-ding downe thofe that were lower: fo that there perifhed at that time (as was fayd) by the fire & the preffe,the number of 800000 people,or more.

The firing of *Mosko* by the *Chrim Tartar*,in the yeare 1571.

5

10

15

20

The *Chrim* thus hauing fired the Citie, and fedde his eyes with the fight of it all on a light flame, returned with his armie, and fent to the *Ruffe* Emperour a knife (as was fayd) to fticke himfelfe withall: obbraiding this loffe,& his defperate cafe,as not daring either to meet his enimy in the fielde,nor to truft his friends,or fubiects at home. The principall caufe of this continual quarell,be-

25

30

K 2   twixt

(4) the greatest part of the citie/the whole Citie   (20) 800000/600000

twixt the *Russe* and the *Chrim*, is for the right
of certeine border parts claimed by the *Tartar*, but posseffed by the *Russe*. The *Tartar* al-
leageth that befides *Aftracan*, & *Cazan* (that
are the ancient poffefsió of the Eaft *Tartar*)
the whole countrie from his bounds North
and Weftward, fo farre as the citie of *Mosko*,
and *Mosko* it felfe, perteineth to his right.
Which feemeth to haue bene true by the report of the *Russes* thefelues, that tell of a certeine homage that was done by the *Russe* Emperour euery yeare, to the Gteat *Chrim* or
Cham, the *Russe* Emperour ftanding on foote
& feeding the *Chrims* horfe, (himfelfe fitting
on his back) with oates out of his owne cap,
in ftead of a boule or maunger, & that within
the caftle of *Mosko*. And this homage (they
fay) was done til the time of *Bafileus* grandfather to this man. Who furprifing the *Chrim*
Emperor by a ftratagem, done by one of his
Nobilitie (called *Iuan Demetrowich Belfchey*)
was content with this raunfome, vz: with the
chaunging of this homage into a tribute of
furres: which afterwards alfo was denied to
be paied, by this Emperours father.

Hereupon they continue the quarrell,
the *Russe* defending his countrie, and that
which he hath wonne, the *Chrim Tartar* inuading him once or twife euery yeare, fometime about Whitfontide, but oftener in Harueft

margin: Homage done by the *Russe* to the *Chrim* Tartar.

line numbers: 5, 10, 15, 20, 25, 30

(4–5) besides *Astracan* . . . East *Tartar*) *omitted.* (8) to his right/vnto him (11–
16) was done . . . in stead of a boule/was yearlie doon by the Russe Emperour him
self, feeding the *Chrims* horse with oats owt of his own capp, in stead of a bowl (21)
Iuan Demetrowich Belschey/Ivan Demetriwich Belskoy (27–29) the *Russe* . . . once
or twise/the *Russe* onlie defending his Countrey, and the *Chrim Tartar* invading hi
borders once or twise

ueſt. What time if the great *Cham* or *Chrim*
come in his owne perſon, he bringeth with
him a great armie of 100000, or 200000.
men. Otherwiſe they make ſhorte, and ſud-
den roads into the countrie with leſſer numbers, running about the liſt of the border as
wild geeſe fl..,inuading and retiring where
they ſee aduantage.

Their common practiſe(being very popu-
lous)is to make diuers armies,& ſo drawing
the *Ruſſe* to one,or two places of the frontiers, to inuade at ſome other place, that is
left without defence. Their manner of fight,
or ordering of their forces, is much after the
Ruſſe manner (ſpoken of before) ſaue that
they are all horſemen,and carrie nothing els
but a bow, a ſheafe of arrowes, and a falcon
ſword after the *Turkiſh* faſhion. They are very
expert horſmē,& vſe to ſhoot as readily back-
ward, as forward Some wil haue a horſmans
ſtaffe like to a bore ſpeare, beſides their o-
ther weapons. The cōmon ſouldier hath no
other armour then his ordinary apparel,vz:
a blacke ſheeps skin with the wooll ſide outward in the day time, & inward in the night
time,with a cap of the ſame.But their *Morſeys*
or Noblemen imitate the *Turke* both in apparel,& armour. When they are to paſſe ouer
a riuer with their armie, they tie three or
foure horſes together, & taking long poles

The man-
ner of the
Tartars
fight,and
armour.

5

10

15

20

25

30

K 3   or

(21-24) to a bore speare . . . sheeps skin/to a bore spear. Their armour is nothing els
but a black sheeps skinne

or pieces of wood, bind them faſt to the tails of their horſe: ſo ſitting on the poles they driue their horſe ouer. At handie ſtrokes (when they come to ioyne battaile)they are accounted farre better men then the *Ruſſe* people, fearſe by nature, but more hardie & blouddy by continuall practiſe of warre: as men knowing no artes of peace, nor any ciuill practiſe.

The ſubtiltie of the *Tartar.* Yet their ſubtiltie is more then may ſeeme to agree with their barbarous condition. By reaſon they are practiſed to inuade continually, and to robbe their neighbours that border about them, they are very pregnant, and ready witted to deuiſe ſtratageams vpō the ſuddaine for their better aduantage. As in their warre againſt *Beala* the fourth king of *Hungarie,* whome they inuaded with 500000. men, & obteined againſt him a great victorie. Where among other, hauing ſlaine his Chauncellor, called *Nicholas Schinick,* they founde about him the Kings priuie ſeale. Whereupon they deuiſed preſently to counterfait letters in the Kings name, to the cities and townes next about the place, where the field was fought; with charge that in no caſe they ſhould conuey themſelues, and their goods out of their dwellings, where they might abide ſafely without all feare of daunger, and not leaue

---

(10) Yet their ſubtiltie . . . [to end of paragraph on p. 68v line 12] *omitted.*

leaue the coūtrie defolate to the poffefsion
of fo vile & barbarous an enimie, as was the
Tartar nation, terming themfelues in all re-
prochfull manner. For notwithftanding he
had loft his carriages, with fome fewe ftrag-   5
lers that had marched diforderly, yet hee
doubted not but to recouer that loffe, with
the acceffe of a notable victorie, if the fa-
uage *Tartar* durft abide him in the fielde.
To this purpofe hauing written their letters   10
in the *Polish* character, by certaine young
men whom they tooke in the field, & figned
them with the Kings feale, they difpatched
them foorth to all the quarters of *Hunga-*
rie, that lay neare about the place. Where-   15
upon the *Ungarians*, that were now flying a-
way with their goods, wiues, & children, vpō
the rumour of the Kings ouerthrow, taking
comfort of thefe counterfait letters, ftayed
at home. And fo were made a pray, being   20
furprifed on the fuddaine by this huge number of thefe *Tartars* that had cōpaffed them
about before they were aware.

   When they befiege a towne or fort, they
offer much parle, and fende many flattering   25
meffages to perfwade a furrendry : promi-
fing all things that the inhabitants will require : but beyng once poffeffed of the place,
they vfe all manner of hoftilitie, and crueltie. This they doo vppon a rule they   30
                  K 4   haue,

haue, vz : that Iuſtice is to be practiſed but
towardes their owne. They encounter not
lightly, but they haue ſome ambuſh, where‑
vnto (hauing once ſhewed themſelues, and
made ſome ſhort côflict,they retire as repul‑
ſed for feare, and ſo draw the enimie into it
if they can.But the *Ruſſe* being wel acquain‑
ted with their practiſe,is more warie of them.
When they come a rouing with ſome ſmall
number , they ſet on horſebacke counterfáit
ſhapes of men, that their number may ſeeme
greater.

When they make any onſet,their man‑
ner is to make a great ſhoote, crying all out
together *Olla Billa* , *Olla Billa*, *God helpe vs*,
*God helpe vs.*They contemne death ſo much,
as that they chuſe rather to die,then to yeeld
to their enimie, and are ſeene when they are
ſlaine to bite the very weapon, when they
are paſt ſtriking, or helping of themſelues.
Wherein appeareth how different the *Tar‑
tar* is in his deſperate courage from the
Ruſſe,and *Turke*. For the *Ruſſe* Souldier if
he begin once to retire putteth all his ſafety
in his ſpeedie flight,And if once he be taken
by his enemie , he neyther defendeth him‑
ſelfe, nor intreateth for his life , as recko‑
ning ſtraight to die. The *Turke* commonly
when he is paſt hope of eſcaping, falleth to
intreatie , and caſteth awaie his weapon,
offereth

offereth both his handes, and holdeth them
vp, as it were to be tyed: hoping to faue his
life, by offering himfelfe bondflaue.

The chiefe bootie the *Tartars* feeke for
in all their warres, is to get ftore of captiues,
fpecially yong boyes, and girls, whom they
fell to the *Turkes*, or other their neighbors.
To this purpofe they take with them great
baskets made like bakers panniers to carrie
them tenderly, and if any of them happen to
tyer, or to be ficke on the way, they dafh
him againft the ground, or fome tree, and
fo leaue him dead : The fouldiers are not
troubled with keeping the captiues, and the
other bootie, for hindering the execution
of their warres, but they haue certein bands
that intend nothing els, appointed of purpofe to receiue and keepe the captiues and
the other praye.

The *Rufse* borders (being vfed to their in-
uafions lightly euery yeere in the fommer)
keepe fewe other cattel on the border parts,
faue fwine onely, which the *Tartar* will not
touch, nor driue away with him: for that he
is of the *Turkifh* religion, and will eate no
fwines flefh. Of Chrift our Sauiour they con-
feffe afmuch as doeth the *Turke* in his Alka-
ron, vz. that hee came of the Angell *Gabriel*,
and the Virgin *Marie*, that hee was a great
Prophet, and fhalbe the Iudge of the world
at

5

10

15

The *Tartar* 20
religion.

25

30

(1–3) *omitted.* (13–19) The souldiers . . . praye *omitted.*

at the laſt day. In other matters likewiſe, they are much ordered after the manner and direction of the *Turke* : hauing felt the *Turkiſh* forces when hee wonne from them *Azou*, & *Caffa*, with ſome other townes about the *Euxine*, or *Blacke ſea*, that were before tributaries to the *Chrim* T*artar*. So that now the Emperour of the *Chrims* for the moſt part is choſen ſome one of the Nobilitie whom the T*urke* doeth commend : whereby it is brought nowe to that paſſe, that the *Chrim* T*artar* giueth to the *Turke* the tenth part of the ſpoyle, which hee getteth in his warres againſt the Chriſtians.

Herein they differ from the T*urkiſh* religion, for that they haue certeine idole puppets made of ſilke, or like ſtuffe, of the faſhion of a man, which they faſten to the doore of their walking houſes, to be as *Ianuſſes* or keepers of their houſe. And theſe idols are made not by all, but by certeine religious women, which they haue among them for that, & like vſes. They haue beſides the image of their King or great *Cham*, of an huge bignes which they erect at euery ſtage; when the army marcheth: & this euery one muſt bend and bowe vnto as hee paſſeth by it, bee he T*artar*, or ſtranger. They are much giuen to witchcraft, & ominous coniectures, vpon euery accident which they heare, or ſee,

In

---

(10) doeth/doth   (14) against the Christians *omitted.*   (15–30) *Paragraph omitted.*

In making of mariages they haue no
regard of alliance or confanguinitie. Onely
with his mother, fister, and daughter a man
may not marrie, and though hee take the
woman into his houfe, and accompany with
her, yet hee accounteth her not for his wife,
till he haue a childe by her. Then he beginneth to take a dowrie of her friendes of
horfe, fheepe, kyne, &c. If fhe be batren after
a certeine time, he turneth her home againe.

Vnder the Emperour they haue certeine
Dukes, whome they call *Morfeis* or *Diuoy-* The *Tartar*
morfeis: that rule ouer a certeine number of Nobilitie.
10000. 20000. or 40000. a piece, which they
call *hoords.* When the Emperour hath any
vfe of them to ferue in his warres, they are
bound to come, & to bring with them their
fouldiers to a certeine nomber, euery man
with his two horfe at the leaft, the one to
ride on, the other to kill, when it commeth
to his turne to haue his his horfe eate. For
their chiefe vittaile is horfe flefh, which they The *Tartar*
eate without bread, or any other thing with dyet.
it. So that if a *Tartar* be taken by a *Ruffe,* he
fhall be fure lightly to finde a horfe legge, or
fome other part of him at his faddle bow.

This laft yeere when I was at the *Mofko,*
came in one *Kiriach Morfey,* nephewe to the
Emperour of the *Chrims* that now is (whofe
father was Emperour before) accompanied
with

with 300. *Tartars*, and his two wiues, whereof one was his brothers widdow. Where being intertained in very good fort after the
Russe manner, hee had fent vnto his lodging
for his welcome, to bee made ready for his
fupper and his companies, two very large
and fatte horfes, ready flawed in a fledde.
They preferre it before other flefh, becaufe the meate is ftronger (as they fay)
then beefe, mutton, and fuch like. And
yet (which is marueile) though they ferue all
as horfemen in the warres, and eate all of
horfe flefh, there are brought yeerely to the
Mosko to be exchanged for other cōmodities 30. or 40. thoufand *Tartar* horfe, which
they call *Cones*. They keepe alfo greet heards
of kine, and flockes of blacke fheepe, rather
for the skins and milke (which they carry
with them in great bottels) then for the vfe
of the flefh, though fometimes they eate of
it. Some vfe they haue of ryfe figs, and other
fruites. They drinke milke or warme blood,
and for the moft part carde them both together. They vfe fometimes as they traueile
by the way, to let their horfe blood in a
vain, and to drinke it warme, as it commeth
from his body.

The *Tar-*   Townes they plant none, nor other ftan-
tars dwel-   ding buildings, but haue walking houfes
ling.   which the Latines call *Veij*, built vpon
                                     wheeles

(30) which the Latines call *Veij* omitted.

wheeles like a shepheards cottage. These they drawe with them whithersoeur they goe, driuing their cattaile with them. And when they come to their stage, or standing place, they plant their carthoufes very orderly in a ranke: and so make the forme of streetes, and of a large towne. And this is the manner of the Emperour himselfe, who hath no other seat of his Empire but an *Agora,* or towne of wood, that moueth with him whitherfoeuer hee goeth. As for the fixed and standing building vsed in other countreys, they say they are vnwholfome and vnpleafant.

They beginne to mooue their houses and cattaile in the spring time from the South part of their Countrey towards the North parts. And so driuing on til they haue grafed all vp to the farthest part Northwarde, they returne backe againe towardes their South countrey(where they continue all the winter) by ten or twelue miles a stage: in the meane while the graffe being sprung vp againe, to serue for their cattaile as they returne. From the border of the *Shalcan* towards the *Cafpian* fea, to the *Ruffe* frontiers, they haue a goodly Countrey, specially on the South and Southeast partes, but lost for lacke of tillage.

Of money they haue no vse at all, and therefore

(1-2) a shepheards cottage . . . drawe with them/a shepards cottage sett vpon a cart, though it bee much larger, which they draw with them (11-14) As for . . . pleasant *omitted.* (24-27) returne . . . Countrey/retourn. Their Countrey is verie large abowt 2000. verse long from the border of the *Shalcan* to the Russ frontiers.

therefore preferre braffe and fteele before other mettals, fpecially bullate, which they vfe for fwords, kniues, and other neceffaries. As for golde and filuer they negle&t it of ve-ry purpofe, (as they doe all tillage of their ground)to be more free for their wandring kinde of life , and to keepe their Countrey leffe fubie&t to inuafiós. Which giueth them great aduantage againft all their neighbors, euer inuading,& neuer being inuaded. Such as haue taken vpon them to inuade their Countrey (as of olde time *Cyrus* and *Darius Hyftafpis*, on the Eaft and Southeaft fide) haue done it with very ill fucceffe:as we find in the ftories written of thofe times. For their manner is when any will inuade them, to allure and drawe them on by flying and reculing (as if they were afraide) till they haue drawen them fome good way within their countrey. Then when they beginne to want vittaile and other neceffaries (as needs they muft where nothing is to bee had)to ftoppe vp the paffages , and inclofe them with multitudes. By which ftratagem (as we reade in *Laonicus Chalcacondylas* in his *Tur-kifh* ftorie) they had welnigh furprifed the great aud huge armie of *Tamerlan*,but that hee retyred with all fpeede hee coulde, to-wardes the riuer *Tanais*, or *Don*, not with-out great loffe of his men,and carriages.

In

---

(8) subiect to inuasions/subject to invasions. Whearin they have been happie beefore all other Nations (8–30) Which giueth them . . . [to end of paragraph] *omitted.*

In the ftorie of *Pachymerius* the *Greeke* (which he wrote of the Emperours of *Con-ftantinople* from the beginning of the reigne of *Michael Palæologus* to the time of *Andro-nicus* the elder) I remember hee telleth to the fame pourpofe of one *Nogas* a *Tartari-an* captaine vnder *Cazan* the Emperour of the Eaft *Tartars* (of whome the Citie and kingdome of *Cazan* may feeme to haue ta-ken the denomination) who refufed a pre-fent of Pearle and other iewels fent vnto him from *Michael Palæologus:* asking with-all, for what vfe they ferued, and whither they were good to keepe away ficknefle, death, or other misfortunes of this life, or no. So that it feemeth they haue, euer or long time bene of that minde to value things no further, then by the vfe, and necefsitie for which they ferue.

For perfon and complexion they haue broad and flatte vifages, of a tanned colour into yellowe and blacke, fearfe and cruell lookes, thin haired vpon the vpper lippe, and pitte of the chinne, light and nimble bodied, with fhort legges, as if they were made naturally for horfemen: whereto they practife themfelues from their childehood, feldome going afoote about any bufinefle. Their fpeach is very fuddaine and loude, fpeaking as it were out of a deepe hollowe throate.

Entire page omitted.

throate. When they fing you woulde thinke a kowe lowed , or fome great bandogge howled. Their greateft exercife is fhooting, wherein they traine vp their children from their very infancie , not fuffering them to eate,til they haue fhot neere the marke within a certein fcãtling. They are the very fame that fometimes were called *Scythæ Nomades*,or the *Scythian Shepheards*, by the *Greeks* and *Latines*. Some thinke that the *Turkes* tooke their beginning from the nation of the *Chrim Tartars*. Of which opinion is *Laonicus Chalcocondylas* the *Greeke* Hiftoriographer , in his firft booke of his *Turkiſh* ftorie. Wherein hee followeth diuers very probable coniectures : The firft taken from the very name it felfe , for that the worde *Turke* fignifieth a fhepheard, or one that foloweth a vagrant and wilde kinde of life By which name thefe *Scythian Tartars* haue euer bene noted , being called by the *Greekes* σκύθαι νόμαδες or the *Scythian* fhepheards.His fecond reafon, becaufe the *Turks* (in his time) that dwelt in *Afia the leſſe* , to wit,in *Lydia, Coria, Phrygia*, and *Cappadocia,* fpake the very fame language that thefe *Tartars* did, that dwelt betwixt the riuer *Tanais* or *Don*,and the countrey of *Sarmatia*,which (as is well knowen) are thefe *Tartars* called *Chrims*. At this time alfo the whole nation of

---

(1–7) throate . . . scantling *omitted.* (10) Some thinke . . . [to end of paragraph on p. 73] *omitted.*

of the T*urkes* differ not much in their common ſpeach from the T*artar* lãguage. Thirdly becauſe the T*urke* and the *Chrim* T*artar*
agree ſo well together, aſwell in religion as
in matter of traffique neuer inuading, or
iniurying one another: ſaue that the T*urke*
(ſince *Laonicus* his time)hath encroached vpon ſome Townes vpon the *Euxin* ſea, that
before perteined to the *Chrim* T*artar.*
Fourthly, becauſe *Ortogules* ſonne to *Ogu-
zalpes*, & (father to *Otoman* the firſt of name
of the T*urkiſh* nation) made his firſt roads
out of thoſe partes of *Aſia*, vpon the next
borderers, till he came towardes the countreys about the hill T*aurus*, where hee ouer-
came the *Greeks* that inhabited there: and ſo
enlarged the name and territorie of the
T*urkiſh* nation,til he came to *Eubæa* and *At-
tica*,and other partes of *Greece*. This is the
opinion of *Laonicus*, who liued among the
T*urks* in the time of *Amurat* the ſixt T*urkiſh*
Emperour, about the yeere 1400. when the
memorie of their originall was more freſh:
and therefore the likelier hee was to hit the
trueth.

There are diuers other T*artars* that border *vpon Rusſia*, as the *Nagaies*, the *Chere-
miſſens*, the *Mordwites*, the *Chircaſses*, and
the *Shalcans*, which all differ in name more
then in regiment, or other condition, from

L   the

the *Chrim Tartar* except the *Chircaſſes* that border Southweſt, towardes *Lituania*, and are farre more ciuil then the reſt of the *Tartars*, of a comely perſon, and of a ſtately behauiour, as applying themſelues to the faſhion of the *Polonian.* Some of them haue ſubiected themſelues to the kings of *Poland*, & profeſſe Chriſtianitie. The *Nagay* lyeth Eaſtwarde, and is reckoned for the beſt man of warre among all the *Tartars*, but verie ſauage, and cruell aboue all the reſt. The *Cheremiſin Tartar*, that lieth betwixt the *Ruſſe* & the *Nagay*, are of two ſorts, the *Lugzuoy* (that is of the valley) and the *Nagornay*, or of the hillie countrey. Theſe haue much troubled the Emperours of *Ruſſia.* And therfore they are content now to buy peace of thē, vnder pretence of giuing a yeerely penſion of *Ruſſe* commodities, to their *Morſeis*, or *Diuoymorſeis*, that are chiefe of their tribes For which alſo they are boūd to ſerue thē in their wars, vnder certeine conditions. They are ſaide to be iuſt & true in their dealings: and for that cauſe they hate the *Ruſſe* people, whom they account to be double, & falſe in all their dealing. And therfore the common ſort are very vnwilling to keep agreement with them, but that they are kept in by their *Morſeis*, or Dukes for their penſions ſake.

The moſt rude & barbarous is coūted the *Morduite*

Mordwit Tartar, that hath many felffafhiôs, & ftrange kinds of behauiour, differing frô the reft. For his religiô, thogh he acknowlege one god, yet his maner is to worfhip for god, that liuing thing, that he firft meeteth in the morning & to fweare by it al that whole day whether it be horfe, dogge, catte, or whatfoeuer els it be. When his friend dieth, he killeth his beft horfe, and hauing flayed off the skin, he carrieth it on high vpon a long pole, before the corpes to the place of buriall. This hee doeth (as the *Rußhe* fayeth) that his friend may haue a good horfe to carie him to heauen: but it is likelier to declare his loue towardes his dead friende, in that hee will haue to die with him the beft thing that hee hath.

The *Mordwite Tartar* the moft barbarous of the reft.

Next to the kingdome of *Aftracan*, that is the fartheft part Southeaftward of the *Rußhe* dominion, lyeth the *Shalcan*, and the countrey of *Midia*: whither the *Rußhe* marchants trade for raw filks, fyndon, faphion, skins, and other commodities. The chiefe townes of *Media* where the *Rußhe* tradeth, are, *Derbent* (built by *Alexander* the great, as the inhabitauntes faye) and *Zamachie* where the ftaple is kept for rawe filkes. Their manner is in the Spring time to reuiue the filke-wormes (that lye dead all the Winter) by laying them in the warme funne,

— 2

5
10
15
20
25
30

(18-30) Next to the kingdome . . . [to end of chapter on p. 75] *omitted.*

funne, and (to haſten their quickening that they may ſooner goe to worke) to put them into bags, and ſo to hang them vnder their childrens armes. As for the worme called *Chriniſin* (as we call it *chrymſon*) that maketh coloured ſilke, it is bred not in *Media*, but in *Afsyria*. This trade to *Derbent* and *Sama-chie* for rawe ſilkes, and other commodities, of that countrey, as alſo into *Perſia*, and *Bougharia*, downe the riuer *Volgha*, and through the *Caſpian* ſea, is permiteed aſwell to the Engliſh, as to the *Ruſſe* marchants, by the Emperours laſt Graunt at my being there. Which hee accounteth for a very ſpeciall fauour, and might prooue in deede very beneficiall to our Engliſh marchants, if the trade were wel, and orderly vſed.

The whole nation of the *Tartars* are vtterly voyde of all learning, and without written Lawe. Yet certeine rules they haue which they holde by tradition, common to all the *Hoords* for the practiſe of their life. Which are of this ſort. *Firſt*, T*o obey their Emperour and other Magiſtrates, whatſoeuer they commaunde about the publique ſeruice.* 2. *Except for the publique behoofe, euery man to be free and out of controlement.* 3. *No priuate man to poſſeſſe any lands, but the whole countrey to be as a common.* 4. *To neglect all daintineſſe and varietie of meates, and to content them-*

Entire page omitted.

themselues with that which commeth next to
hand, for more hardneſſe, and readineſſe in the
executing of their affaires. 5. *To weare any*
baſe attire, and to patch their clothes, whether
there bee anie neede or not: that when there
is neede, it bee no ſhame to weare a patcht coate.
6 To take, or ſteale from anie ſtranger whatſoe-
uer they can gette, as beeyng enemies to all
men, ſaue to ſuch as will ſubiect themſelues to
them. 7. *Towardes their owne hoorde and na-*
tion to be true in word, and deede. 8. *To ſuffer no*
ſtranger to come within the Realme. If
any doe, the ſame to bee bondſlaue to
him that firſt taketh him, ex-
cept ſuch marchants and
other as haue the Tar-
tar Bull, or paſt-
port about
them.

L 3. Of

Of the Permians Samoites,
and Lappes.

The 20. Chapter.

He *Permians* &
Samoits that lye
frō *Ruſſia*, north
& Northeaſt, are
thought like-
wiſe to haue ta-
kē their begin-
ning from the
Tartar kind. And
it may partly be
geſſed by the faſhion of their countenance,
as hauing all broade, & flat faces, as the *Tar-*
tars haue, except the *Chirchaſſes.* The *Permi-*
ans are accounted for a very ancient people.
They are now ſubiect to the *Ruſſe.* They liue
by hunting, and trading with their furres, as
doth alſo the *Samoyt,* that dwelleth more towardes the North ſea. The *Samoyt* hath his
name (as the *Ruſſe* ſaith) of eating himſelfe:
as if in times paſt, they liued as the Canni-
bals, eating one another. Which they make
more probable, becauſe at this time they eat
all kind of raw fleſh, whatſoeuer it bee, euen
the very carion that lieth in the ditch. But
as

The *Per-*
mans.

The *Sa-*
moites.

5

10

15

20

25

30

(18–20) all broade . . . *Permians*/all broad and flatt faces, save that the *Chirchasse*
is of a better countenance and visage then the rest. The *Permians* (21) subiect to the
Russe/subiect to the Russe & speak the Russ language

as the *Samoits* themselues wil say, they were called *Samoie*, that is of themselues, as though they were *Indigenæ*, or people bredde vpon that very soyle, that neuer changed their seat from one place to another, as most nations haue done. They are subiect at this time to the Emperour of *Russia*,

I talked with certeine of them, and finde that they acknowledge one God: but repre- sent him by such things as they haue most vse and good by. And therfore they worship the Sun, the Ollen, the Losh, and such like. As for the storie of *Slata Baba*, or the *Golden hagge*, (which I haue read in some mappes, and de- scriptions of these countries, to bee an idole after the forme of an olde woman) that be- ing demaunded by the Priest, giueth them certeyne Oracles, concerning the suc- cesse, and euent of thinges, I founde it to bee but a verye fable. Onelie in the Pro- uince of *Obdoria* vpon the Sea side, neare to the mouth of the great riuer *Obba*, there is a rocke, which naturally (beeing some- what helped by imagination) may seeme to beare the shape of a ragged woman, with a child in her armes (as the rock by the North cape the shape of a Frier) where the *Ob- dorian Samoites* vse much to resort, by rea- son of the commoditie of the place for fishing: and there sometime (as their man-

L 4   ner

The margin notes:

The *Sa- moites* reli- gion.   5   10

Slata Baba or the gol- den Hag.   15

20

25

30

(8–9) I talked with certeine of them, and finde that *omitted*.   (12–30) As for the storie . . . [to end of paragraph on p. 76v] *omitted*.

ner is)conceiue,and practise their sorceries,
and ominous coniecturings about the good,
or bad speed of their iourneies, fishings,hun-
tings,and such like,

The *Samoits* habite and behauiour. They are clad in Seale skins,with the hea-
rie side outwards downe as low as the knees,
with their breeches and netherstocks of the
same , both men and women. They are all
blacke haired, naturally beardlesse. And
therefore the men are hardly discerned from
the women by their looks: saue that the women weare a lock of haire down along both
their eares.They liue in a maner a wilde and
a sauage life,rouing stil from one place of the
countrey to another,without anie proper-
tie of house or land more to one then to an
other. Their leader or directer in euery companie,is their *Papa* or Priest.

The *Lappes.*   On the North side of *Russia* next to *Corelia*,lieth the countrey of *Lappia*, which reacheth in length from the fartheft poynt
Northward, (towardes the Northcape) to
the fartheft part Southeaft (which the *Russe*
calleth *Sweetnesse* or Holie nose, the English
men *Capegrace*)about 345.verft or miles.Frõ
Sweetnesse to *Candelox* by the way of *Versega*
(which measureth the breadth of that countrey) is 90,miles or there abouts. The whole
countrey in a manner is eyther lakes , or
mountaines,which towardes the Sea side
are

(1–4) *omitted.* (7–15) with their breeches . . . to another/both men and women and
live in a manner a wilde and savage life, roving still from on place of their Countrey
to an other (15–30) without anie . . . [to end of chapter on p. 78] *omitted.*

are called T*ondro*,becaufe they are all of hard
and craggy rocke, but the inland partes are
well furnifhed with woods, that growe on
the hilles fides, the lakes lying betweene.
Their diet is very bare & fimple. Bread they
haue none, but feed onely vpon fifh & fowle.
They are fubieƈt to the Ëmperour of *Ruffia*,
and the two Kings of *Sweden*, and *Denmark* :
which all exaƈt tribute and cuftome of them
(as was faid before) but the Emperour of
Ruffia beareth the greateft hand ouer them,
and exaƈt of them farre more then the reft.
The opinion is that they were firft termed
Lappes of their briefe and fhort fpeach. The
Ruffe deuideth the whole natiō of the *Lappes*
into two forts. The one they call *Nowremanf-*
koy Lapary, that is,the *Noruegian Lappes:* becaufe they be of the *Danifh* religion . For the
Danes and *Noruegians* they account for one
people . The other that haue no religion at
all,but liue as brute and Heathenifh people,
without God in the world , they call *Dikoy*
Lopary,or the wild *Lappes* .

The whole nation is vtterly vnlearned,
hauing not fo much as the vfe of any Alpha-
bet, or letter among them . For praƈtife of
witchcraft and forcery,they paffe all nations
in the world. Though for the enchaunting of
fhippes that faile along their coaft (as I haue
heard it reported)and their giuing of winds
good

Entire page omitted.

good to their friends, and contrary to other, whom they meane to hurt by tying of certein knots vpon a rope (somewhat like to the tale of *Æolus* his windbag) is a very fable, deuised (as may seeme) by themselues, to terrifie sailers for comming neare their coast. Their weapons are the long bow, and handgunne, wherein they excell, aswell for quicknes to charge and discharge, as for nearnesse at the marke, by reason of their continuall practise (wherto they are forced) of shooting at wild fowle. Their manner is in Sommer time to come downe in great companies to the sea side, to *Wardhuyse, Cola, Kegor,* and the bay of *Vedagoba,* & there to fish for Codd, Salmon, & But-fish, which they sell to the *Russes, Danes,* & *Noruegians,* and now of late to the English mē that trade thither with cloth, which they exchaunge with the *Lappes* and *Corelians* for their fish, oile, and furres, whereof also they haue some store. They hold their mart at *Cola* on S. *Peters* day: what time the Captain of *Wardhuyse* (that is resiant there for the king of *Denmarke*) must be present, or at least send his deputie to set prices vpon their stockfish, traine oile, furres, and other commodities: as also the *Russe* Emperours customer, or tribute taker, to receiue his custome, which is euer payed before any thing can be bought, or sold. When their fishing is done, their māner

Entire page omitted.

ner is to drawe their carbaffes, or boates on
fhoare, & there to leaue them with the keele
turned vpwardes, till the next fpring tide.
Their trauaile too & fro is vpon fleds, draw-
en by the Olen deer:which they vfe to turne
a grafing all the Sommer time,in an iland called *Kilden* (of a very good foile compared
with other partes of that countrie) and towards the winter time ,when the fnow beginneth to fall, they fetch them home again,
for the vfe of their fledde.

Of their Ecclefiafticall ftate , with their Church offices.

The 21. Chapter.

Oncerning the
gouernement of
their Churche, it
is framed altoge-
ther after the mā-
ner of the Greek:
as being a part of
that Church, and
neuer acknowled-
ging the iurifdi-
ction of the Latine Church, vfurped by the
Pope. That I may keepe a better meafure in
defcri-

(1–11) *omitted.* (26–30) that Church . . . That I may keepe/that Church when it was at the woorst and hadd corrupted it self aswell in doctrine as in discipline. That I may keep

describing their ceremonies, thẽ they in the vfing them (wherein they are infinite) I will note briefly: Firft, what Ecclefiafticall degrees, or offices they haue with the iurifdiction, and practife of them. Secondly, what doctrine they holde in matter of religion. Thirdly, what leiturgie, or forme of feruice they vfe in their Churches, with the manner of their adminiftring the Sacramẽts. Fourthly, what other ftraunge ceremonies, and fuperftitious deuotions are vfed among them.

Thechurch officers.

Their offices, or degrees of Churchmen, are as many in number, and the fame in a manner both in name and degree, that were in the Wefterne churches. Firft they haue their *Patriarch*, then their *Metropolites*, their *Archbifhops*, their *Vladikey* or *Bifhops*, their *Protopapes* or *Archpriefts*, their *Papes* or *Priefts* their *Deacons, Friers, Monkes, Nunnes,* and *Eremites.*

The Patriarch.

Their *Patriarch*, or chiefe directer in matter of religion vntill this laft yeare, was of the citie of *Conftantinople* (whom they called the *Patriarch* of *Sio*) becaufe being driuen by the *Turke* out of *Conftantinople* (the feate of his Empire) he remoued to the Ile *Sio*, fometimes called *Chio*, and there placed his Patriarchiall fea So that the Emperours, and clergie of *Ruffia*, were wont yearely to fend gifts thither and to acknowledge a fpirituall kind of homage, and fubiection due to him, and

---

and to that Church . Which cultome they
haue held (as it feemeth) euer fince they pro-
feffed the Chriftian religiō. Which how long
it hath bene I could not well learne, for that
they haue no ftorie,or monument of antiquitie (that I could heare of) to fhewe what
hath bene done in times paft within their
countrie,concerning either Church,or common wealth matters. Onely I heare a report
among them , that about three hundred
yeares fince , there was a marriage betwixt
the Emperour of *Conftantinople*, & the kings
daughter of that countrie : who at the firft
denied to ioyne his daughter in marriage
with the *Greeke* Emperour,becaufe he was of
the Chriftian religion . Which agreeth well
with that I finde in the ftorie of *Laonicus
Chalcacondylas* concerning Turkifh affaires
in his fourth booke : where hee fpeaketh of
fuch a marriage betwixt *Iohn* the Greeke
Emperour , and the Kings daughter of *Sarmatia.* And this argueth out of their owne
report , that at that time they had not receyued the Chriftian religion: as alfo that they
were conuerted to the faith,and withall per-
uerted at the very fame time, receyuing the
doctrine of the gofpell,corrupted with fuperftitions euen at the firft when they tooke it
from the *Greeke* Churh , which it felfe then
was degenerate, and corrupted with many
fuper-

(17–22) I finde . . . And this argueth/I finde in the storie of *Nicephorus* that speaketh of such a marriage with the Kings daughter of *Sarmatia* abowt the time of *Andron-
icus* the younger which was abowt the year 1300. And this argueth

superstitions,and fowle errours, both in doctrine and discipline:as may appeare by the story of *Nicephorus Gregoras*, in his 8.and 9. bookes. But as touching the time of their conuersion to the christiã faith,I suppose rather that it is mistaken by the *Russe*, for that which I find in the *Polonian* storie,the secõd booke the third chapter;where is said that about the yeare 990.*Vlodomirus* Duke of *Russia*,married one *Anne* sister to *Basilius*,and *Constantinus* brothers,& Emperours of *Constantinople*.Wherupon the *Russe* receiued the faith & profession of Christ. Which though it be somewhat more auncient then the time noted before out of the *Russe* report ,yet it falleth out al to one reckoning,touching this point,vz: in what truth and sinceritie of doctrine the *Russe* receiued the first stampe of religion: for asmuch as the *Greeke* church at that time also was many waies infected with errour,and superstition.

The translation of the Patriarchicall sea from *Constantinople* or *Sio*, to *Mosko.*

At my being there,the yere 1588 came vnto the *Mosko* the *Patriarch* of *Constātinople*,or *Sio*)called *Hieronomo* being banished as some said)by the *Turke*,as some other reported by the *Greeke* clergie depriued. The Emp. being giueu altogether to superstitious deuotions, gauehim great intertainment. Before his cõming to *Mosko*,he had bene in *Italy* with the Pope,as was reported ther by some of his cõpany.

(3-4) story of *Nicephorus Gregoras*, in his 8. and 9. bookes/storie of *Nicephorus* and hath so continued ever since. And that they receaved this form aswell of doctrine as of the Church government from the Greek church, thear are manie evident reasons to induce a man to think, which might hear bee sett down, but that it would draw this breif note into over great length. (4-21) But as touching . . . [to end of paragraph] omitted. (24) called *Hieronomo* omitted.

pany. His arrād was to cōsult with the Emp. concerning these points. Firſt about a league to paſſe betwixt him & the king of *Spaine*, as the meeteſt Prince to ioyne with him in op-poſition againſt the *Turke*. To which purpoſe alſo Ambaſſages had paſſed betwixt the *Ruſſe* & the *Perſian*. Likewiſe from the *Geor-gians* to the Emperour of *Ruſſia*, to ioyne league together, for the inuading of the *Turke* on all ſides of his dominion: taking the aduantage of the ſimple qualitie of the *Turke* that now is. This treatie was helped forward by the Emperours Ambaſſadour of Almaine, ſent at the ſame time to ſolicite an inuaſion vpon the parts of *Polonia*, that lie towards *Ruſland*, and to borrow mony of the *Ruſſe* Emperour, to purſue the warre for his brother *Maximilian*, againſt the *Swedens* ſon now king of *Poland*. But this conſultation concerning a league betwixt the *Ruſſe* & the *Spaniard*, (which was in ſome forwardnes at my comming to *Mosko*, and already one ap-pointed for Ambaſſage into *Spaine*) was mar-red by means of the ouerthrow giuen to the *Spaniſh* king by her Maieſtie, the Queene of England, this laſt yeare. Which made the *Ruſſe* Emperour and his Counſell, to giue a ſadder countenance to the Engliſh Ambaſſa-dour at that time: for that they were diſap-pointed of ſo good a policie, as was this con- iunction

5

10

15

20

25

30

(7) Likewise/And this year (12–19) This treatie . . . now king of *Poland* omitted.

iunction suppofed to bee betwixt them and the *Spanifh.*

His fecond purpofe (whereto the firft ferued as an introduction) was in reuenge of the Turke and the Greeke cleargie, that had thruft him from his feat, to treate with them about the reducing of the *Ruffe* church vnder the Pope of Rome. Wherein it may feeme that comming lately from Rome, he was fet on by the Pope, who hath attempted the fame many times before, though all in vaine: and namely in the time of the late Emperour *Iuan Vafilowich*, by one *Anthony* his Legate. But thought this belike a farre better meane to obteine his purpofe by treatie and mediation of their owne Patriarch. But this not fucceeding, the Patriarch fell to a third point of treatie, concerning the refignation of his Patriarchfhip, & tranflation of the Sea from *Conftantinople*, or *Sio*, to the citie of *Mosko*. Which was fo well liked, and intertained by the Emperour (as a matter of high religion, & pollicie) that no other treatie (fpecially of forrein Ambaffages) could be heard or regarded, till that matter was concluded.

The reafon wherewith the Patriarch perfwaded the tranflating of his Sea to the citie of *Mosko* were thefe in effect. Firft, for that the Sea of the Patriarch was vnder the *Turk*

that

that is enemie to the faith. And therefore to bee remoued into ſome other countrie of Chriſtian profeſsion . Secondly, becauſe the *Ruſſe* church was the only naturall daughter of the Greeke at this time , and holdeth the fame doctrine & ceremonies with it:the reſt being all ſubiect to the Turke, and fallen a-way from the right profeſsion. Wherein the ſubtill Greeke to make the better market of his broken ware , aduaunced the honour that would growe to the Emperour,and his countrie: to haue the Patriarches ſeat , tranſlated into the chiefcitie,and ſeat of his Empire. As for the right of tranſlating the ſea, and appointing his ſucceſſour , hee made no doubt of it , but that it perteyned wholy to himſelfe.

So the Emperour,& his Counſell,with the principall of his cleargie being aſſembled at the *Moſko*, it was determined that the *Metropolite* of *Moſko,* ſhould become Patriarch of the whole Greeke Church , and haue the fame full authoritie,& iuriſdiction that perteined before to the Patriarch of *Conſtantinople*, or *Sio* . And that it might bee done with more order,& ſolemnitie, the 25.of *Ianuary,,* 1588.the Greeke Patriarch accompanied with the *Ruſſe* Cleargie,went to the great Church of *Precheſte,*or our Ladie , within the Emperours caſtle (hauing firſt wandred thorough

The Patri-archſhip of Conſtantino-ple tranſla-ted to Moſ-ko.

M   the

(22) of the whole Greeke Church *omitted.*

the whole citie in manner of a procefsion, and blefsing the people with his two fingers) where hee made an Oration, and deliuered his refignation in an inftrument of writing, and fo laied downe his Patriarchicall ftaffe. Which was prefently receiued by the Metropolite of *Mosko*, and diuers other ceremonies vfed about the inauguration of this new Patriarch.

The day was holden very folemne by the people of the citie, who were cõmaunded to forbeare their workes, and to attend this folemnitie. The great Patriarch that day was honoured with rich prefents fent him from the Emperour and Emprefse, of plate, cloth of gold, furres, &c: carried with great pompe thorough the ftreats of *Mosko* and at his departing receiued many giftes more, both from the Emperour, Nobilitie, and Cleargie. Thus the Patriarchfhip of *Conftantinople*, or *Sio*, (which hath continued fince the Counfell of *Nice*) is now tranflated to *Mofko*, or they made beleeue that they haue a Patriarch with the fame right and authoritie that the other had. Wherin the fubtil *Greeke* hath made good aduantage of their fuperftition, and is now gone away with a rich bootie into *Poland*, whither their Patriarchfhip be currant or not.

The matter is not vnlike to make fome fchifme

---

(13) great Patriarch/Greek Patriarch   (22) Counsell . . . is now translated/Counsell of Niece (though subiect to the Turk for a 100 yeares and more) is now translated (28) into *Poland* omitted.

schisme betwixt the *Greeke* & *Russe* Church, if the *Russe* holde this Patriarchship that he hath so well payed for, and the Greekes e-lect an other withall as likely they will, whi-ther this man were banished by the Turke, or depriued by order of his owne Cleargie. Which might happen to giue aduantage to the Pope, & to bring ouer the *Russe* Church to the sea of Rome (to which end peraduen-ture he deuised this stratageam, and cast in this matter of schisme among them) but that the Emperours of *Russia* know well enough, by the exaple of other christian Princes, what inconuenience would grow to their state & coûtrie, by subiecting themselues to the Ro-mish sea. To which ende the late Emperour *Iuan Vasilowich* was very inquisitiue of the Popes authority ouer the Princes of christen-dome, & sent one of very purpose to Rome, to behold the order, & behauior of his court.

With this Patriarch *Hieronimo* was driuen out at the same time by the great Turke, one *Demetrio* Archbishop of *Larissa*: who is now in England, & pretendeth the same cause of their banishment by the Turke (to wit) their not admitting of the Popes new Kalender, for the alteration of the yeare. Which how vnlikely it is, may appeare by these circum-stances. First, becavse there is no such affe-ction, nor friendlie respect, betwixt the

M 2 Pope

(12–16) the Emperours . . . To which ende/the Emperours of Russia have learned the inconvenience that would grow to their state, by letting in that Beast. For which end (19) one *omitted*. (21) With this Patriarch . . . [to end of paragraph, p. 82v] *omitted*.

Pope & the Turke as that he ſhould baniſh a
ſubieᐧᵗ for not obeying the Popes ordināce,
ſpecially in a matter ot ſome ſequele for the
alteration of times within his owne countries. Secondly, for that he maketh no ſuch
ſcruple in deduᐧᵗing of times, and keeping
of a iuſt and preciſe account from the incar-
natiō of Chriſt: whom he doth not acknowledge otherwiſe then I noted before. Thirdly, for that the ſaid Patriarch is now at *Na-*
ples in Italy, where it may be gheſſed he would
not haue gone within the Popes reach, and
ſo neare to his noſe, if he had bene baniſhed
for oppoſing himſelfe againſt the Popes de-
cree.

The Patri-
arches iu-
riſdiᐧᵗion.
This office of Patriarchſhip now tranſla-
ted to *Mosko,* beareth a ſuperiour authoritie
ouer all the Churches, not onely of *Ruſſia,* &
other the Emperours dominions, but thorough out all the churches of Chriſtendome
that were before vnder the Patriarch of *Cō-*
ſtantinople, or *Sio:* or at leaſt the *Ruſſe* Patriarch imagineth himſelfe to haue the ſame
authoritie. Hee hath vnder him as his proper dioceſſe the Prouince of *Mosko,* beſides other peculiars. His court, or office is
kept at the *Mosko.*

The Me-
tropolites.
Before the creatiō of this new Patriarch,
they had but one *Metropolite,* that was called the *Metropolite* of *Mosko.* Now for more
ſtate

(1–15) *omitted.* (19–20) thorough out/throughowt (22–24) or *Sio* . . . Hee hath/
Sio, or at the least they must suppose it to bee soe, except they will graunt that they
have made a badd bargain, and bought that of the Greek, that him self had not right
to sell. He hath

ſtate to their Church, and newe Patriaich,
they haue two Metropolites,the one of *No-*
ubgrod velica , the other of *Roſtoue .* Their
office is to receiue of the Patriarch ſuch Ec-
clefiaſticall orders, as he thinketh good,and
to deliuer the charge of them ouer to the
Archbifhops : befides the ordering of their
owne dioceſſe.

Their Archbifhops are foure:of *Smolenſ-*
ko,Cazon,Vobs'o, and *Vologda.* The partes of
their office is all one with the Metropolits:
ſaue that they haue an vnder iurifdiction,
as Suffraganes to the Metropolites , and ſu-
periours to the Bifhops. The next are the
Vladikeis , or Bifhops, that are but fixe in
all : of *Crutirska ,* of *Rezan ,* of *Orfer* and
Torſhock, of *Collomenska ,* of *Volodemer ,* of
Suſdalla . Theſe haue euery one a very large
dioceſſe : as diuiding the reſt of the whole
countrie among them.

   The matters perteyning to the Ecclefi-
aſticall iurifdiction , of the Metropolites,
Archbifhops, and Bifhops are the ſame in a
manner that are vſed by the Cleargie in o-
ther partes of Chriſtendome . For befides
their authoritie ouer the Cleargie ,and ordering ſuch matters as are meare Ecclefi-
aſhca l,their iurifdiction extendeth to all te-
ſtamentarie cauſes , matters of marriage ,
and diuorcementes, ſome pleas of iniu-

       M 3   ries,

Marginal notes:
5
Archbi-
fhops. 10
Bifhops. 15
20
Ecclefiaſti-
call iurifdi-
ction.
25
30

(22) iurisdiction . . . Metropolites/iurisdiction, first of the Patriarch, then of the *Metropolits* (24) vsed/claimed (25) of Christendome. For besides/of Christendoom by the Canon Law. For (bysides (27–29) meare Ecclesiastical . . . causes/mear ecclesiasticall) they usurp manie things that belong to the Civill magistracie, as all testamentarie cawses

ries, &c. To which purpofe alfo they hane
their Officials, or Commiffaries (which
Their Gen- they call *Boiaren Vladitskey*) that are Lay-
tlemen có- men of the degree of Dukes, or Gentle-
miffaries. men, that keepe their Courtes and execute
their iurifdiction. Which befides their o-
ther opprefsions ouer the common people, raigne ouer the Prieftes: as the Dukes
& Diacks doo ouer the poore people, within their precinĉts, As for the Archbifhop or
Bifhop himfelfe, he beareth no fway in deciding thofe caufes, that are brought into
his Court. But if hee would moderate any
matter, hee muft doo it by intreatie with
his Gentleman officiall. The reafon is, becaufe thefe *Boiarskey*, or Gentlemen officials, are not appointed by the Bifhops, but
by the Emperour himfelfe, or his Counfell,
and are to giue account of their doings to
none but to them. If the Bifhoppe can intreat at his admifsion to haue the choice of
his owne officiall, it is accounted for a fpeciall great fauour ⋅ But to fpeake it as it is,
the Cleargie of *Ruffia*, afwell concerning
their landes and reuenues, as their authoritie and iurifdiction, are altogether ordered
and ouer ruled by the Emperour, and his
Counfell, and haue fo much, and no more of
both as their pleafure doth permit thē, They
haue alfo their afsiftants or feuerall Coun-
fels

5

10

15

20

25

30

(8) the Priestes/the pore Priests   (9) the poore people/the other people
p. 84
(4) twentie . . . aduise/.24. a piece, to whome thear is allotted owt of their livings
the summe of Fortie Rubbells. These advise (16–17) the Metropolite of *Nouograde*
. . . apparell/the Metropolite of *Novagorod*. But the Emperours of late have well abated
their revenues, which notwithstanding wear large if they received it clear, and had it

fels (as they call them)of certeine Priefts that are of their dioceffe, refiding within their cathedrall cities,to the number of foure and twentie a piece. Thefe aduife with them about the fpeciall and neceffarie matters belonging to their charge.

Concerning their rentes and reuenues to mainteyne their dignities, it is fomewhat large. The Patriarches yearely rents out of his landes(befides other fees)is about 3000. rubbels, or markes. The Metropolites and Arch bifhops about 2500. The Bifhops fome a 1000.fome 800.fome 500,&c. They haue had fome of them (as I haue heard fay) ten or twelue thoufand rubbels a yeare : as had the Metropolite of *Nonograde.*

Their habite or apparell (when they fhewe themfelues in their Pontificalibus after their folemneft manner) is a miter on their heades , after the popifh fafhion, fette with pearle and pretious ftone , a cope on their backes , commonly of cloth of golde, embrodered with pearle , and a Crofiers ftaffe in their handes , layed ouer all with plate of filuer double guilt , with a croffe or fheepheardes crooke at the vpper ende of it . Their ordinarie habite otherwife when they ride or goe abroad , is a hood on their heads of blacke colour , that hangeth downe their backes, and ftandeth out like a

M 4   bongrace

margin notes:
The church reuenues.

The habite of their clergy men.

line numbers: 5, 10, 15, 20, 25, 30

all at their own disposicion to spend as they listed. But their Steward is ever of the Emperours appointing, and hath a Commission both to receive all their rents, and to expend what is necessarie abowt their howsholld provision. If anie thing bee left at the yeares end, hee giveth account to the Emperours Officers. The *Patriarch, Metropolits, Arch-Bishopps,* and *Bishopps* are allowed onlie to their privat purse, for the expenses of their persons abowt 200. or 300. Rubbells a piece by the year. Their habitt or apparell

bongrace before. Their vpper garment (which they call *Ress*) is a gowne or mantell of blacke Damaske, with many liftes or gardes of white Sattin layed vpon it, euerie garde about two fingers broad, and their Crofiers ftaffe carried before them. Themfelues followe after, blefsing the people with their two forefingers, with a marueilous grace.

The election of Bifhops. The election, and appointing of the Bifhops and the reft, perteyneth wholy to the Emperour himfelfe. They are chofen euer out of the Monafteries: fo that there is no Bifhop, Archbifhop, nor Metropolite, but hath bene a Monke, or Friet before. And by that reafon they are, and muft all bee vnmaried men, for their vow of chaftitie when they were firft fhorne. When the Emperour hath appointed whom hee thinketh good, he is inuefted in the Cathedrall church of his dioces, with many cerenronies, much after the manner of the Popifh inauguration. They haue alfo their Deanes, & their Archdeacons.

The learning & exercife of the *Ruffe* Clergie. As for preaching the worde of God, or any teaching, or exhorting fuch as are vnder them, they neyther vfe it, nor haue any skill of it : the whole Cleargie beyng vtterlie vnlearned bothe for other knowledge, and in the word of God. Onely their manner

---

(22–25) of the Popish inauguration . . . As for preaching/of the Popish inauguracion. To this purpose they have their deanes, and Archdeacons, after the order of the Popish Churches. And if it bee asked, what vse they have in their Churche of their Patriarch Metropolites, Archbishopps etc. I can note nothing save that among so manie dead Idolls as they woorshipp, they may have soom a live to furnish their Church withall. As for preaching

manner is twife euery yeere, vz. the firft of
September (which is the firft day of their
yere)and on S. *Iohn* Baptifts day, to make an
ordinarie fpeach to the people, euery Metropolite, Archbifhop, and Bifhop in his Ca-   5
thedrall Church, to this or like effect: That
if anie be in malice towardes his neighbour,
hee fhall leaue off his malice : if any haue
thought of treafon or rebellion againft his
Prince, he beware of fuch practife : if he haue   10
not kept his fafts, and vowes, nor done his
other dueties to the holie Church, he fhal a-
mend that fault, &c. And this is a matter of
forme with them, vttered in as many words,
and no more, in a manner, then I haue heere   15
fet downe. Yet the matter is done with that
grace and folemnitie, in a pulpit of purpofe
fet vp for this one Acte, as if he were to dif-
courfe at large of the whole fubftance of diuinitie. At the *Mosko* the Emperour him-   20
felfe is euer prefent at this folemne exhorta-
tion.

   As themfelues are voyde of all maner of
learning, fo are they warie to keepe out all
meanes that might bring any in : as fearing   25
to haue their ignorance, and vngodlineffe
difcouered. To that purpofe they haue perfwaded the Emperours, that it would breed
innouation, and fo danger to their ftate, to
haue anie noueltie of learning come within   30
the

(18-20) as if he were to discourse at large of the whole substance of diuinitie *omitted.*

the Realme. Wherein they say but trueth,for that a man of spirit and vnderstãding,helped by learning and liberal education,can hardly indure a tyrannicall gouernment. Some yeres past in the other Emperors time,there came a Presse and Letters out of *Polonia*, to the citie of *Mosko*, where a printing house was set vp, with great liking & allowance of the Emperour himselfe. But not long after, the house was set on fire in the night time, and the presse and letters quite burnt vp, as was thought by the procurement of the Cleargy men.

Priests.

Their Priestes (whom they call *Papaes* are made by the Bishops,without any great triall for worthinesse of giftes, before they admit them, or ceremonies in their admission: saue that their heades are shorne (not shauen for that they like not)about an hand bredth or more in the crowne, and that place annoynted with oyle by the Bishop: who in his admission putteth vpon the priest, first his surplesse, and then setteth a white crosse on his brest of silke, or some other matter, which he is to weare eight dayes, and no more: and so giueth him authoritie to say and sing in the Church, and to administer the Sacraments.

They are men vtterly vnlearned,which is no marueile,forasmuch as their makers, the Bishops

(1–5) Wherein they say . . . Some yeres past/Wherein they say but truth, for that sound learning and wisdoom, speciallie godlie wisdom will not well indure a tirannicall government. Soom years past (12–13) by the procurement . . . Cleargymen/by procurement of the Bishopps and other of the Cleargie

Biſhops themſelues (as before was ſaide) are
cleere of that qualitie, and make no rarther
vſe at al of any kindof learning, no rot of the
ſcriptures themſelues, ſaue to reade and to
ſing them. Their ordinary charge & functiõ   5
is to ſay the Leiturgie, to adminiſter the Sacraments after their maner, to keepe & deck
their idoles, and to doe the other ceremonies vſuall in their Churches. Their number
is great, becauſe their townes are parted in-   10
to many ſmal pariſhes, without any deſcreti-
on for deuiding them into competent numbers of houſholds, and people for a iuſt con-
gregation: as the manner in all places where
the meanes is neglected, for increaſing of   15
knowledge, and inſtruction towardes God.
Which cannot well be had, where by means
of an vnequall partition of the people, and
pariſhes, there followeth a want and vn-
equalitie of ſtipend for a ſufficient mini-   20
ſterie.

For their prieſts, it is lawful to marrie for
the firſt time. But if the firſt wife dye, a ſecond hee cannot take, but hee muſt looſe
his Prieſthood, and his liuing withall. The   25
reaſon they make out of that place of Saint
Paul to *Timothie* 1. 3. 2. not well vnderſtood, thinking that to bee ſpoken of diuers
wiues ſucceſsiuely, that the Apoſtle ſpeaketh
of at one and the ſame time. If he will needs   30
marrie

(14–17) as the manner . . . Which cannot well be had/as is the manner in all places,
whear thear is an idolatrous or ignorant miniſtrie, whear the people are content to want
the preaching of the woord which can not bee well had   (27) not well/corruptlie

marry againe after his firſt wife is dead, hee is no longer called *Papa*, but *Roſpapa*, or *Prieſt quondam*. This maketh the Prieſtes to make much of their wiues, who are accounted as the matrones, and of beſt reputation among the women of the pariſh.

For the ſtipend of the Prieſt, their manner is not to pay him any tenthes of corne, or ought els: but he muſt ſtand at the deuotion of the people of his pariſh, and make vp the incommes towards his maintenance, ſo wel as he can, by offerings, ſhriftes, marriages, burials, dirges, and prayers for the dead and the liuing. (which they call *Molitua*) For befides their publike feruice within their Churches, their manner is for euery priuate man to haue a prayer ſaide for him by the Prieſt, vpon any occaſion of buſineſſe whatſoeuer, whether he ride, goe, ſaile, plough, or whatſoeuer els he doeth. Which is not framed according to the occaſion of his buſineſſe, but at randome, being ſome of their ordinarie and vſuall Church-prayers. And this is thought to be more holy, and effectuall, if it be repeated by the Prieſts mouth, rather then by his owne. They haue a cuſtome befides to folemnize the Saints day, that is patrone to their Church once euery yeere, What time al their neighbours of their coūtrey, and pariſhes about, come in to haue prayers

---

(14) *Molitua*/which they call *Molytva* or praier for remiſſion of ſinnes (29–30) of their countrey/of their Town & Countrey

prayers ſaide to that Saint for themſelues,
and their friendes: and ſo make an offering
to the Prieſt for his paines. This offering
may yeeld them ſome ten poundes a yeere,
more or leſſe , as the patrone, or Saint of
that Church is of credite, and eſtimation a-
mong them. The manner is on this day
(which they keep anniuerſarie) for the prieſt,
to hire diuers of his neighbour prieſtes to
helpe him : as hauing more diſhes to dreſſe
for the Saint, then he can wel turne his hand
vnto. They vſe beſides to viſite their pariſhi-
oners houſes, with holy water, and perfume,
commonly once a quarter : and ſo hauing
ſprinckled, and beſenſed the goodman and
his wife, with the reſt of their houſhold, and
houſhold ſtuffe, they receiue ſome deuotion more or leſſe, as the man is of abilitie. This
and the reſt laid altogether, may make vp
for the prieſt towardes his maintenaunce, a-
bout thirtie or fourtie rubbels a yere. wherof he payeth the tenth part to the Biſhop of
the Dioces.

The *Papa* or Prieſt is knowen by his long
tufts of haire, hanging downe by his eares,
his gowne with a broad cape, and a walking
ſtaffe in his hand. For the reſt of his habite,
he is apparelled like the common ſort. When
he ſaith the Leiturgie or ſeruice, within the
Church, he hath on him his ſurpleſſe, and
ſometimes

marginal notes:
The prieſts mainte- nance.

The prieſts attire.

line numbers: 5, 10, 15, 20, 25, 30

ſometimes his coape, if the day be more ſolemne. They haue beſides their *Papaes* or
Prieſtes , their *Churnapapaes* (as they call
them) that is, *Blacke Prieſtes* : that may
keepe their Benefices , though they bee admitted Friers withall within ſome Monaſterie. They ſeeme to bee the verie ſame
that were called Regular Prieſtes in the Popiſh Church. Vnder the Prieſt, is a Deacon
in euery Church, that doeth nothing but the
office of a pariſh Cleatke. As for their *Pro-*
topapaes, or Archeprieſtes , and their Arch-
deacons(that are next in election to be their
Protopopas) they ſerue onely in the cathedral
Churches.

Friers. Of Friers they haue an infinit rabble, farre
greater thē in any other countrey, where po-
pery is profeſſed. Euery city, & good part of
the countrey, ſwarmeth ful of them. For they
haue wrought (as the popiſh Friers did by
their ſuperſtition and hypocriſie)that if any
part of the Realme bee better and ſweeter
then other, there ſtandeth a Friery, or a monaſtery dedicated to ſome Saint.

The number of them is ſo much the greater, not onely for that it is augmented by
the ſuperſtition of the countrey , but becauſe the Fryers life is the ſafeſt from the
oppreſsions, and exactions, that fall vpon
the Commons. Which cauſeth many to
put

(16–17) Of Friers . . . professed/Of Friars they have a greater number, then in anie
Countrey whear poperie is professed

put on the Fryers weede , as the beſt armour to beare off ſuch blowes. Beſides ſuch
as are voluntarie, there are diuers that are
forced to ſhire themſelues Fryers , vpon
ſome diſpleaſure. Theſe are for the moſt part
of the chiefe Nobility. Diuers take the Monaſteries as a place of Sanctuary , and there
become Friers, to auoyde ſome puniſhment,
that they had deſerued by the lawes of the
Realme. For if hee gette a Monaſtery ouer
his head, and there put on a coole before
hee be attached , it is a protection to him
for euer againſt any law, for what crime ſoeuer: except it be for treaſon. But this *Prouiſo*
goeth withal, that no man commeth there,
(except ſuch as are commanded by the Emperour to be receiued) but hee giueth them
lands, or bringeth his ſtock with him, & putteth it into the common Treaſurie. Some
bring a 1000 rubbels, & ſome more. None is
admitted vnder 3. or 4. hundred.

The manner of their admiſsion is after
this ſort. Firſt, the Abbot ſtrippeth him of
all his ſecular or ordinarie apparell . Then
hee putteth vpon him next to his skinne, a
white flannel ſhirt, with a long garment o-
uer it down to the ground, girded vnto him
with a broade leather belt. His vppermoſt
garment is a weede of *Garras*, or *Say*, for colour and faſhion, much like to the vpper

Their ma-
ner of ſhi-
ring Friers.

weed

weed of a Chimney-sweeper . Then is his
crown shorne a hand breadth, or more close
to the very skinne, and these, or like wordes
pronounced by the Abbot, whiles hee clip-
peth his haire: *As these haires are clipped of, & taken from thy head, so now we take thee, and separate thee cleane from the worlde, and worldly thinges, &c.* This done, hee annoynteth his
crowne with oyle, and putteth on his coole:
and so taketh him in among the Fraternitie.
They vowe perpetuall chastitie, and absti-
nence from flesh.

Besides their landes, (that are verie great)
they are the greatest marchants in the whole
countrey, and deale for all manner of commodities. Some of their monasteries dispēd
in landes, one thousande, or two thousande
rubbels a yeere. There is one Abbey called
Troits, that hath in lands & fees, the summe
of 100000. rubbels, or marks a yeere . It is
built in maner of a Castle, walled rounde a-
bout, with great ordinance planted on the
wall, and conteineth within it a large bredth
of grounde, and great varietie of building.
There are of Friers within it, (besides their
officers, and other seruants) about 700. The
Empresse that now is, hath many vowes to
Saint Sergius, that is patrone there: to intreat
him to make her fruitful, as hauing no children by the Emperour her husband. Lightly
euery

5

10

15

20

25

30

(16–18) dispend . . . a yeere/dispend in Lands 10000, soom 20000 Rubbells a year
(19–21) that hath . . . in maner of a Castle/that hath in Lands & fees to the summe
of 100000 Rubbells a year. This is manie times visited by the Emperours for devotion,
soomtimes allso they visitt their purse withowt anie devotion. It is built in manner of a
Castle (29–30) to make her fruitful . . . her husband/to make hir fruitfull for children (30) Lightly *omitted.*

euery yeere fhe goeth on pilgrimage to him
from the *Mosko*, on foote, about 80 Englifh
miles, with fiue or fixe thoufand women attending vpon her, all in blewe liueries, and
foure thoufand fouldiers for her garde. But
Saint Sergius hath not yet heard her prayers,
though (they fay) he hath a fpeciall gift and
facultie that way.

What learning there is among their Fryers, may be knowen by their Bifhops, that
are the choyce men out of all their monafteries. I talked with one of them at the Citie
of *Vologda*, where (to trie his skill) I offered him a *Ruffe* Teftament, and turned him
to the firft Chapter of Saint *Mathewes* Go-
fpel. Where hee beganne to reade in verie
good order. I asked him firft what part of
fcripture it was, that hee had read? hee an-
fwered, that hee coulde not well tell. Howe
manie Euangeliftes there were in the newe
Teftament? Hee fayde he knew not. Howe
manie Apoftles there were? Hee thought
there were twelue. Howe he fhoulde be faued? Whereunto he anfweared mee with a
piece of *Ruffe* doctrine, that hee knew not
whether he fhoulde bee faued or no : but if
God woulde *Pofhallonate* him, or gratifie
him fo much, as to faue him, fo it was, hee
would be glad of it : if not, what remedie.
I asked him, why he fhoare himfelfe a Fryer?

The Friers
learning.

5

10

15

20

25

30

N   He

---

(1) euery yeere she goeth/A year or two since shee went   (3) thousand women/hun-
dredth women   (13–16) Vologda . . . beganne to reade/*Vologda* by an interpreter.
Thear was brought vnto him a Russ testament whear hee tourned to the first Chapter
of St. Mathiews Ghospell, whear hee beegann to read   (21) he knew not/hee knew
not well

He anſwered,becauſe he would eat his bread with peace. This is the learning of the Friers of *Ruſſia*, which though it be not to bee meaſured by one, yet partly it may bee geſſed by the ignorance of this man, what is in the reſt.

Nunneries.   They haue alſo many Nunneries, whereof ſome may admitte none but Noblemens widowes, and daughters, when the Emperour meaneth to keepe them vnmarried, from continuing the blood or ſtocke,which he would haue extinguiſhed. To ſpeak of the life of their Friers,and Nunnes,it needes not, to thoſe that know the hypocriſie, and vncleanneſſe of that Cloyſter-broode. The *Ruſſe* himſelfe (though otherwiſe addicted to all ſuperſtition) ſpeaketh ſo fowlly of it, that it muſt needes gaine ſilence of any modeſt man.

Eremites.   Beſides theſe, they haue certeyne *Eremites*, (whome they call *Holy men*) that are like to thoſe *Gymnoſophiſts*, for their life and behauiour : though farre vnlike for their knowledge,& learning. They vſe to go ſtarke naked,ſaue a clout about their middle,with their haire hanging long,and wildely about their ſhoulders, and many of them with an iron coller,or chaine about their neckes, or middes, euen in the very extremity of winter.Theſe they take as Prophets,and men of great

great holines,giuing them a liberty to ſpeak what they liſt,without any cŏtroulmĕt,thogh it be of the very higheſt himſelfe, So that if he reproue any openly, in what ſort ſoeuer, they anſwere nothing, but that it is *Po gra-* 5
*cum,*that is, for their ſinnes, And if anie of them take ſome piece of ſale ware from anie mans ſhop,as he paſſeth by,to giue where he liſt, hee thinketh himſelfe much beloued of God,and much beholding to the holy man, 10
for taking it in that ſort,

Of this kinde there are not many, be-cauſe it is a very harde and colde profeſsion, to goe naked in *Ruſſia*, ſpecially in Winter, Among other at this time, they haue one 15
at *Mosko*, that walketh naked about the ſtreetes, and inueyeth commonly againſt the ſtate,and gouernment, eſpecially againſt the *Godonoes*, that are thought at this time to bee great oppreſſours of that Common 20
wealth. An other there was, that dyed not many yeeres agoe (whome they called *Baſi-* *Baſileo the* *leo*) that would take vpon him to reprooue *Ermite.* the olde Emperour, for all his crueltie, and oppreſsions, done towards his people, His 25
body they haue trăſlated of late into a ſump-tuous Church,neere the Emperours houſe in *Mosko*, and haue canonized him for a Saint, Many miracles he doth there (for ſo the Fri-ers make the people to beleeue) and manie 30
N 2 offrings

offrings are made vnto him, not only by the people,but by the chiefe Nobilitie, and the Emperour, and Empreſſe theinſelues which viſite that Church with great deuotion. But this laſt yeere, at my beeing at *Mosko*, this Saint had ill lucke, in working his miracles. For a lame man that had his limmes reſtored (as it was pretended by him) was charged by a woman that was familiar with him (being then fallen out) that hee halted but in the day time , and coulde leape merily when he came home at night. And that hee had intended this matter ſixe yeeres before. Nowe he is put into a Monaſtery, and there rayleth vpon the Fryers , that hyred him to haue this counterfaite miracle, practiſed vpon him. Beſides this diſgrace, a litle before my comming from thence , there were eyght ſlaine within his Church by fire in a thunder. Which cauſed his belles (that were tingling before all day and night long as in triumph of the miracles wrought by *Baſileo* their Saint) to ring ſomewhat ſoftlier, and hath wrought no little diſcredite to this Miracle-worker. There was another of great account at *Plesko*, (called *Nichôla* of *Plesko*) that did much good, when this Emperours father came to ſack the towne,vpon ſuſpition of their reuolting and rebellion againſt him. The Emperour, after hee had ſaluted

Nicôla the *Eremite.*

(16–19) counterfaite miracle . . . eyght ſlaine/counterfaut miracle. Again a fiew dayes beefore I cam owt of the Countrey, thear wear eight ſlaine (26) great account at *Plesko*/great account not long since at *Plesko* (27) much good/ſoom good

luted the *Eremite*, at his lodging, fent him a
reward. And the *Holy man* to requite the
Emperour, fenthim a piece of rawe flefhe,
beyng then their Lent time. Which the Emperour feeing, bid one to tell him, that hee
marueiled that the *Holy man* woulde offer
him flefh to eat in the Lent, when it was for-
bidden by order of holie Church. And doth
Euasko, (which is as much to faye, as Iacke)
thinke (quoth *Nicôla*)that it is vnlawfull to
eate a piece of beafts flefh in Lent and not to
eate vp fo much mans flefh,as hee hath done
already. So threatning the Emperour with
a prophecy of fome hard aduenture to come
vpon him, except hee left murdering of his
people, and departed the towne: he faued a
great many mens liues at that time.

This maketh the people to like very well
of them,becaufe they are as *Pafquils*,to note
their great mens faults, that no man els dare
fpeake of. Yet it falleth out fometime, that
for this rude libertie, which they take vpon
them, after a counbrfeite mannerin imita-
tion of prophets, they are made away in fecret: As was one or two of them,in the
iaft Emperours time, for beyng o-
uer bolde in fpeaking againft
his gouernment.

N 3   *Of*

Of their Leiturgie, or forme of
Church-seruice, and their manner of
adminiſtring the Sacraments.

The 22. Chapter.

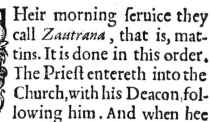

Heir morning ſeruice they call *Zautrana*, that is, mattins. It is done in this order. The Prieſt entereth into the Church, with his Deacon, following him. And when hee is come to the middle of the Church, he beginneth to ſay with a loude voyce : *Blasſlaney Vladika* (that is) *Bleſſe vs heauenly Paſtor :* meaning, of Chriſt. Then he addeth, *In the name of the Father, and of the Sonne, and of the holy Ghoſt, one very God in Trinitie: and Aſpody Pomeluy*, or, *Lorde haue mercy vpon vs, Lorde haue mercie vpon vs, Lorde haue mercie vpon vs :* repeated three times. This done, hee marcheth on towardes the Chauncell, or *Sanctum Sanctorum*, (as they vſe to call it) and ſo entreth into the *Scharſuey Dwere*, or the heauenly doore: which no man may enter into, but the Prieſt only. Where ſtanding at the altar, or table (ſet neere to the vpper wall of the chauncell) hee ſayeth the Lordes prayer, and then againe *Aſpody Pomeluy*,

or

or *Lord haue mercie vpon vs, Lorde haue mer-*
cie vpon vs, &c: pronounced twelue times.
Then prayfed be the *Trinitie, the Father, the*
Sonne, and holie Ghoſt for euer and euer. Wherto the Deacons, and people fay, *Amen.* Next
after, the Prieſt addeth the Pfalmes for that
day, and beginneth with *O come let vs wor-*
ſhippe, and fall downe before the Lorde, &c. and
therewithall himfelfe, with the Deacons, &
people, all turne themfelues towardes their
Idoles, or Images, that hang on the wall and
crofsing themfelues, bowe downe three
times, knocking their heades to the veric
ground After this, he readeth the ten com-
mandements and *Athanaſius* Creed, out of
the Seruice booke.

This being done, the Deacon that ſtandeth without the heauenly doore, or chaun-
cel readeth a piece of a Legéd, out of a written booke, (for they haue it not in print) of
fome Saints life, miracles, &c. This is diuided
into manie partes, for euerie day in the
yeere, and is read by them with a playne
finging note, not vnlike to the Popiſh tune,
when they foung their Gofpels. After all
this (which reacheth to an houre, and an
halfe, or two houres of length) hee addeth
certeyne fette Colle&es or prayers vpon
that which hee hath read out of the Le-
gend before : and fo endeth his Seruice.

N 4　　All

All this while ſtand burning before their I-
doles, a great many of waxe candles, (wherof ſome are of the bigneſſe of a mans waſt)
vowed, or enioyned by penance, vpon the
people of the pariſh.

About 9. of the clock in the morning, they
haue an other ſeruice, called *Obeidna*, (or
Compline) much after the order of the Popiſh Seruice, that bare that name. If it bee
ſome high, or Feſtiuall day, they furniſh
their Seruice beſide, with *Bleſſed bee the
Lorde God of Iſrael, &c.* and *We prayſe thee O
God, &c:* Sung with a more ſolemne, and curious note.

Their Eue-
ning ſer-
uice. Their Euening ſeruice, is called *Vecherna*,
where the Prieſt beginneth with *Blaſlauey
Vladika*, as hee did in the morning, and
with the Pſalmes appointed for the *Vecherna*. Which beyng read, hee ſingeth, *My ſoule
doeth magnifie the Lorde, &c.* And then the
Prieſt, Deacons, and people, all with one
voice, ſing, *Aſpody pomelui,* or *Lord haue mercie vpon vs,* thirty times together. Whereunto the boyes that are in the Church, anſwere
all with one voyce, rowling it vp ſo faſt, as
their lippes can goe : *Verij, Verij, Verij, Verij,*
or, *Prayſe, Prayſe, Prayſe, &c.* thirty times together, with a very ſtraunge noyſe. Then is
read by the prieſt, & vpō the holidaies ſung,
the firſt Pſalme: *Bleſſed is the man, &c.* And in
the

the end of it, is added *Alleluia* repeated ten
times. The next in order is some part of the
goſpell read by the Prieſt, which hee endeth
with *Alleluia* repeated three times. And ſo
hauing ſaid a collect in remembrance of the
Saint of that day, he endeth his euening ſeruice. All this while the Prieſt ſtandeth aboue
at the altar or high table, within the Chancel,
or *Sanctum Sanctorum*, whence he neuer moueth al the ſeruice time. The Deacon, or Deacons (which are many in their cathedrall
Churches) ſtand without the chancell by the
Scharſuey dwere, or heauenly doore: for within they may not be ſeene all the ſeruice time,
though otherwiſe their office is to ſweepe,
and keepe it, and to ſet vp the waxe candels
before their Idols. The people ſtand together the whole ſeruice time in the body of
the Church, and ſome in the church porch,
for piew, or ſeate they haue none within
their churches.

The Sacrament of baptiſme they admini- The man-
ſter after this manner. The child is brought ner of the
vnto the Church (& this is done within eight *Ruſſe* bap-
daies after it is borne) if it bee the childe of tiſme.
ſome Nobleman, it is brought with great
pomp in a rich ſled or wagō, with chaires &
cuſhiōs of cloth of gold, & ſuch like ſumptu-
ous ſhew of their beſt furniture. When they
are come to the Church, the Prieſt ſtandeth
readie

5

10

15

20

25

30

ready to receiue the child within the church porch, with his tub of water by him. And the beginneth to declare vnto them, that they haue brought a little Infidell to be made a Chriftian, &c. This ended, he teacheth the witneffes (that are two or three) in a certeine fet forme out of his booke, what their dutie is in bringing vp the childe after hee is baptifed vz. That he muft be taught to know God, and Chrift the Sauiour . And becaufe God is of great maieftie, and wee muft not prefume to come vnto him without mediatours (as the manner is when wee make any fuit to an Emperour, or great Prince) therefore they muft teach him what Saints are the beft, & chiefe mediatours, &c. This done, he cōmandeth the diuell in the name of God after a coniuring manner, to come out of the water: & fo after certeine praiers he plungeth the childe thrife ouer head, & eares. For this they holde to be a point neceffary , that no part of the childe be vndipped in the water.

The words that beare with the the forme of baptifme vttered by the Prieft, when he dippeth in the childe , are the very fame that are prefcribed in the gofpell, & vfed by vs, vz: *In the name of the Father, & of the Sonne, & of the Ghoſt*. For that they fhould altar the forme of the words, and fay *by the holy Ghaſt*, (as I haue heard that they did(folowing certein

tein heretikes of the Greeke church, I found to be vntrue, aſwell by report of them that haue bin often at their baptiſmes, as by their booke of *Leiturgie* it ſelfe, wherein the order of baptiſme is preciſely ſet downe.

When the childe is baptiſed, the Prieſt laieth oile and ſalt tempred together vpon the forehead, and both ſides of his face, and then vppon his mouth, drawing it along with his finger ouer the childes lippes (as did the Popiſh prieſtes) ſaying withall certeine prayers to this effect: that God will make him a good Chriſtian, &c: all this is done in the Church porch. Then is the childe (as being now made a Chriſtian, and meet to be receiued within the church dore) carried into the church, the Prieſt going before, and there he is preſented to the chiefe Idoll of the Church, being layd on a cuſhion before the feete of the image, by it(as by the mediatour) to bee commended vnto God. If the child be ſick, or weake(ſpecially in the winter) they vſe to make the water luke warme. After baptiſme the manner is to cut of the haire from the childes head, and hauing wrapped it within a piece of wax to lay it vp, as a relique, or monument in a ſecret place of the church.

This is the maner of their baptiſme, which they accout to be the beſt & perfecteſt form.

AS

(22–28) If the child be sick . . . [to end of paragraph] *omitted.*

Of their Leiturgie.

As they doo all other parts of their religion, receiued (as they say) by tradition from the best church, meaning the Greeke, And therfore they will take great paynes to make a proselite, or couert, either of an infidell, or of a forrein Christian, by rebaptizing him after the *Russe* manner. When they take any *Tartar* prisoner, commonly they will offer him life, with condition to be baptized. And yet they perswade very few of them to redeeme their life so: becaufe of the naturall hatred the *Tartar* beareth to the *Russe*, and the opinion he hath of his falshood, and iniustice. The yere after *Mosko* was fired by the *Chrim Tartar*, there was taken a *Dinoymorsey*, one of the chiefe in that exploit with 300. *Tartars* more: who had all their liues offered thē, if they would be baptized after the *Russe* manner. Which they refufed all to doo, with many reproches against thofe that perfwaded them. And fo beyng carried to the riuer *Mosko* (that runneth through the citie) they were all baptized after a violent manner: being thruft downe with a knock on the head into the water, through an hole made in the yfe for that purpofe. Of *Lieslanders* that are captiues, there are many that take on thē this fecōd *Russe*, baptifme to get more libertie, & fomwhat befides towards their liuing, which the Emperour ordinarily vfeth to giue them.

Of

OF Engliſhmen ſince they frequented the countrie there was neuer any found, that ſo much forgot God,his faith,and countrie,as that he would bee content to be baptized *Ruſſe*, for any reſpect of feare, preferment, or other meanes whatſoeuer: ſaue onely *Richard Relph*,that following before an vngodly trade,by keeping a *Caback*(againſt the order of the countrie) and being put of from that trade, & ſpoiled by the Emperours officers of that which he had,entred himſelf this laſt yeare into the *Ruſſe* profeſsion: & ſo was rebaptiſed,liuing now aſmuch an idolater as before he was a rioter, and vnthrifty perſon.

Such as thus receiue the *Ruſſe* baptiſme, are firſt carried into ſome Monaſterie to be inſtructed there in the doctrine and ceremonies of the church.Where they vſe theſe ceremonies. Firſt, they put him into a new and freſh ſuite of apparell, made after the *Ruſſe* faſhion, and ſet a coronet or (in Sommer) a garland vpon his head. Then they annoint his head with oile,& put a waxe candle light into his hand: and ſo pray ouer him foure times a day,the ſpace of ſeuen daies.All this while he is to abſtaine from fleſh,and white meats.The ſeuen daies being ended,he is purified and waſhed in a bathſtoue, and ſo the eight day hee is brought into the church, where he is taught by the Friers how to behaue

(11) which he had/which hee had gott by vnlawfull meanes   (18–30) of the church . . . how to behaue/of their church, whear the Friars take them privatlie into the monasterie church, and thear teach them how to beehave

Of their Leiturgie.

haue himfelfe in prefence of their idols, by ducking downe, knocking of the head, croffing himfelf, and fuch like geftures, which are the greateft part of the *Ruffe* religion.

The facrament of the Lordes fupper they receiue but once a yeare, in their great Lent time, a litle before Eafter. Three at the moft are admitted at one time, and neuer aboue. The manner of their cōmunicating, is thus. Firft they cōfeffe themfelues of all their fins to the Prieft (whō they call their ghoftly father. Then they come to the Church, & are called vp to the Cōmunion table, that ftandeth like an altar, a little remoued frō the vpper end of the Church, after the Doutch maner. Here firft they are asked of the Prieft whither they be cleane or no, that is, whither they haue neuer a finne behind that they left vnconfeffed. If they anfwere, *No*, they are taken to the table. Where the Prieft beginneth with certeine vfuall prayers, the communicants ftanding in the meane while with their armes foulded one within an other, like penitentiaries, or mourners. When thefe prayers are ended, the Prieft taketh a fpoone, and filleth it full of claret wine Then he putteth into it a fmall piece of bread, and tempereth them both together: and fo deliuereth them in the fpoone to the Communicants, that ftande in order, fpeaking the vfuall

---

(1–5) [be]haue himselfe . . . they/beehave themselves in presence of their idolls, by ducking down, knocking of the head, signing them selves with the Cross & such like gestures, which are the greatest part of the Russ relligion. Soomtimes they baptize within privat howses. The Sacrament of the Lords supper they

vſuall wordes of the Sacrament. *Eat this &c.*
Drinke this &c. both at one time without a-
ny pauſe.

After that he deliuereth them againe
bread by it ſelf, and then wine carded together with a little warme water, to repreſent
bloud more rightly (as they thinke) and the
water withall, that flowed out of the ſide of
Chriſt Whiles this is in doing the communicants vnfold their armes. And then foul-
ding them againe, follow the Prieſt thriſe
round about the communion table, and ſo
returne to their places againe, Where hauing ſaid certeine other prayers, he diſmiſ-
ſeth the communicants, with charge to bee
meary, and to cheere vp themſelues for the
ſeuen daies next following. Which being ended, he enioyneth them to faſt for it as long
time after. Which they vſe to obſerue with
very great deuotion, eating nothing els but
bread and ſalt, except a little cabbage, and
ſome other hearbe or roote, with water or
quaſſe mead for their drinke.

This is their manner of adminiſtring the
Sacraments. Wherein what they differ from
the inſtitution of Chriſt, and what ceremonies they haue added of their owne, or rather borrowed of the Greekes, may eaſily
be noted,

Of

Of the doctrine of the Ruſſe church, and what errours it holdeth.

The 23, Chapter.

5

The *Ruſſe*
errours.
1. Their
diſallowing
of certeine
parts of the
Canonicall
ſcriptures.

10

Heir chiefeſt errours in matter of faith I find to be theſe. Firſt concerning the word of God it ſelf they will not read publiquely certeine bookes of the Canonicall ſcripture, as the bookes of *Moſes*: ſpecially the foure laſt, *Exodus*, *Leuiticus*, *Numeri*, and *Deuteronomie*, which they ſay are al made diſauthentique, and put out of vſe by the comming of Chriſt: as not able to diſcerne the difference betwixt the morall, and the ceremoniall law. The bookes of the prophets they allow of, but read thē not publikely in their churches for the ſame reaſon: becauſe they were but directers vnto Chriſt, & proper (as they ſay) to the nation of the Iewes. Onely the booke of Pſalmes they haue in great eſtimation and ſing and ſay them dayly in their Churches, Of the new Teſtament they allow, and read all, except the *Reuelation*: which therefore they read not (though they allow it) becauſe they vnderſtand it not, neither haue the like occaſion, to know the fulfilling of the prophecies

15

20

25

30

(10–11) they will not read publiquely certaine bookes/they refuse certein books

phecies conteyned within it, concerning e-
ſpecially the apoſtaſie of the Antichriſtian
Church, as haue the Weſterne Churches.
Notwithſtanding they haue had their Anti-
chriſts of the Greeke Church, and may finde
their owne falling of, and the puniſhments
for it by the Turkiſh inuaſion in the prophecies of that Booke.

Secondly(which is the fountain of the reſt
of al their corruptiõs both in doctrine & ceremonies) they holde with the Papiſtes,that
their church *Traditions* are of equall authoritie with the written worde of God.Wherein
they prefer thēſelues before other churches:
affirming that they haue the true and right
traditions deliuered by the Apoſtles to the
Greeke church, and ſo vnto them.

2. Traditi-
ons equall
to the holy
Scripture.

3. That the church meaning the Greeke
and ſpecially the Patriarch and his Synod,as
the head of the reſt) haue a ſoueraigne authoritie to interpret the Scriptures, and that
all are bound to holde that interpretation as
found,and authentique.

3. The
Church to
haue ſoue-
raigne au-
thoritie in
interpre-
ting the
Scriptures.

4. Concerning the diuine nature & the
three perſons,in the one ſubſtance of God,
that the holy Ghoſt proceedeth from the
Father onely,and not from the Sonne.

4. The ho-
ly Ghoſt to
proceed frõ
the Father
onely.

5. About the office of Chriſt,they holde
many fowle errours, and the ſame almoſt as
doth the Popiſh church : namely that hee is

5. Chriſt
not ſole
mediator of
interceſſiõ.

O   the

(1–4) [pro]phecies . . . Notwithſtanding/prophecies of it concerning Antichrist and
the rest, as have the western Churches, notwithstanding (6–9) and the punishments
. . . Secondly/and punishments for it foretolld them by God, in the phrophecies of that
book. Secondlie (24–28) 4. Concerning . . . 5. About the office/.4. Concerning the di-
vine nature & the three persons in on substance, they are free from the errours of *Arrius*,
Macedonius, *Manichie* and the rest. But abowt the office

the fole mediatour of redemption, but not of intercefsion. Their chiefe reafon(if they bee talked withall)for defence of this errour, is that vnapt and foolifh comparifon, betwixt God and a Monarch or Prince of this world, that muft bee fued vnto by Mediatours about him:wherein they giue fpeciall preferment to fome aboue others, as to the bleffed *Virgin* whom they call *Precheſte*, or vndefiled, and S.*Nicôlas*, whom they call *Scora pomofnick*, or the *Speedy helper*, and fay that he hath 300.angels of the chiefeft appointed by God to attend vpon him, This hath brought them to an horrible exceffe of idolatry,after the groffeft & prophaneft maner,giuing vnto their images al religious worfhip of praier,thankfgiuing,offerings,& adoration,with proftrating and knocking their heads to the ground before the,as to God himfelf.Which becaufe they doo to the picture, not to the portraiture of the Saint, they fay they worfhip not an idol,but the Saint in his image,& fo offend not God:forgetting the comandement of God, that forbiddeth to make the image or likenes of any thing,for any religious worfhip,or vfe whatfoeuer.Their church walles are very full of them,richly hanged & fet forth with pearle & ftone vpô the fmooth table.Though fome alfo they haue emboffed, that ftick from the board almoft an inch outwards,

wards. They call them *(hudouodites,* or their miracle workers : and when they prouide them to ſet vp in their Churches, in no caſe they may ſay that they haue bought the image, but exchaunged monie for it.

6. For the means of iuſtification, they agree with the Papiſts, that it is not by faith only apprehēding Chriſt, but by their works alſo. And that *Opus operatum,* or the worke for the worke ſake, muſt needes pleaſe God. And therefore they are all in their numbers of praiers, faſtes, vowes, & offrings to ſaints, almes deeds, croſsings & ſuch like, and carrie their numbring beads about with them cōtinually, aſwel the Emperour & his Nobilitie as the cōmon people not only in the church, but in all other publike places, ſpecially at any ſet or ſolemne meeting, as in their faſtes, lawe courts, common conſultations, intertainement of Ambaſſadours, and ſuch like.

7. They ſay with the Papiſts that no man can be aſſured of his ſaluation, til the laſt ſentence be paſſed at the day of iudgement.

8. They vſe auricular confeſsion, & thinke that they are purged by the very action frō ſo many ſinnes, as they confeſſe by name, and in particular to the Prieſt.

9. They hold three ſacramentes, of *Baptiſme,* the *Lords ſupper,* and *the laſt annoiling,* or *vnction.* Yet concerning their Sacrament

O 2   of

of extreame vnction, they holde it not fo neceffarie to faluation as they do baptifme, but thinke it a great curfe and punifhment of God, if any die with out it.

10. All dã-ned that die without baptifme.

10. They thinke there is a necefsitie of baptifme, and that all are condemned that die without it.

11. Ana-baptifme.

11. They rebaptife as many Chriftians (not being of the Greek church) as they con-uert to their *Ruffe* profefsion : becaufe they are diuided from the true Church, which is the Greeke, as they fay.

12. Diffe-rence of meates.

12. They make a difference of meates & drinks, accounting the vfe of one, to be more holy then of an other. And therefore in their fet faftes they forbeare to eate flefhe, and white meats (as we call them) after the man-ner of the Popifh fuperftition : which they obferue fo ftrictly, & with fuch blinde deuo-tion, as that they will rather die, then eat one bit of flefh, egges, or fuch like, for the health of their bodies in their extreme ficknefle.

13. Marri-age for fome per-fons vnlaw-full.

13. They hold marriage to be vnlawfull for all the Clergie men, except the priefts on-ly, and for them alfo after the firft wife, as was faid before. Neither doo they well allow of it in Lay men after the fecond marriage. Which is a pretence now vfed againft the Emperours only brother, a child of fix yeres old : Who therefore is not praied for in their churches

churches (as their manner is otherwife for
the Princes bloud) becaufe hee was borne of
the fixt marriage,and fo not legitimate This
charge was giuen to the priefts by the Emperour himfelfe, by procurement of the
*Godonoes:*who make him beleeue that it is a
good pollicie to turne away the liking of the
people from the next fucceffour.

Many other falfe opinions they haue in
matter of religion, But thefe are the chiefe,
which they holde partly by meanes of their
traditions (which they haue receiued from
the Greeke church) but fpecially by ignorance of the holy Scriptures Which notwithftanding they haue in the *Polonian* tongue,
(that is all one with theirs fome few wordes
excepted)yet fewe of them read them with
that godly care which they ought to doo:
neither haue they(if they would bookes fuf-
ficient of the old and new Teftament for the
common people,but of their Leiturgie onely, or booke of common feruice, whereof
there are great numbers.

All this mifchief commeth from the clergie,who being ignorant and godleffe themfelues, are very warie to keepe the people
likewife in their ignorance and blindneffe,
for their liuing and bellies fake : partly alfo
frō the manner of gouernment fetled among
them: which the Emperours (whom it fpeci-

O 3 ally

5

10

15

20

25

30

(28) partly also . . . [to end of sentence on p. 99v:] agreeth with it *omitted*.

ally behoueth) lift not to haue chaunged by any innouation, but to retaine that religion that beft agreeth with it. Which notwithstanding it is not to be doubted, but that hauing the word of God in fome fort (though without the ordinarie meanes to attaine to a true fenfe and vnderftanding of it) God hath alfo his number among them. As may partly appeare by that which a *Ruffe* at *Mosko* faid in fecret to one of my feruaunts, fpeaking againft their images and other fuperftitions: That God had giuen vnto England light to day, and might giue it to morrow (if he pleafed) to them.

As for any inquifition or proceeding againft men for matter of religion, I could heare of none: faue a few yeares fince againft one man and his wife, who were kept in a clofe prifon the fpace of 28. yeares, till they were ouer growen into a deformed fafhion, for their hayre, nailes, collour of countenance, and fuch like, and in the end were burned at *Mosko*, in a fmall houfe fet on fire. The caufe was kepte fecrete, but like it was for fome part of truth in matter of religion: though the people were made to beleeue by the Priefts and Friers, that they held fome great, and damnable herefie.

Of

Of the manner of solemnizing
their Marriages.

The 24. Chapter.

He manner of making & solemnizing their marriages is different frō the maner of other countries . The man (though he ne-
uer saw the woman before) is not permitted
to haue any fight of hir al the time of his wo-
ing:which he doth not by himself,but by his
mother or some other ancient woman of his
kin,or acquaintance. When the liking is taken (aswell by the parents as by the parties
théselues,for without the knowledge & consent of the parents,the cótract is not lawful)
the fathers on both sides,or such as are to thē
in steede of fathers, with their other chiefe
friends,haue a meeting & conference about
the dowrie,which is comonly very large after the abilitie of the parents:so that you shal
haue a market man (as they call them) giue a
1000.rubbels, or more with his daughter.

As for the man it is neuer required of him,
nor stādeth with their custome to make any
iointer in recompence of the dowrie. But in
case he haue a child by his wife,she enioieth a
thirde deale after his disease . If hee haue
two children by hir or more , shee is to haue

The man-
ner of in-
dowment
for wiues.

O 4 &

a courtesie more, at the discretion of the husband. If the husband depart without issue
by his wife, shee is returned home to hir
friends without any thing at al, saue only hir
dowrie: if the husband leaue so much behind
him in goods When the agreement is made
cócerning the dowrie, they signe bonds one
to the other, aswell for the paiment of the
dowrie, as the performing of the mariage by
a certein day. If the woman were neuer married before hir father and friends are bound
besides to assure hir a maiden. Which breedeth many brabbels and quarrels at Law, if
the man take any conceipt concerning the
behauiour, and honestie of his wife.

Thus the contract being made, the parties
begin to send tokés the one to the other, the
woman first, then afterwards the mã, but yet
see not one an other till the marriage be so-
lemnized. On the eaue before the marriage
day, the bride is carried in a *Collimago*, or
coach, or in a sledde (if it be winter) to the
bridegromes house, with hir marriage apparell and bedstead with hir, which they are to
lie in. For this is euer prouided by the Bride,
and is commonly very faire, with much cost
bestowed vpon it. Here she is accompaned
all that night by hir mother, and other women: but not welcommed, nor once seene by
the Bridegrome himselfe.

When

---

(1) a courtesie more, at the discretion/a courtisie more, but at the discreation (20)
eaue/daye

When the time is come to haue the marriage folemnized, the Bride hath put vpon her a kind of hood, made of fine knitworke, or lawne that couereth her head, and all her body downe to the middle. And fo accompanied with her friends, & the bridegroome with his , they goe to Church all on horfebacke, though the Church bee neere hande, and themfelues but of very meane degree. The wordes of contract, and other ceremonies in folemnizing the marriage, are much after the order, and with the fame wordes that are vfed with vs: with a ring alfo giuen to the Bride. Which beeing put on, and the wordes of contract pronounced : the Brides hand is deliuered into the hand of the Bride groome, which ftandeth al this while on the one fide of the altar or table, and the Bride on the other . So the marriage knot beeing knitte by the Prieft, the Bride commeth to the Bridegroome (ftanding at the end of the altar or table) and falleth downe at his feete, knocking her head vpon his fhooe , in token of her fubiection, and obedience . And the Bridegroome againe cafteth the lappe of his gowne, or vpper garment, ouer the Bride, in token of his duetie to protect, and cherifh her.

Then the Bridegroome, and Bride, ftanding both together at the tables ende, commeth

Ceremonies in mariages.

5

10

15

20

25

30

meth

meth firſt the father, and the other friends of the Bride, and bowe themſelues downe low to the Bridegroome : and ſo likewiſe his friends bow themſelues to the Bride, in tokē of affinity & loue, euer after betwixt the two kinreds. And withall, the father of the Bridegroome offreth to the prieſt, a loafe of bread, who deliuereth it ſtraight again to the father, & other friends of the Bride, with atteſtatiō before God and their idols, that hee deliuer the dowry wholly and truely at the day appointed, & hold loue euer after, one kinred with another. Wherupon they break the loaf into pieces, & eate of it, to teſtifie their true & ſincere meanings, for performing of that charge, and thenceforth to become as grains of one loafe, or men of one table.

Theſe ceremonies being ended, the Bridegroome taketh the Bride by the hand, and ſo they goe on together, with their friendes after them, towardes the Church porche. Where meete thē certein with pots, & cups in their handes, with meade and *Ruſſe* wine. Whereof the Bridegroome taketh firſt a charke, or little cuppe full in his hand, and drinketh to the Bride : who opening her hood, or vale below, and putting the cup to her mouth vnderneath it (for beeing ſeene of the Bridegroome) pleadgeth him againe. Thus returning altogether from the

Church,

Church, the Bridegroome goeth not home to his owne, but to his fathers houfe, and fhe likewife to hers, where either intertayn their friends apart. At the entring into the houfe, they vfe to fling corne out of the windowes, vpon the Bridegroome, and Bride, in token of plentie, and fruitfulnes to bee with them euer after.

When the Euening is come, the Bride is brought to the Bridegrooms fathers houfe, and there lodgeth that night, with her vale or couer ftill ouer her head. All that night fhe may not fpeak one word (for that charge fhe receiueth by tradition from her mother, and other matrones her friendes) that the Bridegroome muft neither heare, nor fee her, till the day after the marriage. Neither three dayes after, may fhee bee hearde to fpeake, faue certeyne fewe wordes at the table, in a fet forme with great manners, and reuerence to the Bridegroome. If fhe behaue her felfe otherwife, it is a great preiudice to her credite, and life euer after : and will highly be difliked of the Bridegroome himfelfe.

After the third day, they depart to their owne, and make a feaft to both their friends together. The marriage day, and the whole time of their feftiuall, the Bridegroome hath the honour to bee called *Moloday Knez,* or or yong Duke, and the Bride *Moloday Kne-zay*, or young Dutcheſſe.

In liuing with their wiues, they ſhewe themſelues to be but of a barbarous condition : vſing them as ſeruaunts, rather then wiues. Except the Noble-women, which are, or ſeeme to be of more eſtimation with their husbands then the reſt of meaner ſort. They haue this fowle abuſe, contrary to good order, and the worde of God it ſelfe, that vpon diſlike of his wife, or other cauſe whatſoeuer, the man may goe into a Monaſterie, and ſhire himſelfe a Frier, by pretence of deuotion: and ſo leaue his wife to ſhift for her ſelfe ſo well as ſhe can.

Of the other Ceremonies of the Ruſſe Church.

The 25. Chapter.

The ſigne of the croſſe.

He other ceremonies of their Churche, are manie in number : eſpecially, the abuſe about the ſigne of the Croſſe, which they ſet vp in their high wayes, in the tops of their Churches, and in euery doore of their houſes, ſig-ning

---

(25–26) in number . . . the ſigne/in number, and fowl for superstition. That which a man shalbee forced most to see is the abuse abowt the signe

ning themſelues continually with it, on their
foreheads and breſts, with great deuotion,
as they will ſeeme by their outward geſture.
Which were leſſe offence, if they gaue not
withall, that religious reuerence and woor-
ſhip vnto it, which is due to God onely, and
vſed the dumbe ſhewe, and ſigning of it in-
ſteede of thankſgiuing, and of all other dueties which they owe vnto God . When they
riſe in the morning, they goe commonly in
the ſight of ſome ſteeple, that hath a croſſe
on the toppe: and ſo bowing themſelues towardes the croſſe, ſigne themſelues withal on
their foreheads and breſts. And this is their
thankſgiuing to God for their nightes reſt,
without any word ſpeaking, except peraduenture they ſay, *Aſpody Pomelxy*, or, *Lorde
haue mercie vpon vs* . When they ſitte downe
to meate, and riſe againe from it, the thankſgiuing to God, is the croſsing of their foreheads and breſts. Except it be ſome few that
adde peraduenture, a worde or two of ſome
ordinarie prayer, impertinent to that purpoſe. When they are to giue an oath for the
deciding of anie controuerſie at Lawe, they
doe it by ſwearing by the Croſſe, and kiſsing
the feet of it, making it as God, whoſe name
onely is to bee vſed in ſuch triall of iuſtice.
When they enter into any houſe (where e-
uer there is an idole hanging on the wall)
they

they figne themfelues with the croffe, & bow themfelues to it. When they begin any work, bee it little, or much they arme them felues firft with the figne of the croffe. And this cō-monly is all their prayer to God, for good fpeede of their bufineffe. And thus they ferue God with croffes, after a croffe and vaine maner : not vnderftanding what the croffe of Chrift is, nor the power of it. And yet they thinke all ftrangers Chriftians, to be no better then Turkes, in comparifon of themfelues (and fo they wil fay) becaufe they bow not themfelues, when they meete with the croffe, nor figne themfelues with it, as the *Ruffe* maner is.

Holy water. They haue holie water in like vfe, and e-ftimation, as the Popifh Church hath. But herein they exceede them, in that they doe not onely hallow their holie water ftockes, and tubbes ful of water, but all the riuers of Hallowing the countrey once euery yeere. At *Mosko* it of riuers. is done with great pompe, and folemnitie: the Emperour himfelfe being prefent at it, with all his Nobility, marching through the ftreets towards the riuer of *Moskua*, in man-ner of procefsion in this order as followeth. Firft goe two Deacons, with banners in their hands, the one of *Prechefte* (or our Ladie) the other of *S. Michael*, fighting with his dragō. Then follow after, the reft of the Deacons & the

the prieſts of *Mosko*, two & two in a ranke,
with coaps on their backs, and their idols at
their breſts, carried with girdles or ſlinges,
made faſt about their necks. Next the prieſts
come their Biſhops in their pontificalibus: 5
then the Friers, Monks, and Abbots: and after, the Patriarches, in very rich attire, with a
ball, or ſphere on the top of his myter, to ſig-
nifie his vniuerſalitie ouer that Church. Laſt
commeth the Emperor with all his nobility. 10
The whole traine is of a mile long, or more.
When they are come to the riuer, a great
hole is made in the yſe, where the market is
kept, of a rod and a halfe broad, with a ſtage
round about it to keepe off the preſſe. Then 15
beginneth the Patriarch to ſay certaine praiers, and coniureth the diuel to come out of
the water: and ſo caſting in ſalt, and cenſing
it with frankincenſe, maketh the whole riuer
to become holy water. The morning before, 20
all the people of *Mosko* vſe to make croſſes
of chawlke ouer euerie doore, and window
of their houſes: leaſt the Diuell beyng coniu-
red out of the water, ſhoulde flye into their
houſes. 25

When the ceremonies are ended, you ſhal
ſee the black Gard of the Emperours houſe,
and then the reſt of the Towne, with their
pailes and buckets, to take off the hallowed
water for drinke, and other vſes. You ſhall 30
alſo

(7) the Patriarches/the Patriarch (15-20) Then beginneth . . . The morning before/
Then beginneth the Patriarch to say certain prayers and those beeing ended, hee coniureth the divell to coom owt of the water, and so casting in salt and censing it with
franckencence, and manie other circumstances, maketh the River as holie water as that
within the Church. The morning beefore

alſo ſee the women dippe in their children o-
uer head and eares, and many men and women leape into it, ſome naked, ſome with
their clothes on, when ſome man woulde
thinke his finger woulde freeſe off, if hee
ſhould but dippe it into the water. When
the men haue done, they bring their horſe
to the riuer, to drinke of the ſanctified water: and ſo make them as holie as a horſe.
Their ſet day for this ſolemne action of hallowing their riuers, is that we cal *Twelfthday*.
The like is done by other Biſhops, in al parts
of the Realme.

Their maner is alſo to giue it to their ſick,
in their greateſt extremitie: thinking that it
will eyther recouer them, or ſanctifie them
to God. Whereby they kill many, through
their vnreaſonable ſuperſtition, as did the
Lord Borris his onely ſonne. at my beyng at
the *Moſko*: whom he killed (as was ſaid by
the phiſitions) by powring into him, colde
holie water, and preſenting him naked into the Church, to their Saynt *Baſileo*, in the
colde of the Winter, in an extremitie of ſick-
neſſe.

They haue an image of Chriſt, which
they call *Neruchi*, (which ſignifieth as much
as *Made without hands*) for ſo their prieſts, &
ſuperſtition with al. perſwadeth them it was.
This in their proceſsions, they carry about
with

(margin) Drinking of holy wa-ter.

(9–10) as holie as a horse. Their set day/as holie as a horse, and them selves not much
holier. The like is doon by other Bishopps in all parts of the Realm. The sett day
(12–13) The like . . . Realme *omitted*. (26) They haue an image . . . [to end of
paragraph on p. 105] *omitted*.

with them on high vpon a pole, enclofed
within a Pixe, made like a lanthorn, and doe
reuerence to it, as to a great myfterie.

At euery brewing, their maner is likewife,
to bring a difh of their woort to the Prieft,
within the Church : which beyng hallowed by him, is powred into the brewing, and
fo giueth it fuch a vertue, as when they drink
of it, they are feldome fober. The like they
doe with the firft fruites of their corne in
Harueft.

They haue an other ceremonie on Palm-
funday, of auncient tradition: what time the
Patriarch rideth through the *Mosko*, the Emperour himfelf holding his horfe bridle, and
the people crying *Hofanna*, & fpreding their
vpper garmentes vnder his horfe feete. The
Emperour hath of the Patriarch for his good
feruice of that day 200. rubbels of ftanding
penfion. Another pageant they haue much
like to this, the weeke before the natiuitie
of Chrift: When euery Bifhop in his Cathedral Church fetteth forth a fhew of the three
children in the Ouen. Where the Angell is
made to come flying from the roofe of the
Church, with great admiration of the loo-
kers on, and many terrible flafhes of fire, are
made with rofen, and gun-powder, by the
Chaldeans (as they call them) that run about
the towne all the twelue dayes, difguifed in

P   their

Brewing
with holy
water.   5

10

Palmfun-
day.

15

20

25

30

(1–3) *omitted.* (9) seldome sober. The like/seldoom sober which is no dispraise
after the Russ diett. The like

their plaiers coats,&make much good sport for the honour of the Bishops pageant. At the *Mosko*,the Emperour himselfe, and the Empresse neuer faile to be at it, though it be but the same matter plaid euery yeere, without any new inuention at all.

Besides their fastes on Wednesdayes,and Fridayes throughout the whole yeere , (the one becaufe they say Christ was solde on the Wednesday, the other becaufe he suffered on the Friday) they haue foure great Fastes, or Lentes euery yeere . The first, (which they call their great Lent) is at the same time with ours. The fecond, about Midsommer.The third,in Haruest time.The fourth,about Hallontide: which they keepe not of pollicie,but of meere superstition. In their great Lent for the first weeke,they eate nothing but bread and salt, and drinke nothing but water, neither meddle with anie matter of their vocation,but intende their shriuing,and fasting only.They haue also 3. *Vigils*, or *Wakes* in their great Lent, which they cal *Stoiania* & the last Friday their great *Vigil*,as they cal it.What time the whole parish must bee present in the Church , and watch from nine a clocke in the Euening, til sixe in the morning, all the while standing, saue when they fall downe, and knock their heads to their idoles,which must be an hundred dred

Fasts.

Vigils.

(17) superstition/devotion

dred and feuentie times, iuft through the whole night.

About their burials alfo, they haue ma- Burials. nie fuperftitious and prophane ceremonies: as putting within the finger of the corpes, a 5 letter to Saint *Nicôlas* : whome they make their chiefe mediatour, and as it were, the porter of heauen gates, as the Papiftes doe their *Peter.*

In Winter time, when all is couered with 10 fnow, and the ground fo hard frozen, as that no fpade, nor pikeaxe can enter their man- ner is not to burie their dead, but to keepe the bodies (fo many as die all the Winter time)in an houfe, in the fuburbs, or outparts 15 of the towne, which they call *Bohfedom,* that is, *Gods houfe:* where the dead bodies are py- led vp together, like billets on a woodftack, as hard with the froft as a very ftone, till the Springtide come & refolueth the froft : what 20 time euery man taketh his dead friend, and committeth him to the ground.

They haue befides their yeeres and mo- Moneths neths mindes, for their friendes departed. mindes. What time they haue praiers faide ouer the 25 graue by the Prieft : who hath a penie ordi- narie for his paines. When any dieth, they haue ordinary women mourners, that come to lament for the dead party: and ftand how- ling ouer the bodie, after a prophane, and 30 P 2 heathe-

---

(5) the finger/the little finger (10-22) In Winter time . . . [to end of paragraph] *omitted.* (27) for his paines. When any dieth/for his paines, and to stick upp candells abowt the grave when anie dieth

heatheniſh manner (ſometimes in the houſe,
ſomtimes bringing the bodie into the back-
ſide asking him what hee wanted,and what
he meant to die.They bury their dead,as the
party vſed to goe,with coate, hoſe, bootes,
hat,and the reſt of his apparell.

Many other vaine and ſuperſtitious ceremonies they haue, which were long and tedious to report.By theſe it may appeare,how
farre they are fallen from the true knowledge,and practiſe of Chriſtian religion: hauing exchanged the worde of God,for their
vaine traditions,and brought al to external,and ridiculous ceremonies,
without any regard of ſpirite
and trueth,which God re-
quireth in his true
worſhip.

Of

(3–4) asking him what hee wanted, and what he meant to die *omitted.*

Of the Emperours domestike or priuate behauiour.

The 26. Chapter.

HE Emperours priuate behaui-our so much as may bee, or is meete to bee known, is after this maner. Hee riseth comonly about 4 a clock in the morning. After his apparrelling, and washing, in commeth his ghostly father, or priest of his chãber, which is named in their tongue, *Otetz Duhouna*, with his crosse in his hand, wherwith he blesseth him, laying it first on his forehead, then vpon his cheekes, or sides of his face, and then offreth him the ende of it to kisse. This done, the Clearke of the crosse (called *Chresby Deyack Profery*) bringeth into his chamber, a painted image, represen-ting the Saint for that day. For euery day with them hath his seuerall Saint, as it were the patrone for that day. This he placeth a-mong the rest of his image gods, wherewith-all

His priuate prayer.

P 3

(17) and washing/and washing his hands

all his chamber is decked, as thicke almoſt as the wall can beare, with lampes and waxe candles burning before them. They are very coſtly and gorgeouſly decked with pearle, and precious ſtone. This image being placed before him, the Emperour beginneth to croſſe himſelfe after the *Ruſſe* manner, firſt on the forehead, then on both ſides of his breaſte, with *eAſpody Pomeluy, Pomeluy mena hoſpody, ſacroy mena greſnick Syhodeſtua:* which is as much to ſay, as, *Helpe me O Lorde my God, Lorde comfort me, defende and keepe me a ſinner from doing euill, &c.* This hee directeth towardes the image, or Saynt for that day, whom hee nameth in his prayer, together with our Lady (whom they call *Precheſte) Saint Nicholas,* or ſome other, to whome he beareth moſt deuotion, bowing himſelf proſtrate vnto them, with knocking his head to the verie ground. Thus he continueth the ſpace of a quarter of an houre, or thereabouts.

Then cōmeth againe the ghoſtly father, or chāber prieſt, with a ſiluer bowle full of holy water, which they call in *Ruſſe, Sweta Voda,* & a ſprinkle of Baſill (as they call it) in his hād: & ſo al to beſprinckleth firſt the image gods, and then the Emperour. This holy water is brought freſh euery day from the Monaſteries, farre and neere, ſent to the Emperour
from

from the Abbot or Prior, in the name of the
Saint, that is patrone of that Monaſtery, as a
ſpeciall token of good wil from him.

Theſe deuotions being ended, he ſendeth
in to the Empreſſe, to aske whether ſhe hath
reſted in health, &c. And after a little
pawſe goeth himſelfe to ſalute her in a middle roome betwixt both their chambers.
The Empreſſe lieth apart from him, and keepeth not one chamber, nor table with the
Emperour ordinarily, ſaue vpon the eaue of
their Lentes, or common Faſtes : what time
ſhe is his ordinarie gheſt at bedde and
boorde . After their meeting in the morning, they goe together to their priuate
Churche or Chappell, where is ſayde, or
ſoung a morning Seruice (called *Zautrana*)
of an houre long or thereabouts. From
the Church hee returneth home, and ſitteth
him downe in a great chamber, to be ſeene
and ſaluted by his Nobilitie, ſnch as are in
fauour about the Court . If hee haue to
ſay to anie of them, or they to him, then
is the time. And this is ordinarie, except
his health, or ſome other occaſion alter the
cuſtome.

About nine in the morning, he goeth to
another Church within his Caſtle : where
is ſoung by Prieſts, and Choriſters, the high
Seruice (called *Obeadna* or *Complin*) which

The Empe-
rour giueth
preſence e-
uery mor-
ning.

P 4   common-

commonly lasteth two houres: the Emperour in the meane time, talking commonly
with some of his Councell, Nobilitie, or
captaines, which haue to say to him, or he to
them . And the Councell likewise conferre
together among themselues, as if they were
in their councell house. This ended, he returneth home, and recreateth himselfe vntill it
be dinner time.

He is serued at his table on this manner.
First, euery dish(as it is deliuered at the dres-
ser) is tasted by the Cooke, in the presence
of the high Stewarde, or his Deputie. And
so is receyued by the Gentlemen wayters
(called *Shulshey*) and by them carried vp to
the Emperours table, the high Stewarde or
his Deputie going before. There it is receiued by the Sewer (called *Erastnoy*) who
giueth a taste of euerie dishe to the Taster,
and so placeth it before the Emperour. The
number of his dishes for his ordinarie seruice is about seuenty: dressed somwhat grose-
ly, with much garlicke, & salt, much after the
Doutch manner. When hee exceedeth vpon
some occasion of the day, or entertainment
of some Ambassador, he hath many more dishes. The seruice is sent vp by 2. dishes at a
time, or three at the most that he may eate it
warme, first the baked, then the rost meats, &
last the brothes. In his dyning chamber is an
                                          other

*The Empe-
rours ser-
uice at his
Table.*

other table: where fit the chiefe of his Nobilitie that are about his Court, and his
ghoftly father, or Chapleine. On the one
fide of the chamber ftandeth a cubbard or
table of plate, very fayre and riche with a
great cefterne of Copper by it full of yfe
and fnow, wherein ftande the pottes that
ferue for that meale. The tafter holdeth the
cup that he drinketh in all dinner time and
deliuereth it vnto him with a fay, when hee
calleth for it. The manner is to make many
difhes out of the feruice after it is fet on
the table, and to fend them to fuch Noblemen and officers, as the Emperour liketh
beft. And this is counted a great fauour, and
honour.

After dinner hee layeth him downe to
refte, where commonly hee taketh three
houres fleepe, except he employ one of the
houres to bathing, or boxing. And this cuftome for fleeping after dinner, is an ordinary matter with him, as withall the *Ruffes*.
After his fleepe he goeth to euenfong (called *Vechurna*) and thence returning, for the
moft parte recreateth himfelf with the Empreffe till fupper time, with iefters, and
dwarfes, men and women, that tumble before him, and fing many fongs after the *Ruffe*
manner. This is his common recreation
betwixt meales, that hee mofte delightes in.

On

On other speciall recreation is the fight with wilde Beares, which are caught in pittes, or nets, and are kepte in barred cages for that purpofe, againft the Emperour be difpofed to fee the paftime. The fight with the Beare is on this fort. The man is turned into a circle walled round about, where he is to quite himfelfe fo well as he can:for there is no way to flie out. When the Beare is turned loofe he commeth vpon him with open mouth. If at the firft pufhe hee miffe his aime,fo that the Beare come within him, hee is in great daunger. But the wilde Beare being very fearfe,hath this qualitie, that giueth aduantage to the Hunter. His manner is when he affaileth a mã, to rife vp right on his two hinder legges, and fo to come roaring with open mouth vpon him. And if the Hunter then can pufhe right into the very breft of him betwixt his forelegges (as commonly hee will not miffe) refting the other ende of their boarefpeare at the fide of his foote,& fo keeping the pike ftill towards the face of the Beare, he fpeedeth him cõmõly at one blow. But many times thefe Hunters come fhort, and are either flaine,or miferably torne with the teeth & talents of the fierce beaft. If the partie quite himfelfe well in this fight with the Beare, he is carried to drinke at the Emperours feller doore:where he drinketh himfelfe

(1) On other speciall recreation . . . [to p. 110, line 7:] on the holy daies *omitted*.

felfe drunke for the honor of *Hofpodare*. And this is his rewarde for aduenturing his life, for the Emperours pleafure. To maintain this paftime the Emperor hath certein huntfmen that are appointed for that purpofe to take the wild Beare. This is his recreation commonly on the holy daies. Somtimes he fpendeth his time in looking vpō his goldfmiths, and Iewellers,tailers embroderers, painters, & fuch like,& fo goeth to his fupper. When it draweth towacds bed time,his prieft faieth certein praiers:and then the Emperour bleffeth and croffeth himfelfe, as in the morning for a quarter of an houre or thereaboutes, and fo goeth to his bedde.

The Emperour that now is (called *Theodore Iuanowich*) is for his perfon of a meane ftature, fomewhat lowe and groffe, of a fallowe complexion, and inclining to the dropfie, hawke nofed, vnfteady in his pafe by reafon of fome weakenes of his lims,heauie and vnaftiue, yet commonly fmiling almoft to a laughter. For qualitie otherwife, fimple and flowe witted, but verie gentle, and of an eafie nature,quiet,mercifull,of no martiall difpofition,nor greatly apt for matter of pollicie,very fuperftitious,and infinite that way. Befides his priuate deuotions at home,he goeth euery weeke cōmonly on pilgrimage to fome Monafterie, or other that

is

5

10

15

20

25

30

(1-7) [him]selfe drunke . . . holy daies *omitted.*

is neareſt hand. He is of 34. yeares old, or thereaboutes, and hath reigned almoſt the ſpace of ſixe yeares.

Of the Emperours priuate, or houſe-holde Officers.

The 27. Chapter.

Maiſter of the Horſe.

He chiefe officers of the Emperours houſhold, ar theſe which follow. The firſt is the office of the *Boiaren Coneſheua*, or maiſter of the Horſe. Which côteineth no more then is expreſſed by the name, that is. to be ouerſeer of the Horſe, and not *Magiſter equitum*, or Maſter of the Horſemen. For he appointeth other for that ſeruice, as occaſion dothe require (as before was ſaid.) He that beareth that office at this time, is *Borris Federowich Godonoe*, brother to the Empreſſe. Of Horſe for ſeruice in his warres (beſides other for his ordinary vſes) he hath to the number of 10000. which are kept about *Mosko*.

The

The next is the Lord Stewarde of his
houſhold at this time, one *Gregorie Uaſilo-*
wich Godonoe. The third is his Treaſurer, that
keepeth all his monies, iewels, plate, &c:
now called *Stepan Uaſilowich Godonoe.* The
fourth his Controller, now *Andreas Petro-*
wich Cleſinine. The fift his Chamberlaine.
He that attendeth that office at this time, is
called *EStoma Biſabroza PaStelniſchay.* The
fixt his Taſters, now *Theodore Alexandro-*
wich, and *Iuan Vaſilowich Godonoe.* The ſe-
uenth his Harbengers, whieh are three Noble men, and diuers other Gentlemen that
doo the office vnder them. Theſe are his ordinarie officers, and offices of the chiefeſt
account.

Of Gentlemen beſide that wait about
his chamber, & perſon (called *Shilſey Strap-*
ſey) there are two hundred, all Noblemens
ſonnes. His ordinary Garde is 2000, Hagbutters ready with their pieces charged, and
their match lighted, with other neceſſarie
furniture, continually day and night: which
come not within the houſe, but wait without in the court or yard, where the Emperour is abiding. In the night time there lodgeth next to his bedchamber the chiefe
Chamberlaine, with one or two more of beſt
truſt about him. A ſecond chamber of, there
lodge ſixe other of like account, for their
truſt

Marginal notes:
The L. Ste-
ward.

The L. Tre-
ſurer.

5

Controller.

Chamber-
laine.

Taſters.

10

Harbégers.

15

Gentlemen
of the chã-
ber.

The Gard.

20

25

30

(7) *Cleſinine/Cleſnine*

truſt and faithfulneſſe . In the third chamber lie certeine young Gentlemen, of theſe
two hundred , called *Shilſey Strapſey* , that
take their turnes by forties euery night .

Grooms. There are Grooms beſides that watch in their
courſe,and lie at euery gate and doore of the
Court,called *Eſtopnick* .

The Hagbutters or Gunners, whereof
there are two thouſand (as was ſaid before)
watch about the Emperours lodging, or bed
chamber by courſe two hundred and fiftie
euery night ,and two hundred & fiftie more
in the Court yarde , and about the Treaſure
houſe . His court or houſe at the *Mosko* is
made Caſtle wiſe , walled about with great
ſtore of faire ordinance planted vpon the
wall , and conteyneth a great breadth of
ground within it , with many dwelling
houſes . Which are appointed for
ſuch as are knowen to be ſure,
and truſtie to the
Emperour.

Of

(16) faire *omitted*.

Of the priuate behauiour, or qualitie
of the Ruſſe people.

The 28. Chapter.

He priuate behaui- *Conſtituti-*
our and qualitie of *on of their*
the *Ruſſe* people, *bodies.*
may partly be vn-
derſtood by that
whiche hath beene
ſaid cócerning the
publique ſtate and
vſage of the coun-
trie. As touching
the naturall habite of their bodies, they are
for the moſt parte of a large fiſe, and of very
fleſhly bodies: accounting it a grace to bee
ſomewhat groſſe and burley, and therefore
they nouriſh and ſpread their beardes, to
haue them long and broad. But for the moſt
part they are very vnweldy & vnactiue withall. Which may bee thought to come partly
of the climate, and the numbnes which they
get by the cold in winter, and partly of their
diet that ſtandeth moſt of rootes, onions,
garlike, cabbage, and ſuch like things that
breed groſſe humors, which they vſe to eate
alone, and with their other meates,

Their

10

15

20

25

30

Their diet.

Their diet is rather much, then curious.
At their meales they beginne commonly
with a *Chark* or finall cuppe of *Aqua vitæ*,
(which they call *Ruſſe* wine)and then drinke
not till towardes the ende of their meales,
taking it in largely, and all together, with
kiſsing one another, at euery pledge . And
therefore after dinner there is no talking
with them,but euery man goeth to his bench
to take his afternoones ſleepe, which is as
ordinary with them as their nightes reſte.
When they exceede,and haue varietie of
diſhes the firſt are their baked meates (for
roſte meates they vſe little)and then their
broathes,or pottage. To drinke drunke, is
an ordinary matter with them euery day in
the weeke. Their common drinke is *Mead*,
the poorer fort vſe water,and thinne drinke
called *Quaſſe*, which is nothing els (as wee
ſay but water turned out of his wittes,with
a little branne meaſhed with it.

This diet would breede in them many
diſeaſes,but that they vſe bathſtoues, or hote
houſes in ſteede of all Phiſicke, commonly
twiſe or thriſe euery weeke . All the winter
time and almoſt the whole Sommer, they
heat there *Peaches*, which are made lyke the
Germane bathſtoaues, and their *Potlads* like
ouens,that ſo warme the houſe that a ſtraun-
ger at the firſt ſhall hardly like of it, Theſe
two

two extremities, fpecially in the winter of heat within their houfes, and of extreame colde without, together with their diet, maketh them of a darke, and fallow complexion, their skinnes beyng tanned and parched both with colde and with heate: fpecially the women, that for the greater parte are of farre worfe complexions, then the men. Whereof the caufe I take to bee their keeping within the hote houfes, and bufying themfelues about the heating, and vfing of their bathftoues, and peaches.

The *Ruffe* becaufe that hee is vfed to both thefe extremities of heat and of cold, can beare them both a great deale more patiently, then ftraungers can doo. You fhal fee them fometimes (to feafon their bodies) come out of their bathftoues all on a froth, and fuming as hote almoft as a pigge at a fpitte, and prefently to leape into the riuer ftarke naked, or to powre colde water all ouer their bodies, and that in the coldeft of all the winter time. The women to mende the bad hue of their skinnes, vfe to paint their faces with white and redde colours, fo vifibly, that euery man may perceyue it. Which is made no matter, becaufe it is common, and liked well by their husbandes: who make their wiues and daughters anordinarie allowance to buy them colours to paint their faces withall,

Q   and

5

10

15

20

25

30

and delight themſelues much to ſee them
ot fowle women to become ſuch faire images. This parcheth the ſkinne, and helpeth to
deforme them when their painting is of.

The Noble mans at-tire. They apparell themſelues after the
Greeke manner. The Noblemans attire is
on this faſhion. Firſt a *Taffia* or little night
cappe on his head, that couereth little more
then his crowne, commonlie verie riche
wrought of ſilke and gold thread, & ſet with
pearle & pretious ſtone. His head he keepeth
ſhauen cloſe to the very ſkin, except he be in
ſome diſpleaſure with the Emperour. Then
hee ſuffereth his haire to growe and hang
downe vpon his ſhoulders, couering his face
as vgly and deformedly as he can, Ouer the
Taffia he weareth a wide cap of black Foxe
(which they account for the beſt furre) with
a *Tiara* or long bonnet put within it, ſtanding vp like a *Perſian* or *Babilonian* hat. A-
bout his neck (which is ſeene al bare) is a coller ſet with pearle and pretious ſtone, about
three or foure fingers broad. Next ouer his
ſhirt, (which is curiouſly wrought, becauſe he
ſtrippeth himſelfe into it in the Sommer
time, while he is within the houſe) is a *Shepon*,
or light garment of ſilke made downe to the
knees, buttoned before; & then a *Caftan* or a
cloſe coat buttoned, and girt to him with a
Perſian girdle, whereat he hanges his kniues
and ſpoone. This commonly is of cloth of
gold,

gold, and hangeth downe as low as his an-
kles, Ouer that he weareth a lofe garment of
fome rich filke, furred and faced about with
fome gold lace,called a *Ferris.* An other ouer
that of chamlet,or like ftuffe called an *Alkaben,*fleeued & hanging low, and the cape   5
commonly brooched and fet all with pearle.
When heé goeth abroad, he cafteth ouer all
thefe (which are but fleight (though they
feeme to be many) an other garment called
an *Honoratkey,* like to the *Alkaben,* faue that   10
it is made without a coller for the neck. And
this is commonly of fine cloth, or Camels
haire His buskins(which he weareth in ftead
of hofe, with linnen folles vnder them in
fteed of boot hofe) are made of a *Perfian* lea-   15
ther called *Saphian,*embrodered with pearle.
His vpper ftockes commonly are of cloth of
gold. When he goeth abroad, he mounteth
on horfebacke, though it be but to the next
doore : which is the manner alfo of the *Boi-*   20
*arskey,*or Gentlemen.

The *Boiarskey* or Gentlemans attire is The Gen-
of the fame fafhion, but differeth in ftuffe: tlemans
and yet he will haue his *Caftan* or vndercoat apparell.
fometimes of cloth of gold, the reft of cloth,   25
or filke.

The Noble woman (called *Chyna Boi-* The Noble
arfhena) weareth on hir head, firft a caull of womans at-
fome foft filke (which is commonly redde) tire.
and ouer it a fruntlet, called *Obrofa* of white   30
Q 2   colour.

colour . Ouer that hir cap(made after the coife fashion of cloth of gold) called *Shapka Zempska*, edged with some riche furre, and set with pearle and stone. Though they haue of late begonne to disdaine embrodering with pearle about their cappes, becaufe the Diacks, and some Marchants wiues haue taken vp the fashion. In their eares they weare earerings (which they call *Sargee*) of two inches or more compaffe, the matter of gold set with Rubies, or Saphires, or some like pretious stone. In Sommer they goe often with kerchieffes of fine white lawne, or Cambricke, faftned vnder the chinne, with two long taffels pendent. The kerchiefe spotted and set thicke with rich pearle. When they ride or goe abroad in raynie weather, they weare white hattes with coloured bands(called *Stapa Zemskoy*). About their necks they were collers of three or foure fingers broad, set with riche pearle and pretious stone. Their vpper garment is a loofe gowne called *Opoſhen* commonly of skarlet, with wide loofe sleeues, hanging downe to the ground buttened before with great gold buttons, or at least siluer and guilt, nigh as bigge as a walnut. Which hath hanging ouer it faftned vnder the cappe, a large broad cape of some riche furre, that hangeth downe almoft to the middes of their backes. Next vnder the *Oposken* or vpper garment, they weare another

other called a *Leitnick* that is made clofe before with great wide fleeues, the cuffe or half
fleeue vp to the elbowes, commonly of cloth
of golde: and vnder that a *Ferris Zemskoy,*
which hangeth loofe buttoned throughout
to the very foote. On the hand wrefts they
weare very faire brafelets, about two fingers
broad of pearle and pretious ftone. They
go all in buskins of white, yellow, blew,
or fome other coloured leather, embrodered with pearle. This is the attire of the No-
blewoman of *Ruffia*, when fhee maketh the
beft fhew of hir felfe. The Gentlewomans
apparell may differ in the ftuffe, but is all
one for the making or fafhion.

As for the poore *Moufick* and his wife
they go poorely cladde. The man with his
Odnoratkey, or loofe gowne to the fmall of
the legge, tyed together with a lace before, of
courfe white or blew cloth, with fome *Shube*
or long waftcoat of furre, or of fheepskinne
vnder it, and his furred cappe, and buskins.
The poorer fort of them haue their *Odnorat-*
key, or vpper garment, made of Kowes haire.
This is their winter habite. In the fommer
time, commonly they weare nothing but
their fhirts on their backes, and buskins on
their legges. The woman goeth in a redde or
blew gowne, when fhe maketh the beft fhew,
and with fome warme *Shube* of furre vnder
it in the winter time. But in the Sommer, no-

Q 3 thing

The *Mou-
ficks* or có-
mon mans
attire.

thing but her two fhirts(for fo they call the)
one ouer the other, whetherthey be within
doores, or without. On their heades,they
weare caps of fome coloured ftuffe, many of
veluet,or of cloth of golde: but for the moft
part kerchiefes.Without earings of filuer or
fome other mettall,and her croffe about her
necke you fhal fee no *Ruffe* woman, be fhee
wife,or maide.

Their wits
and capaci-
ties.

   As touching their behauiour,and quality
otherwife they are of reafonable capacities,
if they had thofe means that fome other nations haue to traine vp their wittes in good
nurture,and learning. Which they might
borrowe of the *Polonians*, and other their
neighbours, but that they refufe it of a very
felf pride,as accounting their owne fafhions
to be far the beft.Partly alfo(as I faid before)
for that their manner of bringing vp (voide
of all good learning,and ciuill behauiour) is
thought by their gouernours moft agreable
to that State, and their manner of gouernment. Which the people would hardely
beare,if they were once ciuilled, & brought
to more vnderftanding of God, and good
policie. This caufeth the Emperours to keep
out al meanes of making it better,and to be
very warie for excluding of all peregrinitie,
that might alter their fafhions. Which were
leffe to bee difliked, if it fet not a print into
the very mindes of his people. For as themfelues

---

(9) wife, or maide/wife or maide [*In the manuscript here follows the passage reproduced in the 1591 edition from page 14 (line 20):* Their howses are of wood . . . *to
page 14v (line 9):* is most skant   (30) not a print into/not a woorse print vpon

felues are verie hardlie and cruellie dealte
withall by their chiefe Magiftrates, and o-
ther fuperiours, fo are they as cruell one a-
gainft an other, fpecially ouer their inferiours, and fuch as are vnder them. So that
the bafeft & wretchedeft *Chriftianoe* (as they
call him) that ftoupeth and croucheth like a
dogge to the Gentleman, and licketh vp the
duft that lieth at his feete, is an intollerable
tyrant, where he hath the aduantage. By this *Crueltie of*
meanes the whole Countrie is filled with *the Ruffe*
rapine, and murder. They make no account *people.*
of the life of a man. You fhall haue a man
robbed fometime in the very ftreats of their
townes, if hee goe late in the euening: and
yet no man to come forth out of his doores
to refcue him, though hee heare him crie
out. I will not fpeake of the ftraungeneffe
of the murders, and other cruelties committed among them, that would fcarfly bee
beleeued to bee done among men, fpecially fuch as profeffe themfelues Chriftians.

The number of their vagrant and beg-
ging poore is almoft infinite : that are fo
pinched with famine and extreame neede,
as that they begge after a violent and defperate manner, with *giue mee and cut mee,*
giue mee and kill mee, and fuch like phrafes.
Whereby it may bee gheaffed, what they are
towardes ftraungers, that are fo vnnaturall
and cruell towardes their owne. And yet it
may

5

10

15

20

25

30

(3-6) as cruell . . . the basest/as cruell over their inferiours, and such as are under
them. So that the basest

may bee doubted whither is the greater, the crueltie or intemperancie that is vsed in that countrie. I will not speake of it, becaufe it is fo foule and not to bee named. The whole countrie ouer floweth with all finne of that kinde. And no marueile, as hauing no lawe to reftraine whoredomes, adulteries, and like vncleannesse of life.

As for the truth of his word, the *Ruffe* for the moft part maketh fmall regard of it, fo he may gaine by a lie, and breache of his promife. And it may be faide truely (as they know beft that haue traded moft with them) that from the great to the fmall (except fome fewe that will fcarcely be founde) the *Ruffe* neither beleeueth any thing that an other man fpeaketh, nor fpeaketh any thing him-felfe worthie to be beleeued. Thefe quali-ties make the very odious to all their neigh-bours, fpecially to the *Tartars*, that account themfelues to be honeft and iuft, in compa-rifon of the *Ruffe*. It is fuppofed by fome that doe well confider of the ftate of both countries, that the offence they take at the *Ruffe* gouernment and their maner of be-hauiour, hath beene a great caufe to keepe the *Tartar* ftill Heathenish, and to mif-like (as he doeth) of the Chriftian profefsion.

FINIS.

---

(10) for the most part *omitted*.

APPENDIX A

Fletcher's Report on His Embassy

Fletcher's report on his embassy submitted in September, 1589. The manuscript is in the British Museum, Landsdowne MS 60, Burghley Papers No. 59, Folios 157r–160v. First published by Sir Henry Ellis in *Original Letters of Eminent Literary Men* (London, 1843), pp. 79–85, and then in E. A. Bond, ed., *Russia at the Close of the Sixteenth Century* (London, 1856), pp. 342–351, and most recently in Lloyd E. Berry, *The English Works of Giles Fletcher, the Elder* (Madison, Wisconsin, 1964), pp. 367–375. The text which follows is based on the original manuscript and collated with the edition by Berry.

The summe of my Negotiation.
  I. My intertainment.
 II. The causes of my hard intertainment.
III. What is doon and brought to effect.
 IV. What could not bee obteined on the beehalf of the marchants.

1. *My intertainment.*

My whole intertainment from my first arrivall till towards the very end was such as if they had divised meanes of very purpose to shew their vtter disliking both of the trade of the Marchants, and of the whole English nation.

1. At my arriving at the *Mosko* thear was no man to bidd mee wellcoom, not so much as to conduct mee vpp to my lodging.

2. After I had stayed two or three dayes, to see if anie well-coom or other message would coom from the Emperour, or the Lord *Boris Federowich Godonove,* I sent my Interpreter to the saied Lord *Boris,* to desier him to bee a meanes for audience to the Emperour, that having doon my Ambassage to the Emperour, I might doe my message, and deliver my Lettres likewise to him. My Interpriter having attended him two or three dayes, withowt speaking with him, was commaunded by the Chauncellour to coom no more at the Court, nor to the howse of the saied L. *Boris.*

3. The Counsell was commaunded, not to conferr with mee, nor I to send to anie of them.

4. When I had audience of the Emperour, in the verie entrance of my speach, I was cavilled withall by the Chauncellour, bycawse I saied not forth the Emperours whole stile, which of purpose I forbare to doe, bycawse I would not make his stile of two ellnes, and your Highnes stile of a span long, having repeated the first and principall parts of it, and giving him the titles of great *Lord, Duke and Emperour of all Russia, King of Cazan, King of Astracan* &c. I answeared him that the Emperour was a mightie Prince, and had manie Countries which straungers could not, nor wear not bound to know, that I repeated the principall of his stile, to shew my honour to the rest. But it would not serve till all was repeated.

5. The Presents sent by your Highnes to the Emperour, and delivered to him in his own presence, wear the day following retourned to mee, and very contemptuouslie cast down beefore mee.

6. My articles of petition delivered by woord of mouth, and afterwards by writing, with all other writings wear altered and falsified by the Emperours Interpriter, by meanes of the Chauncellour *Andreas Shalcalove,* speciallie whear it concerned him self, manie things wear putt in, and manie things strook owt,

[44]

which being complained of and the points noted would not bee redressed.

7. I was placed in an howse verie vnhandsoom, and vnholsoom, of purpose (as it seemed) to doe mee disgrace, and to hurt my health whear I was kept as prisoner, not as an Ambassadour.

8. I was not suffred to send anie Lettre into England by the winter way to signifie of my proceedings, not so much as of my health though I desired it earnestlie.

9. My allowance for vittail was so bare and so base, as I could not have accepted it but to avoide cavillation, that I beegan to contend with them abowt so mean a matter.

10. At my retourn, at *Vologda*, open proclamacion was made by the Duke and Diake thear, by order from the Chauncellour *Andreas Shalcalove*, that no man should hier owt horse or boat to anie Englishman: which bredd an opinion in the people thear, that thear was great matter of disliking from the Emperour towards the English nation, which was a cawse of great daunger towards mee and my Companie, and of the firing of the English howse at *Colmigore* (as appeared by the sequeal) whear the Companie of the English Marchants lost to the valiew of 6. or 7. thowsand Marks.

These parts of hard interteinment wear offred mee by the Chauncellour *Andreas Shalcalove* who is allso the Officer for Ambassages, of verie purpose (as it seemed) to move mee to impatience, that hee might have wearwith to disturb this busines. And thearfore I determined with my self to vse all moderation, so farr as might stand with your Highnes honour, that if other meanes of faier treatie prevailed not with them, I might make soom advantage of my hard interteinment towards the end of my negotiation, by layeng it all in on dish beefore them, and applieng it to your Highnes dishonour (as indeed it was) which beeing doon in as earnest and vehement manner as I could divise with discreation, brought them to soom remorse of their former dealings, and so to yeild divers points, and in a manner all that I intreated of them, in recompence of their hard interteinment given mee beefore, whearof they desired mee to make the best to your Highnes at my retourn home.

2. *The causes of my hard intertainment.*

1. Since the loss of the *Narve*, the Russ hath divised by all meanes hee could to dissolve the trade that way (whearbie hee thincketh the enimie is enritched) and to bring it over to the Port of St. Nicholas. This had been doon long since in the other Emperours time, but for a speciall affection hee bare towards your Highnes, which staied him from that which otherwise hee intended. This purpose of reducing the whole trade from the Narve to the Port of St. Nicholas, they suppose to bee hindred speciallie and onlie by the Coompanie of the English Marchants, and their privileadged trade, beeing assured by the Hanses, Neitherlanders, and Frenchmen that if the Companie of the English Marchants wear cast of, and their Privileadge dissolved, they should presentlie have a famous and notable trade at their saied Port of St. Nicholas, which should much encrease the Emperours Coustoom. Vpon hope whearof, they have built a Town and Castle abowt xxx miles within the river that falleth into the bay or road of St. Nicholas. And this is the cheefe grownd of their dislike towards the Companie of the English Marchants and their privileadged trade.

2. It was informed to the Emperour and his Counsell, by Lettres and message owt of England, that the saied Companie was vtterlie disliked by your Highnes, by your Counsell, by all the Marchants of England, speciallie of late, having reduced them selves to the nomber of xij, and so beeing now more notable Monopoliers then they wear beefore, that in case they wear cast

of, they showld have a farr greater trade of English marchants, of 20. 30. or 40. sail a year, which would bee content to pay whole Coustoom, and to bee vsed as common men, that on man would trade for asmuch as the whole Companie now doth, that your Highnes would like it better to have the Companie dissolved, and the trade laied open for all your subiects alike, then to have anie Privileadge confirmed to the saied Companie at this time, for that it would increase your Maiesties Coustoom hear, as it doth the Emperours thear. As for your Highnes Lettres written at this time on the Companies beehalf it was informed that the same wear gott by great importunitie, that your Highnes sett your hand to manie things which yow never read over, and for my self that I was sent but as a messinger not as an Ambassadour, that I never spake with your Highnes.

3. I found the Lord *Boris Federowich Godonove* so displeased with the Companie that no reason nor intreatie would reconcile him. The matters that greived him I found to bee these: 1. That Hierom Horsey was so chased away by the Companie (as hee was informed) being sent as a messinger from him with Lettres and Presents to your Highnes. In which respect (hee thincketh) hee should have been forborn at that time, for his sake and accounteth it his dishonour that hee was retourned in that sort. 2. For that hee was not provided of certein particulars, which hee sent for to the Companie, as horse, armour, pearle &c. 3. For that his late Present sent to your Highnes by Hierom Horsey was dishonoured and disgraced by the said Companie, by whose meanes (as he is vntrulie informed) it was divided into two parts, the on from the Emperour (who sent then no Present) the other from him self, whearby the grace and honour of his present was defaced as hee thought.

4. When I arrived at the *Mosko*, I found a League in hand beetwixt the Emperour and the King of *Spain*, about an opposicion against the Turk. To which purpose an Ambassadour was

appointed to goe into Spain, on Peter Ragon, a Slavonian and the Emperours Interpreter. This League was sett forward by the Patriarch of *Constantinople*, who beeing banished by the Turk, had been with the Pope and was sent by him to the Emperour of *Russia*, aswell to treat abowt this niew League beetwixt him and the Spanish K[ing] as to reduce the Russ from vnder the Greek to the Latine Church. For the effecting whearof, hee thought their own Patriarch (beeing thus banished and discontented) to bee the likeliest meanes. This treatie of League with the Spaniard, was a cawse of more sadd countenance towards mee at my first arrivall. But after your Highnes victorie against the King of Spain was well known thear, (which I vnderstood by Lettres sent mee by Sir *Francis Drake* which I cawsed to bee translated into the Russ toongue togeather with your Highnes Oration made to the Armie in *Essex*) all this conceipt of a Spanish League vanished away.

5. I found at the *Mosko* an other Ambassadour sent from the Emperour of *Almaign*, to treat of a confeaderacie with the Russ Emperour against the *Polonian*, that is over mightie for the Russ, by the access of *Sweaden*. This Ambassadour (as if hee had been sent for nothing ells) inveighed against the doings of England, made small account of the Spanish defeat, assuring them, that the King of Spain would sett on again, and make a conquest of your Highnes Realmes. These and like suggestions made them woorse affected then otherwise they would have been, and bycawse they wear desirous to conclude this league with the Emperour of Allmain, having for that purpose sent vnto him for this Ambassage, they wear the more willing to gratifie his Ambassadour with my hard intertainment.

. I .

To the First I answeared them. That to perform this divise was a matter impossible, that the Marchants that vse to trade by the way of the Sound, would never bee brought to leave a knowne, safe, and speedie trade, for so long, tedious, and daungerous a course, as lieth by the way of St. Nicholas. That in case your Highnes wear, and the Companie of Marchants so requited for their discoverie, and other desert, having served the Emperour so manie yeares with necessarie commodities for his warrs &c (when the other way by the Narve was quite shutt vpp) and thus dishonoured by reiecting your petition and Presents, and they should assure them selves neither to have the English nor anie other Marchant to trade that way to the Port of St. Nicholas. That your Highnes both could and would provide for your own honour, and good of your Marchants, by stopping that way, and not suffer them thus to bee spoiled both of their privileadge and goods. And this they might consider, what inconveinence it would grow vnto, if (the Narve passage being shutt vpp by the Sweaden) the other way allso by the Port of St. Nicholas wear debarred from them, so that they showld have no way to vent their own commodities nor to receive in forreign, speciallie powder, saltpeeter, brimstone, lead &c necessarie for the Emperours warrs. With these and like pointes, I did what I could to beat them from that grownd.

. 2 .

To the 2. I assured them that I receaved my charge and instructions from your Maiestie, that your Highnes had a speciall care what was doon at this time on the beehalf of your marchants, whom yow accounted not as Mousickes or base people (as they termed them) but as verie speciall and necessarie members of your common wealth. And thearfore made your suit to the Emperour at this time, as a full experiment of his good will and affection towards your Maiestie. And as for the increasing of your Highnes Coustoom, yow made more account of your Honour and continuing of the graunt made to the Companie of your marchants by your Majestie and your predicessors, for the incouragement of your subiects to the like enterprises for discovering of niew trades &c then yow did of the enlarging of your Coustoomes, or anie matter of commoditie whatsoever. That your Highnes Coustoom could no whitt bee increased by this meanes forasmuch as the whole countrey of *Russia* was not able to receave so much of English commodities, as wear now brought in yearlie by the saied Companie of Marchants, their lead, copper and other commodities lyeng still vpon their Agents hand, and they never vttering past 130. or 140. clothes yearlie, whearas other English Marchants in on small Towne of *Germanie* vent 60. or 80. thowsand Clothes yearlie.

· 3 ·

To the 3. To remove that conceipt owt of the Lord *Boris* I assured him of your Highnes verie speciall affection and great good opinion of him, that your Highnes thought your self allreadie greatlie beeholding to him, that yow desired to bee beeholding to none but to him for this good tourn towards your marchants. That your Highnes beeing the best and thanckfullest Prince in the world would not be vnmindfull of his good desert, whearof yow had given mee a charge to assure him in your name. As for the Companie of Marchants, they should and would bee readie to make him amendes if they had given him anie iust cawse of offence &c.

3. *What is effected in this busines.*

Concerning the matters of League and friendshipp beetwixt your Highnes and the Emperour: it is receaved in verie kinde sort, and profession made of like good will and other correspondencie as was beefore beetwixt your Highnes and the Emperours Father.

Fletcher's Report

1. Thear is remitted of the debt made by on Anthonie Marshe and claimed from the Companie amounting to the summe of twentie three thowsand fyve hundred fiftie and three Marks: two partes of three with an overplus, so that thear remaineth to bee paied by the Marchants but 7800 Marks.

2. Thear is remitted them bysides at this tyme by the Emperour the sume of 1840 Rubbells or Marks, claimed, and exacted beefore of the Agent for Coustoom of the last year.

3. Farther thear is remitted by the Emperour 300 Marks claimed for rent for their howse at the Mosko.

4. Concerning their Privileadge of trade (which I found to bee of no account at my cooming thither) but infringed in all the principall pointes of it (coustoom, howserent &c beeing claimed of them) thear is graunted in effect all that I required on the beehalf of the Companie, save that half Coustoom is claimed hearafter. This beeing doon they promise a continuance of the Privileadge for ever withowt anie revocation. The additionalls now made to the former Privileadge are these.

That the Companie shall trade freelie down the river *Volgha* into *Media, Persia, Bougharia* &c and no stranger shalbee permitted trade that way but they.

That present paiment shalbee made to the Agent hearafter for all commodities that are taken of the Companie for the Emperours vse by his Treasurers and other Officers.

That a great charge shalbee given to all the Emperours Officers, that no exaction bee made hearafter vpon the Companie, contrarie to their Privileadge.

That (to prevent all inconveinence that may happen hearafter) none shalbee accounted to bee of the Companie, or for their affaiers in that Countrey, but such as shalbee enregistred by the Agent in writing, in the Office of the Treasurie, and this is to bee added as an article to the Privileadge.

That such as are so inregistred, and their names stroken owt afterwards by the Agent, shall no longer bee reputed for the Companies servants, or to have to doe in their affaiers.

That no Englishman hearafter shalbee sett on the pudkey, or otherwise tormented, for anie suspition of cryme whatsoever, but onlie safe kept till hir Maiestie bee informed and the truth of the cawse throwghlie knowne.

That all commodities shalbee transported free, save wax to bee bartred for saltpeeter, powder and brimstone.

That the Companie of English Marchants shall not bee hearafter vnder the Office of *Andreas Shalcan*, but pertein to the Office of the Treasurie, so that they may appeal to the Lord *Boris Federowich Godonove* if they thinck they have wrong.

That the Privileadg graunted to the Companie with these addicions, shalbee proclaimed and made knowne to all the Emperours authorized people.

4. *What is not graunted on the Marchants beehalf.*

Bysides the 7800. Marks, which ar exacted of the Companie of Marchants, thear is deteined allso from the saied Companie, the summe of 11000 marks or thearabowtes, which was seazed on and taken away perforce (by *Andreas Shalcalove* Chauncellour to the Emperour) owt of the hands of on *Anthonie Marsh*. The cawse of this iniust deteinment is this. The Chauncellour this last year, had his goods confiscat (to the valiew of 60000. Marks in money bysides other stuff and commodities) in the Emperours name, but indeed to the vse of the L. *Boris* and other of the *Godonoves* that vse the Emperours authoritie at their pleasure. Among which goods was the saied summe of 11000 Rubbells belonging to Anthonie Marsh. Which beeing once possessed by the saied Lord *Boris* and other of his name, not as Marshes goods, but as the Chauncellours due to the Emperour by confiscation could not bee recovered from their hands, the Chauncellour denieng that ever hee receaved anie such goods. Notwithstanding the evident prooves alleadged by mee to the contrarie.

APPENDIX B

Fletcher's Recommendations

A letter by Fletcher, probably addressed to the Queen, written in 1589. The original is in the British Museum, Landsdowne MS 52, No. 37. Its author was first identified in 1848 by M. A. Obolenskii in an introduction to the confiscated translation of Fletcher's book (cf. *O gosudarstve russkom, sochinenie Fletchera,* St. Petersburg, 1906, p. xvi). The identification is confirmed by T. S. Willan, *The Early History of the Russia Company, 1553–1603* (Manchester, 1956), pp. 205–206, and Lloyd E. Berry, *The English Works of Giles Fletcher, the Elder,* pp. 376–381. First published in E. D. Morgan and C. H. Coote, eds., *Early Voyages and Travels to Russia and Persia,* I (Hakluyt Society Publications, vol. 72, London, 1886), pp. cviii–cxiii, but erroneously attributed to Christopher Borough. Reprinted in Lloyd E. Berry, *The English Works of Giles Fletcher, the Elder,* pp. 376–381. The text which follows is based on the original manuscript and collated with the edition by Berry.

Means of Decay of the Russe Trade

1. *The desier the Russ hath to draw a greater trade to the port of St. Nicolas*: beeing the better & surer way to vent his own commodities, and to bring in forrein, then the other wayes by the Narve and Riga, that ar many times stopped vp by reason of the warres with the Polonian & Sweden. This maketh them discontent with our English Marchants and their trade thear: which beeing very small (viz but of 5. or 6. sail a year) keepeth other from trading that way. Whereas they ar made assured by French, Netherlandish & other English Marchants that they shall have great numbers & a flourishing trade at that port to the enhansing of their commodities and the Emperours cous-

[54]

tooms, if they will cast of the English Company and their priviledged trade.

2. *The keeping of their trade & staple at Mosko.* Whearby grow these inconveniences. 1. A great expense by their travail & carriages to & fro by land from the sea side to Mosko which is 1500. verst or miles. 2. An expense of houskeeping at five places, viz at Mosko, Yaruslave, Vologda, Colmigroe, & St. Nicolas. 3. Their commodities ar ever ready at hand for the Emperour & his Nobilitie lyeng within the eye and reach of the Court. By this means much is taken vpon trust by the Emperour and his Nobilitie (which may not bee denied them) and so it beecommeth desperate debt. 4. Their whole stock is still in daunger to bee pulled & seazed on vpon every pretence & picked matter by the Emperour & his Officers. Which cannot bee helped so long as the trade is helld at Mosko: considering the nature of the Russ which cannot forbear to spoil & fliece strangers now and then (as hee doeth his own people) if hee suppose they gain by his Countrey. This hath caused all other Marchants strangers to give over that trade save two only: whearof the one also (beeing a Netherlander) beecam banckrupt this last year, the other (a Frenchman) beeing spoiled by them at my beeing thear, cam away the last year & hath given over that trade. As for our Marchants priviledges (which they wear suffred to enioy when the discovery was first made, and when the olld Emperour was in a dotage about a marriage in England &c) they must not look that they will protect them hearafter against these seazures & spoiles, the Russe having no respect of honour and credit in respect of his profit.

3. *Their servants which* (*though honest beefore*) *ar made ill by these means* 1. The profannes of that Countrey and liberty they have to all kynd of syn. Whearby it commeth to pass that many of them (beeing vnmarried men) fall to ryott, whoredoom &c: which draweth one expenses: so having not of their

own they spend of the Companies. Of this sort they have had to many (as they know). 2. Lack of good discipline among them selves, specially of a preacher to keep them in knowledg & fear of God & in a conscience of their service towards their Maisters. 3. Their wages & allowance is very small, or (if they bee apprentizes) nothing at all: being debarred bysides of all trade for themselves. This maketh them practise other means to mend their estates, first by imbezeling and drawing from the Company, and then following a privat trade for themselves. Whearby divers of them grow ritch and their Maisters poor. Which they make less conscience of, bycause they say they spend their time in so barbarous a Countrey whear they ar made vnfit for all other trades, & service in other countries abroad. 4. Certein of their servants that have soom better conceipt of themselves grow into acquaintance with Noblemen of the Court to countenance their dealings after they ar entred into a privat trade & other disorders. This friendship of great persons in the Russ Court is very dear & hath cost the Company many a thowsand pownd: having gained nothing by it but the protection of their own lewd servants against themselves.

4. *Privat trade by certein of the Company that have their factours thear vpon the common charge.* Who bysides their inland trade (buyeng at one part of the Countrey & selling at the other (as if they wear Russe Marchants to the great dislyke of the Russ) bring in and ship over commodities in Flemmish bottoms at St. Nicolas, Riga and Narve. Which hindereth muche the common trade & profit of the Company.

Means to please the Russe Emperour
for the Marchants beehalf.

1. If the Queen seem willing to ioign with him for drawing

[56]

Fletcher's Recommendations

a greater trade to the port of St. Nicolas from the other wayes of Narve & Riga. 2. If hir Highnes Letters, treaties, & presents sent to him bee so ordered as that they seem indeed to coom from hir self & hir good affection, & not from the Marchants (as hee is perswaded still they doe) & thearfore reiecteth them, & little regardeth the treaties doon in hir name bycause (as hee sayeth) they coom but from the *Mousicks*. 3. If hir Maiestie (when occasion doeth requier) offer hir self ready to mediat beetwixt him & the Polonian & Sweden, whome the Russ ever feareth bycause hee is ever invaded by them, & not they by him. And thearfore is glad to procure his peace by any means with them: the rather bycause hee never wanteth an enimie on the other side viz the *Tartar*.

Remedyes

The remedy for this is to give the Russ soom better content-ment by enlarging the English trade at the port of St. Nicolas so much as may bee. This may bee doon by refourming the trade after the manner of the Adventurers viz: Every man to trade for him self vnder a governours deputy that is to attend & follow their busines on thother side. 2. The number of the Russe Company to bee enlarged, & young men suffred to trade aswell as the rest. This manner of trading after the order of the Adventurers, & drawing a greater trade to the port of St. Nicolas, is lyke to prove much better for the Generallitie of the Company, for common wealth, & the Q[ueen's] coustooms then that which now is, whear all trade togither in one common stock. If it bee obiected that the Russe countrey will bear no such enlargement of trade, nor vent greater quantitie of o[ur] English commod-ities then now it doeth (which is but 1500 English clothes a year, with soom proportionate quantitie of tin, lead, brimston

Appendix B

&c:) It is answeared by the opinion of soom of good experience, that the trade by St. Nicolas hath ben stinted of late, & restrained of pourpose, and by very practise for the benefit of soom fiew & that the sayed trade will vtter far greater quantities then now it doeth, whatsoever is pretended; if the way by St. Nicolas wear ons [once] well inured & frequented in manner (as beefore is noted), specially when troubles grow on the Narve side.

2. *The remedy. To draw their trade & staple from Mosko, & other inland parts to the sea side, whear they shall bee farther of from the ey[e] & reach of the Court.* This will avoyd the seasures doon vpon every pretence & cavillation & takings vp vpon trust by the Emperour & his Nobles. Which is the speciall means that vndoeth our Marchants trade: the rather when every man dealeth severally for himself with his own stock, which will not bee so ready for the Russ to commaund as when all was in the hand and ordering of one Agent. 2. By this means allso the inland privat trades practised by certein of the Company to the hurt of the Generallitie, will bee prevented, when they ar restrained all to one remote placc from the inland parts. 3. The charge of houskeeping & houserents at those 5. severall places will bee cutt of. 4. The charge and trouble of traveiling to and fro with their commodities & carriages (viz. 1500 miles within land) will bee eased. 5. The Russe commodities (that our Marchants trade for) will bee easier provided towards the sea coast then in the inland parts. And as toutching the lykelyhood of obteining the Emperours favour for the removing their trade from Mosko towards the sea side thear ar these reasons to induce it. 1. The pollicie of the Russ to remove strangers out of the inland parts, specially from Mosko (the Emperours seat) towards the outparts of the Countrey for bringing in novelties, & breeding conceipts in their peoples heads by their beehaviour & reports of the governments & fashions of other Countries. To this pourpose the Emperours Counsell consulted at my beeing

thear, & conferred with mee abowt the removing of our Marchants trade from Mosko to Archangell, that lyeth 30. miles from the port of St. Nicolas vpon the river Duyna, to feell how it would bee taken if it wear forced by the Emperour. 2. The desier the Russ hath to draw trade to the port of St. Nicolas for the reasons mencioned beefore. 3. The necessitie of our English commodities will draw the Russe Marchants to follow the Mart or staple whearsoever it bee specially at St. Nicolas for the commoditie of that port. 4. The whole inland trade will then bee the Russe Marchants. Whearas beefore our English Marchants (that kept residence at Mosko, and other inland parts) had trade within land & delt with Bougharians, Medians Turks etc: aswell as the Natives. Which the Russe Marchants very much envyed & mislyked. 5. The Emperour & his Counsells lyking will force the Marchants to frequent that trade though themselves should mislyke it.

3. *Remedy for this.* viz: 1. By removing their trade from Mosko, & by severall trading (noted beefore). Whear every man followeth his busines by himself or his factour. Hearby their servants ill dealing will bee prevented, and if the servant prove ill & vnthriftie, it hurteth but his M[aister]. 2. If they continew their trade (as they doe) by common servants, to allow them better wages, & to give them more contentment by permitting them to have a peculium to a certein stint, & to trade with it for bettering their own estates. This will give their servants better contentment when they see soom care had of them & their own estate to mend aswell as the Companies. 3. To have a preacher thear resident with them that they may learn to know God and so their dueties towards their Maisters. Which will easier bee graunted if the trade bee removed towards the sea side. If they obiect they have no great number of servants thear that should need a preacher (as was answeared mee when I propounded that matter to them at my gooing over) it may bee answeared that if

they have never so fiew in that Countrey (whear they want all good means of instruction towards God) the Company ought in Christian duety to provide that means for them. The preacher (bysides that vse of him) might earn his stipend by advise with their Agent abowt their affaires beeing a man of soom iudgement & discretion.

4. *This inconvenience is prevented.* By removing the trade to the coast, & observing the order mencioned beefore, as the Adventurers doe.

Means to terrifie the Russ & keep him in order.

1. By threatning to stoppe the way to the port of St. Nicolas. Which (howsoever it can bee doon) the Russ is perswaded hir Maiestie can doe it. 2. If hir Highnes shiew any correspondence with the Polonian, Sweden, and Turk, and that shee hath means to incite them &c: 3. If the Russ practise any seazure or violence vpon our Marchants goods (as was lykely beefore my comming thither) revenge may bee made at Pechora by the sea side vpon the Mart thear. Which is helld yearly abowt Midsommer. Whear ar marted of furres of all sortes to the value of 100000£ yearly which may bee surprised by a fiew sail & a small company well appointed comming on a soodain, the Russ having no means to forsee or prevent it.

APPENDIX C

The Merchant's Protest

A petition submitted by the Muscovy Company to Sir William Cecil (Lord Burghley) probably in 1591, protesting the publication of Fletcher's *Of the Russe Commonwealth.* The manuscript is in the British Museum, Landsdowne MS 112, Burghley Papers No. 39, Folios 134r–135v. First published by Ellis, *Original Letters,* pp. 77–79, then by Bond, *Russia,* pp. 352–355, and most recently by Lloyd E. Berry, *The English Works of Giles Fletcher, the Elder,* pp. 150–153. The text which follows is based on the original manuscript and collated with the edition by Berry.

To the right honorable Sir William Cicell knight
Lord Highe Treasurer of England.

The Companie of Merchauntes tradinge Muskouia havinge bene manie waies preiudiced by the errors which have bene Committed by her Maiesties subiectes imploied by the companie in those partes in givinge offence or some smale Color of offence to the g[ov]ernment of the state of the Countrie of Russia, doe greatelie feare that a booke latelie sett out by Mr Doctor Fletcher, dedicated to her Maiestie intituled the Russe Common Wealthe, will turne the Companie to some greate displeasure with the Emperour and endaunger boeth theire people and goodes nowe remayninge there Except some good order be taken by your Lordships honorable Consideration for the Callinge in of all the bookes that are printed, and some Cowrse holden therein signifyinge her Maiesties dislike of the publishinge of the same. In which booke (besides the discowrse of the discripcion of the

Countrie, the militarie government and forces thereof, the Emperours Revenue, and howe yt ryseth (which is offensive to the Russe that anie man should looke into) the person of the Emperour his father, his Brother, and the L: Boris Fedorowich the protector, and generallie the nature of the people, are towched in soe harde tearmes, as that the Companie doubt the revenge thereof will light on theire people, and goodes remayninge in Russia, and vtterlie overthrowe the trade forever. Out of which booke for your L: readines, there is herevnder noted certen places offensive wherof the whole discowrse is full.

In the epistle dedicatorie of the booke he tearmeth the Russe government a straunge face of a tirannycall state.

Fol. 9b. The intollerable exaccions of the Emperour vppon his subiectes maketh them carelesse to laye vp anie thinge, for that yf they have ought yt cawseth them to be spoiled not onlie of theire goodes but of theire lives.

Fol. 16. In shewinge the likelihoode of the ende of the whole race of the Emperour concluded in some one, two or some fewe of the bloud, he saieth there is noe hope of yssue in the Emperour by the Constitution of his bodie, and the barenes of his wief.

He noteth there the death of the Emperoures elder brother murthered by his father in his furie whose death was the murtheringe of the olde Emperour by extreame greefe.

Fol. 16b. He noteth what practisinge there hath bene by such as aspire the succession to distroye the younger brother of the Emperour that is yet livinge, beinge about Sixe yeares olde wherein he seemeth to ayme at Boris fedorowich.

He noteth in that younge infant an inclinacion to Crueltie resemblinge his father, in delight of bloude, for that he beinge but Sixe yeares olde taketh pleasure to looke into the bleedinge throtes of beastes that are killed and to beate geesse and hens with a staffe untill they dye.

Fol. 20a. The Russe government is plaine tirannycall, and

exceadeth all iust measure without regard of Nobilitie or people givinge to the nobilitie a kinde of vniust and vnmeasured libertie, to exact on the baser sorte of people.

Fol. 21b. If the late Emperour in his progresse had mett a man whose person or face he had not liked, or yf he looked vppon him he would commaunde his heade to be stricken of and to be Cast before him.

Fol. 26b. 27a. The practise of the Godonoes to extinguishe the bloude Ryall who seeke to Cut of or keapt downe the best of the Nobilitie.

Fol. 33b. That yt is to be merveled howe the Nobilitie and people will suffer themselues to be brought vnder suche oppression and slaverie.

Fol. 34b. That the desperate state of thinges at home maketh the people to wishe for some forrein invasion.

Fol. 37b. That Boris Godonoe and the Empresse kindred accoumpt all that commeth to the Emperoures treasurie theire owne.

Fol. 41, 42, 43, 44, 45. Divers grosse practises of the Emperour to drawe the wealth of the land into his treasurie, which he Concludeth to be straunge kinde of extortions but that yt agreeth with the qualitie of the Emperour and the miserable subieccion of the poore Countrie.

Fol. 53a. Theire onlie lawe is theire speakinge lawe that is the pleasure of the prince and Magistrates which sheweth the miserable condicion of the people against whose iniustice and extreame oppression they had neede to be armed with manie good lawes.

Fol. 98, 99. The practise of the Godones against the Emperoures brother to prove him not legittimate and to turne awaie the peoples likinge from him as next successor.

Fol. 110. The discripcion of the Emperour, viz meane of stature lowe and grosse, sallowe of Complexion enclyninge to dropsey hawcke nosed insteadie in his pase by reason of the weaknes of his lymes heavie and vnactive commonlie smilinge, almost to a laughter for quallitie simple and slowe witted, but verie gentle and of an easie nature quiet mercifull &c. Fol. 116. It is to be doubted whether is greater the Crueltie or the intemperauncie that is vsed in the Countrie, it is soe foull that is not to be named. The whole Countrie overfloweth with the synne of that kinde and noe mervell as havinge no law to restrayne whoredomes advlteries and like vncleanes of lief.

From the greatest to the smallest except some fewe that will scarcelie be founde the Russe nether beleeveth anie thinge that an other man speaketh nor speaketh anie thinge him self worthie to be beleaved.

BIBLIOGRAPHY

I. EDITIONS OF *Of the Russe Commonwealth*

1. There are three manuscripts extant: one at the University Library, Cambridge (Queens College MS.25), another at University College, Oxford (MS.144), and a third at the University of Minnesota. They are described and analyzed in Lloyd E. Berry, *The English Works of Giles Fletcher, the Elder*, Madison, Wisconsin, 1964, pp. 160–167.

2. The first printed edition, *Of the Russe Common Wealth, or Maner of Governement by the Russe Emperour (commonly called the Emperour of Moscovia) with the manners, and fashions of the people of that Countrey*, London, 1591.

3. A précis in the second edition of Richard Hakluyt's *Principall Navigations, Voyages and Discoveries of the English Nation*, Volume I, London, 1599 [1598], pp. 473–495. Includes chapters 1–4, 6, 15–20 (omitting the last paragraph of Chapter 18), and 27–28. See Robert O. Lindsay, "Richard Hakluyt and *Of the Russe Common Wealth*," *The Papers of the Bibliographical Society of America*, LVII (1963), 312–327.

4. "A Treatise of Russia and the adioyning Region," in Samuel Purchas, *Purchas his Pilgrimes*, London, 1625, Volume III, pp. 413–460. Purchas provided in fairly complete form the 1591 edition, omitting only passages especially offensive to the Russians, so that, as he put it, he might "doe good at home, without harme abroad" (p. 413). This version was reprinted in the edition of Purchas published in 1906 in Glasgow, Volume XII, pp. 499–633.

5. G. Fletcher, *The History of Russia or the Goverment of the Emperour of Muscovia with the manners and fashions of the People of that Countrey*, n.p., 1643. Integral text of the 1591

[65]

Bibliography

edition, without the Dedication. Reprinted under the same title in London, 1657.

6. Excerpts, mostly of geographic nature, in J. Harris' *Navigantium atque itinerantium bibliotheca*, Volume I, London, 1705, pp. 542–550.

7. E. A. Bond, ed., *Russia at the Close of the Sixteenth Century*, London, 1856, pp. 1–152. The integral text of 1591, with minor editorial improvements and an informative introduction.

8. *La Russie au XVIe siécle*, 2 parts, Leipzig-Paris, 1864. French translation by Charles de Bouzet based on the Bond text.

9. *O gosudarstve Russkom, ili obraz pravleniia russkogo tsariia*, n.p., 1867. An émigré Russian edition of the confiscated 1848 translation by Gippius and Kalachov. Probably published in Basel. (See *Russkaia podpol'naia i zarubezhnaia pechat' — bibliograficheskii ukazatel'*, Vypusk I, Moscow, 1935, p. 132.)

10. A bowdlerized version, which omits among other things Fletcher's discussion of religion and church, in Aleksandr Burtsev, *Opisanie redkikh rossiiskikh knig*, Part III, St. Petersburg, 1897, pp. 185–293.

11. *O gosudarstve rossiiskom; sochinenie Fletchera*, St. Petersburg, 1905. The first legal Russian publication; reprints the Gippius-Kalachov translation. This book, brought out by the publishing house of A. S. Suvorin, had two subsequent identical editions: a second also in 1905, a third in 1906. A fourth legal Russian edition appeared in St. Petersburg in 1911.

12. "Of the Russe Commonwealth," in Lloyd E. Berry, *The English Works of Giles Fletcher, the Elder*, Madison, Wisconsin, 1964, pp. 169–306. The edition of 1591 collated with the manuscripts and other editions.

II. WORKS ON FLETCHER AND HIS BOOK

The best life of Fletcher can be found in Lloyd E. Berry, *The English Works of Giles Fletcher, the Elder*, Madison, Wisconsin,

Bibliography

1964, pp. 3–49. See also *Athenae Cantabrigienses*, Vol. III (Cambridge, 1913), pp. 36–37; this brief and now outdated sketch is reprinted, in somewhat abbreviated form, in the *Dictionary of National Biography*, VII, 299–302.

The only work specifically devoted to the *Russe Commonwealth* is S. M. Seredonin's *Sochinenie Dzhil'sa Fletchera 'Of the Russe Commonwealth' kak istoricheskii istochnik*, St. Petersburg, 1891. It analyzes in great detail the factual information supplied by Fletcher in the light of historical scholarship of the late nineteenth century from the position of a Russian nationalist and monarchist. Seredonin praises Fletcher in general terms, but criticizes him when it comes to particulars. The official Russian record of Fletcher's mission has been published in *Vremennik Imperatorskogo Moskovskogo Obshchestva Istorii i Drevnosti Rossiiskikh*, Vol. VIII (1850), Part II, pp. 1–96.

III. GENERAL LITERATURE ON ANGLO-RUSSIAN RELATIONS IN THE SIXTEENTH CENTURY

The best history of the Muscovy Company is T. S. Willan's *The Early History of the Russia Company, 1553–1603*, Manchester, 1956. It relies mainly on English sources, and does not take full advantage of the materials printed from Russian archives. Karl H. Ruffman's *Das Russlandbild im England Shakespeares*, Göttingen, 1952, gives a convincing picture of England's view of Russia in the reign of Elizabeth. See also M. S. Anderson, *Britain's Discovery of Russia, 1553–1815*, London, 1958, Chapter 1, pp. 1–32.

English travel accounts of Russia can be followed in the second edition of R. Hakluyt's *Principall Navigations*, Vol. I [1598], and E. D. Morgan and C. H. Coote, eds., *Early Voyages and Travels to Russia and Persia*, Hakluyt Society Publications, Volumes 72 and 73, London, 1886. Russo-English diplomatic correspondence of the second half of the sixteenth century, usually both in English and Russian, can be studied in the edition of Iurii Tolstoi, *Pervye sorok*

Bibliography

let snoshenii mezhdu Rossiieiu i Anglieiu, 1553–1593, St. Petersburg, 1875.

See also:

J. von Hamel, *England and Russia*, London, 1854.

V. O. Kliuchevskii, *Skazaniia inostrantsev o Moskovskom gosudarstve*, Moscow, 1918.

I. Liubimenko, *Les relations commerciales et politiques de l'Angleterre avec la Russie avant Pierre le Grand*, Paris, 1933.

GLOSSARY–INDEX
to the facsimile text

The glossary-index lists the terms and proper names mentioned by Fletcher, and where pertinent, defines them. Words incorrectly rendered are put into proper Russian. The Library of Congress system of transliteration is used throughout. Place locations (insofar as they can be identified) can be found on the map of "Fletcher's Russia"; the letters and numbers in parentheses which accompany each geographic reference in the index refer to the grid of this map; references designated "A" refer to the inset.

In sixteenth-century Russia the new year began on September 1. Whenever the sources do not state in which month of the Russian (September) year a given event took place, both the January years are given, separated by a bar. Thus, "1585/86" refers to the year extending from September 1, 1585, to August 31, 1586.

[69]

Glossary — Index

Bela IV (King of Hungary, 1235–1270; on the throne when Mongols invaded Hungary in 1241), 67v–68

Belgorod (C3), 62v

Bellougina [Bellouga], see Beluga

Belo-ozero (A:b2), 2, 12, 19

Belschey, Ivan Demetrowich, see Bel'skii, Prince Ivan Fedorovich

Bel'skii, Prince Ivan Fedorovich (entered Moscow service as boiar from Lithuania, 1522; fought Shuiskiis for control of government, 1538–1542; at height of influence, 1540–1541; died in chains, May 1542), 66v

Beluga (white sturgeon), 9v, 11v

Berossus (Babylonian priest-historian, 3rd century B.C.), 12

Beschest'e (dishonor, especially pertaining to quarrels arising over mestnichestvo, i.e., family and service rank), 29

Bestchest, see Beschest'e

Beza (from vezha), see Guliai gorod

Bezan, see Riazan'

Bezobrazov, Istoma (Khariton) Osipovich (postel'nichii or chamberlain from 1582 until his death in 1604), 111

Bilberry (whortleberry, hurtleberry), 6v

Birch trees, 4v, 8

Bisabroza, see Bezobrazov

Black Sea, 1v, 5v, 69v, 73

Blagoslovi nas, otche nebesnyi ("Bless us, Heavenly Father"), 91v, 92v

Blasslavey vladika, see Blagoslovi nas, otche nebesnyi

Blood, Tatars drink, 70v

Boarstva dumna, see Boiarskaia duma

Bōbasey (Bombasey; location unidentified, possibly Umba — D2), 10

Bohsedom, see Bozhii dom

Boiar (general meaning, any Russian noble; specific meaning, one of the nobles granted this title by the Tsar and entitled to sit as a boiar in the Boiarskaia duma), 13, 27v–28v, 29, 34v–36, 44v, 47, 64v, 83v, 114

Boiar in service of Bishop, 83v

Boiaren coneshcua, see Koniushii

Boiaren vladitskey, see Boiar in service of Bishop

Boiarens, see Boiar

Boiarskaia duma (Tsar's council, composed chiefly of nobles — boiars and the lower-ranking okol'nichie — chosen by Tsar plus a few selected d'iaki and courtiers; with advisory and some administrative functions), 20v–21, 21v, 22, 22v, 23, 23v, 27v, 30v, 31, 31v, 32v, 34v–36, 55, 63v, 81, 83v, 108v

Boiarskaia zhena (boiar's wife), 114

Boiarskeis, see Boiar

Boiarskey, see Boiar

Boiuren, see Boiar

Bol'shoi prikhod ("Office of Great Income" having financial competence over state lands, collecting essentially indirect taxes and fees), 36v, 38, 38v, 39, 39v, 40, 40v

Bonfinius, Anton (Hungarian historian, died 1502), 14v

Boristhenes, see Dnepr

Borris, see Godunov, Boris Fedorovich

Bougharia, see Bukhara

Boulgharia, see Bulgaria on the Volga

[71]

Glossary — Index

[74]

Glossary — Index

Glossary — Index

Glossary — Index

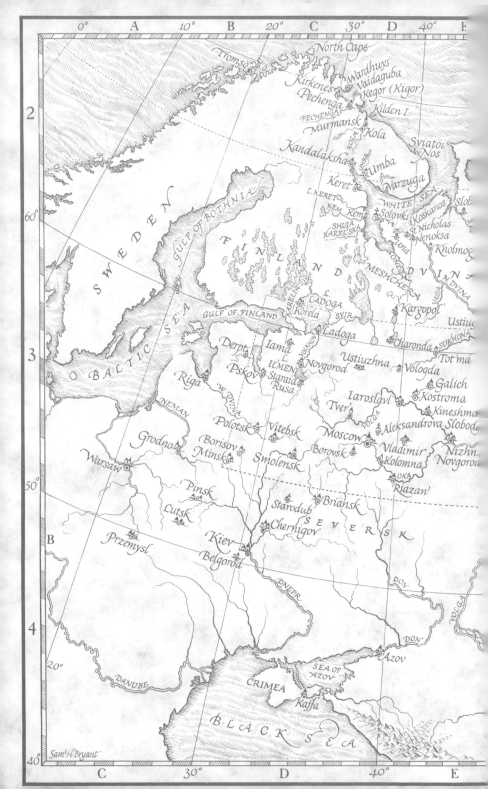